T0179361

Algorithms and Automation

To enact the book's central theme of automation and human agency, the author designed a Bot trained on her book to support dialogue with the content and facilitate discussions. If you like to compare what the author says and Bot 'interprets' or generates, go here https://www.anonette.net/denisaBot/

Algorithms and Automation: Governance over Rituals, Machines, and Prototypes, from Sundial to Blockchain is a critical examination of the history and impact of automation on society. It provides thought-provoking perspectives on the history of automation and its relationship with power, emphasizing the importance of considering the social context in which automation is developed and used. The book argues that automation has always been a political and social force that shapes our lives and futures, rather than a neutral tool. The author provides a genealogy of automation, tracing its development from ancient rituals to modern-day prototypes, and highlights the challenges posed by new technologies such as blockchain and artificial intelligence. The volume argues that we need more democratic and accountable governance over technological innovation to ensure that it respects human rights, political pluralism, legitimacy, and other values we hold dear in our institutions and political processes.

An engaging read on a fascinating topic, this book will be indispensable for scholars, students, and researchers of science and technology studies, digital humanities, politics and governance, public policy, social policy, system design and automation, and history and philosophy of science and technology. It will also be of interest to readers interested in the interactions of the sciences and the social sciences and humanities.

Denisa Reshef Kera is a philosopher and designer, senior lecturer in the Science, Technology and Society at Bar Ilan University, Israel. She is the founder of a Design and Policy lab, Dando.design, which explores innovative and creative ways of embedding ethical program and regulatory norms into the fabric of technical infrastructures. Her commitment to public participation in science and technology is reflected in her unique projects. Her award-winning work *Lithopy* combines a fairy tale with functional code in a smart village that operates via satellites and blockchain services. Her academic career over the past decade includes University of Malta, Tel Aviv University, University of Salamanca, the National University of Singapore, Arizona State University, and Charles University in Prague, her hometown.

Algorithms and Automation

Governance over Rituals, Machines, and Prototypes, from Sundial to Blockchain

Denisa Reshef Kera

LONDON AND NEW YORK

Designed cover image: Cover Illustration provided by Eva Holá. For more of her work, visit www.evahola.com

First published 2024
by Routledge
4 Park Square, Milton Park, Abingdon, Oxon OX14 4RN

and by Routledge
605 Third Avenue, New York, NY 10158

Routledge is an imprint of the Taylor & Francis Group, an informa business

© 2024 Denisa Reshef Kera

The right of Denisa Reshef Kera to be identified as author of this work has been asserted in accordance with sections 77 and 78 of the Copyright, Designs and Patents Act 1988.

British Library Cataloguing-in-Publication Data
A catalogue record for this book is available from the British Library

ISBN: 978-0-367-72226-5 (hbk)
ISBN: 978-1-032-03863-6 (pbk)
ISBN: 978-1-003-18941-1 (ebk)

DOI: 10.4324/9781003189411

Typeset in Sabon
by SPi Technologies India Pvt Ltd (Straive)

Access the BookBot here: https://anonette.net/denisaBot/

For Tsipi and Yair, my joys in the vastness of space and immensity of time

Contents

Governance over Prototypes   89

  8 From Governance over Rituals and Instruments to
     Governance over Prototypes   91

  9 Grassroots Governance over Open Science Hardware   106

10 Public and Open Futures between Labor, Action,
     and Leisure   126

11 Global Prototypes for Local Futures   141

PART IV
Governance over Exploratory Sandboxes   171

12 Experimental Governance over Metaphors, Prototypes,
     and Sandboxes   173

13 Governance 'Trading Zones': Exploratory Sandboxes   192

14 Experimental Algorithmic Citizenship   203

15 Conclusions   218

     Afterword   *223*
     References   *228*
     Index   *245*

Figures

Acknowledgments

I stole the dedication from Carl Sagan's *Cosmos*, a book that inspired a life-long love of reading, learning, and exploring. It is a tribute to every book that defines moments that open minds and hearts, an experience that no language model will ever be able to replicate with a click, no matter how large a dataset it uses. What is a book but a fossil of time spent in solitude, a monument of thoughts and obsessions that connects us to a long line of writers and readers that we will never meet, a unique community of the living, the dead, and the yet unborn? As I finish the book at a time of public excitement about large language models and AI bots, I challenge everyone to compare the book as a community across time and space with content triggered by a model. The book comes with a bot[1] trained on my writings, and anyone is welcome to break the chain of influences and connections with a click, and to explore the variations, triggers, and prompts. I argue that the clicks will never capture the unique history and moments that make a book a unique community and experience of time that Nabokov called a 'memory in making'. My hope for the future is that our models and prototypes will become more like books rather than vice versa, a means of our personal and social agency, public engagement with the future and time.

That every book is a community means that there is an act of dedication, which no bot will ever need, because it has no family or friends, no personal connections to the living and the dead. Bots based on models will never have to explain that there is a family without whose sacrifices the book would never have been finished, or as the joke goes, 'it would have been finished half the time'. Tsipi, Yair, Rumi and Ismail, Esther and Asher, my deepest gratitude goes to you for finding the reasons to support my work. Without your generosity and love, this book would not have been possible, and you are a part of it with your small and large acts of love, kindness, and support. I must also thank many close friends: Amy Sapan, for being one of the first readers and reviewers; Marketa Dolejšová, for being a partner in research adventures and for supporting me through the rough patches of the writing process; Silvia Lindtner, for the long and ongoing discussions and your generous comments; Lior Zalmanson, for providing new perspectives and reasons to finish this work; Petr Šourek, for being my guide and fellow pilgrim through ancient

texts explaining modern issues; Andrej Boleslavsky, for collaborating on prototypes that serve ideas and theory rather than startups; Anetta Mona Chisa
and dear Hugo, for creating my home away from home and allowing me to
be a part of a creative process that probes challenging philosophical ideas
with new materials.

This book is also a unique community directly connected to its content:
hackerspaces, citizen labs, and makerspaces around the world, such as
Hackteria.org, HONF (House of Natural Fiber), Lifepatch.org, Brmlab.cz,
and Tel Aviv hackerspace. Geeks, hackers, and makers inspired me to rethink
the role of the present academic institutions and knowledge, and to blur the
lines between friendship and research, Global North and South, past and
future engagement with crafts and prototypes. In this vernacular cosmopolitan Republic of Artisans, I would like to express my indebtedness to JB, a
true geek diplomat who connects many worlds, disciplines, and environments; Marc Dusseiller aka dusjagr, for showing what nomadic science can
do; Urs Gaudens, for all the open hardware magic that breaks down the silos;
Sachiko Hirosue, for your courage as a scientist to democratize science in
diverse environments; Paula Pin, for the wild explorations that I follow and
admire; Irene Agrivine, for changing the lives of so many people with your
unique projects and networks that continue to inspire. I have also been influenced by the larger open science hardware community, including Gathering
for Open Science Hardware (GOSH), and the work of many makers who are
also brilliant researchers and academics – Stefania Druga, Jenny Molloy,
Tincuta Heinzel, Hannah Perner-Wilson, and Andrew Quitmeyer.

My work would not have been possible without the ongoing support of
Julie Harboe from the CreaLab in Switzerland, who taught me how to connect diverse stakeholders through creative engagements and formats, and
Zohar Messeca-Fara, whose Idiots.io taught me the joy of playing with cir-
cuitry and finding creative ways to resist technocratic rule. Thank you Hermes
Huang and Justyna Ausareny, for supporting the early work on open, citizen,
and decentralized science that played a central role in the endeavor to rethink
governance. Another important catalyst has been Honor Hager, curator, and
artist, who continues to demonstrate how art can help us make sense of the
developments in science and technology. I am immensely grateful to friends
who kept me connected to the efforts to democratize science: Clarissa Reche,
whose creative work on science engagement in the Global South has revolu-
tionized iGEM; Michal Jordan, whose exploratory work on blockchain solutions for decentralized science at the University of Malta I was privileged to
supervise; Vojtěch Jeremiáš Kundrát from the Weizmann Institute of Science,
who continues to provoke me with his impressive work at nanoscale and
helps me imagine the technology we will use in the next century.

Special thanks also go to the Maker Faire Prague team and Prusa Design,
dear colleagues and friends, Jasna Sykorova and Josef Průša, for supporting
my work in Prague; Angelika Dudová and Linette Manuel, for the creative use
cases using emerging technologies; Branislava Kuburovic and Petr Knobloch

from Prague City University, for exploring and testing different ideas of how to teach design and art. I am privileged to be part of the Uroboros.design festival, where I would like to thank Michal Kučerák and Lenka Hámošová for involving me in their art and design provocations. I would also like to thank Pavlina Schultz and Misha Sidenberg for always finding new ways to connect my homeland, the Czech Republic, with my new home, Israel.

The book has been generously supported by academic institutions that were open to the challenges of hackerspaces, makerspaces, and efforts to democratize science and technology. I would like to express my heartfelt gratitude to the Weizenbaum Institute in Berlin, which supported the work on the book with a fellowship, especially Prof. Dr. Gesche Joost and her wonderful team, Dr. Michelle Christensen, Dr. Florian Conradi, and Dr. Bianca Herlo. I will always be thankful for the unique opportunity offered by BISITE at the University of Salamanca, which hosted my Marie Curie Fellowship, especially Prof. Juan M. Corchado, who became a true mentor and role model. I am privileged to have worked with Dr. Joshua Ellul and Dr. Ioannis Revolidis from the Center for Distributed Ledger Technology, University of Malta, who helped me test the ideas about the future of regulation and experimental governance, and I look forward to our future collaborations.

In the present, I would like to acknowledge the inspiring colleagues from the Center for Cyber-Social Dynamics and the collaboration with Prof. John Symons, Dr. Ramón Alvarado, and Brian Rosenblum from the Institute for Digital Research in the Humanities at the University of Kansas. Our ongoing dialogues inspired many themes in the book. Also crucial were the visiting professorship position at the School for the Future of Innovation in Society (SFIS) at Arizona State University and the work of Prof. David Guston and Dr. Cynthia Selin, whose influences are visible throughout the book. I am indebted to my colleagues from the Science, Technology, and Society Research Cluster at the National University of Singapore and their various initiatives, in which I was involved, especially Prof. Gregory Clancey, Prof. Mohan Dutta, Prof. Michael Fischer, and Dr. Lonce Wyse. I would like to thank you for your continued support and trust in my vision.

This brings me to my current academic home, the Science, Technology, and Society program at Bar Ilan University, where my odyssey across disciplines and universities ends and where I have found the right environment to create a Design and Policy lab that explores the future engagements and governance over prototypes. I am very fortunate to have wonderful mentors and colleagues who motivated me to finish the book with their feedback and advice, especially Prof. Noah Efron and Dr. Ido Hartogsohn. I would also like to thank Dana Gordon, whose Speculative Futures Tel Aviv and courses on speculative design continue to inspire my work and bring new ideas for projects. This part should also include artists, academics, and friends in my new home, Israel, whose work I admire and who continue to motivate me to explore new topics and approaches in the study of science, technology, and society: Shira Ansky, Tsila Hassine, Carmel Vaisman, Mushon Zer-Aviv, Amnon Dekel, Galit Wellner, Liat Segal, and Yoav Wald.

I also feel indebted to the unique environment of my alma mater, Charles University in Prague, especially the mentorship of Prof. Miroslav Petříček and Prof. Rudolf Vlasák, who supported my early projects in the New Media Studies program in Prague. Special thanks are addressed to Pavel Sedlák, whose projects in the field of art, science, and technology inspired my early research, and to his parents, Milca and Bohous, who remain my second family in Prague. Last but not the least, we are always indebted to our early teachers, and I would like to mention and express special gratitude to Smilja Marjanović, my first teacher in place with a complicated history and present, Kosovo. She taught me to read and count, but more importantly, she showed me how to overcome divisions, to dare and not lose hope for the future even in the most complicated environments and times. My final note and thanks go to the editors at Routledge, Aakash Chakrabarty and Brinda Sen, whose hard work and support made all the difference.

Note

1 https://anonette.net/DenisaBot

Part I
Introduction

1 Introduction

In our quest to bring order and predictability to an inherently complex and uncertain world, we created a powerful utopia and myth of society governed by automation. The myth of automation emerges as a form of control over time and the future. Enacted through tools as old as sundials and as contemporary as blockchain and machine learning (ML) algorithms, it seeks to eradicate uncertainty from both the natural world and human society. It uses rituals, instruments, and infrastructures not only to control and predict but also to impose cycles, patterns, and data on nature and society.

While promising to optimize every aspect of social life, the myth of automation inadvertently perpetuates existing inequalities and biases and leads to a resignation upon political and social agency. It bypasses the need to transform values, meanings, and practices in society with its promise of control and prediction. Instead of embracing social life as an experience of agency and pursuit of human dignity, governance and society become a matter of cosmology or ontology. The cycles in the past that enabled calendars and clocks together with patterns captured by instruments lead directly to the present data models that impose stability and predictability upon all aspects of social life.

To discuss the ethical, philosophical, and practical implications of automation, we need to capture the origins of the myth that reduces governance to control of patterns, signals, cycles, and more recently also data. We will use personifications of time from ancient Greek mythology, *Chronos* and *Kairos*, to examine the tensions between agency and structure in the concepts of governance and cosmology. Chronos embodies the measurable, linear, and quantitative time of natural cycles and cosmological phenomena that 'govern' the world, such as day and night or the changing of the seasons. These cycles impose stability and predictability as the ideals for society and governance. In contrast, Kairos represents the 'uncontrollable' time of agency, chance, and opportunity in political, social, and natural processes that we will try to rehabilitate.

The myth of automation reduces human action and governance to decisions driven by insights into cosmology or design of new infrastructures. Instead of facing uncertainty, chance, and opportunity that define human

DOI: 10.4324/9781003189411-2

agency as a matter of action, open future, and experience of time as Kairos, we are imposing linear, quantifiable, and predictable time of Chronos as the foundation for governance. The dichotomy of Chronos and Kairos thus summarizes the main problem with the myth of automation – the imbalance between our insights into natural laws (discovery and innovation) and experiences of social norms (values), between structure and agency and between tools of technology and goals of governance.

To solve the various dichotomies and tensions between technology and governance, we will emphasize the importance of prototyping. We will explore how prototyping supports an experimental and participatory approach to technology but also governance (innovation and society). Against the teleology of progress and doom that comes with the myth of automation, we will emphasize the importance of open social and technological transformations and processes. Instead of aligning or embedding any predefined values and goals that support the teleological view of society and innovation, we are advocating experimental practices and environments that depend on engagement and negotiation. We define them as radically open and political and describe them as prototyping and sandboxes for governance. Instead of supporting or refusing some predefined apocalyptic and progressivist agendas, these practices and environments facilitate the negotiation, balancing, and integration of agency and structure, facts and values, Chronos and Kairos. While the beginning of the book follows the uses of rituals and instruments in governance in a genealogy of automation, the later chapters focus on the blockchain and ML infrastructures as more recent attempts to automate governance. On these examples, we will show how to move beyond the myth of automation and preserve the importance of Kairos in governance (society) as much as in technology (innovation).

Fantasy and Anxiety of Automation

The attempts to resist automation are as old as the myth of automation itself, as discussed in Chapters 2–4 on the examples of anecdotes about 'predictive analytics' over olive presses in the 6th century BCE, complaints about the merciless water clock in the 4th century BCE, and the famous curse of the sundial. These classic loci about control of time and the future capture how the fantasy of automation always turns into anxiety about bias, precarity, and loss of agency and sovereignty. To map the fantasies and anxieties of automation, we will start with the early time measuring instrument leading to the technological ideal of governance as innovation and progress in Chapters 5–7. On the examples of instruments, prototypes, and experimental institutions (early academies of sciences and later hackerspaces), we will reflect on the different projects connecting governance with technology. The examples will then inspire the proposal for a sandbox in Chapters 12–14 that opposes the ideal of governance as matter of innovation and automation.

The ideal of governance reduced to innovation originated in Francis Bacon's project of technological and scientific 'restoration' (*Instauratio*) discussed in Chapters 6 and 7. Bacon assumed that innovation and discoveries would automatically restore the power of humanity over creation, lost after the fall, and bring a moral 'restoration'. These teleological and theological ideals do little justice to the actual processes of invention, discovery, and prototyping, but they captured the public imagination, and we still use them when we speak of progress and innovation. Since Bacon's Instauratio, governance is a relentless search for deus ex machina tricks, miraculous contraptions, and devils' bridges. They deliver omnipotent 'gods' and (technological) miracles as crane-like contraptions from the ancient dramas to 'automatically' solve human problems. They also claim to bring a moral 'restoration' and ideal governance that works just like the devil's bridges from the legends – as miracles that turn into curses.

The myth of automation thus appears with every new instrument and infrastructure that claims to improve society and governance. Starting with the rituals, calendars, and clocks to present reputation and scoring systems in predictive AIs, or smart contracts on trustless blockchain ledgers, the ideal of automation promises a frictionless, evidence-based, and politically neutral future. The present computer clocks then amplify and make even more pervasive this form of control over time and the future. Instead of measuring anything external, to which society adapts or defines new relations, with the computer clocks we are directly generating the signals and cycles. With them we synchronize the data across the computers and networks and, by proxy, all the processes in society and concentrate the power in the hands of the few that decide on their design. To reclaim agency and restore the opportunity and time as Kairos in governance as much as in technology, we need to start questioning when and why governance became a matter of cycles, patterns, and data and why it was reduced to a myth of automation.

Rituals, Instruments, and Prototypes

Hidden in the history of the early clocks and instruments discussed in Chapters 3–5 is a forgotten role of instrument-making that defines governance resisting the myth of automation (Chapters 6–8). Governance experiments and visions by mechanical artisans, such as Cornelius Drebbel, embraced the process of prototyping and emphasized time as an experience of human agency and transformation or Kairos. Instead of restoring an ideal past or imposing the teleology of progress, these prototypes transform the expectations about the future and society. Instead of mirroring the insights from cosmology that reduce time to patterns and cycles of Chronos (Chapter 5), the future and governance become a matter of personal and social agency.

The forgotten history of instrument-making thus defines what we will explore as governance based on prototypes in Chapters 5–7. After defining the crucial role of prototyping for governance in Chapter 8, we will use the examples of 'fringe' prototypes in the hackerspaces, makerspaces, and citizen science (Chapters 9–11) to propose a model of governance over sandboxes in Chapters 12–14. Rather than reducing governance to innovation, prototyping for governance emphasizes time as agency and Kairos that oppose the reduction of governance to a matter of ontology, cosmology, or automation.

Prototyping and later sandboxes in the service of governance support embodied, liminal, personal, and social uses of science, technology, and time that challenge the ahistorical, teleological, and universalistic notions of technology as progress or restoration (Chapters 7 and 8). In contrast to the teleological notions of governance and technology (Chapters 5 and 6), prototyping in the service of governance and time as Kairos emphasizes pragmatic and hybrid engagements which remains open-ended and participatory. The prototyping practices and efforts, described in the open science hardware projects in Chapters 9–11, then demonstrate prototyping as a medium of personal and social agency against the technological control and automation.

Participatory engagements with technology and governance in hackerspaces and liminal environments cultivate personal and social agency over prototyping. They offer a novel model for governance of emerging technologies and infrastructures that we will discuss as governance over exploratory sandboxes (from Chapter 12 to 15). Instead of automation and pervasive control, prototyping becomes an opportunity to collaboratively learn, test, tinker, and negotiate emerging technologies and futures. The open, liminal, and fringe prototypes support practices that define time and the future as a matter of Kairos and provide a model for the sandboxes that explicitly work with the future as a public good, 'commons', and challenge of stakeholders' negotiation.

Sandboxes

Since the early instruments and prototypes, there is a vision of governance that resists the myth of automation. The forgotten anxieties about the clocks (Chapters 3–5) together with the genealogy of prototyping and instrument-making in Chapters 6 and 7 present alternatives to the disruptive innovation that reduces governance to progress. Prototypes define governance as a need and opportunity to reconcile personal and social goals with external opportunities and discoveries, to balance nature, history, and politics. Prototyping in the service of personal and social agency then resists the teleological project of progress or Instauratio (restoration), including visions of accelerationism, singularity, solar punk, and luxury communism (Bassett & Roberts, 2020; Bastani, 2020; Gardiner, 2017, 2020; Vostal, 2019; Williams, 2019).

In contrast to the utopian and dystopian futures unleashed upon society by disruptive technologies, prototyping in the service of Kairos preserves personal and social agency as means of tactical decisions about the future. It enacts open, pluralistic, and democratic engagements with technology without any ultimate goals in history, technology, or politics, including the pursuit for social justice. The material, conceptual, and social engagements with prototypes in the sandboxes proposed in Chapters 12–15 enable open experiments with the future. These engagements reject any teleology of final causes in history, society, or the universe, including demands for restoration, progress, and justice. Such prototypes and environments explore agency and practices that

> abstract, appropriate, buy, cheat, choose, colonize, commodify, compress, conquer, control, create, de-contextualize, devise scales, edit, enjoy, experience, fear, hierarchize, impose, kill, live, measure, maintain order, plan, prioritize, quantify, rationalize, reckon, (re-)generate, regulate, relate to, (re-)organize, represent, reproduce, (re-)structure, save, sell, slow down, speed up, steal, synchronize, tell, use and waste time.
>
> (Adam, 2000)

Exploratory sandboxes as liminal environments connect the work on the infrastructures with questions of governance; they connect prototyping with policymaking. Prototyping facilitates personal and collective ideas of new infrastructures that support creative, participatory, and open futures. An essential part of these exploratory and public sandboxes (Chapter 12) is then their genealogy, since only after we identify the forgotten anxieties and fantasies of governance as automation (Chapter 3) can we question the control over the future and time. The emerging blockchain, ML, and Internet of Things (IoT) prototypes thus echo the promises of every magical infrastructure since the clocks and devil's bridges or bewildering cathedrals of the builders' legends: they only work if we sacrifice our firstborn, a metaphor of our personal and social agency over the future.

Prototyping in the public and exploratory sandboxes demystifies the magical control over the future and time by infrastructures promising automation while sacrificing our agency. It exposes the myth of automation beyond every infrastructure that demands personal and collective sacrifices. By slowing down the implementation and decision-making processes, sandboxes support personal, collective, and institutional aspirations and exploratory uses of technology. Sandboxes prevent the reduction of governance to automation and encourage agonistic, plural, and transparent work on the futures. Rather than reducing technology to a ritual that achieves political and social goals automatically and 'by design' (or via alignment), prototyping in the sandboxes engage with technologies and institutions as social and political processes. Rather than becoming an opportunity for a monopoly, the future becomes a personal and shared project that can succeed or fail, but never close itself from the further engagements.

Genealogy of Automation

The ambiguous temporality of prototyping means that opportunity and Kairos expressed as a new instrument or tool often enable the rule of Chronos – control over the future of society (when a unique prototype transforms into disruptive innovation). This ambiguity of Kairos and Chronos, innovation and control, defines the goal for the sandboxes as balancing of these powers. Sandboxes are environments that support personal and social engagements with open, plural, and agonistic futures over prototyping. They emphasize Kairos in governance as much as technology and reconcile the ontology and cosmology of Chronos with the demands for personal and social action. In Chapter 8, we will outline how prototypes support Kairos and Chronos and identify the forgotten practices and aspirations that expanded the possibilities of engagement with time, technology, and governance. Based on these practices, we outline a model for exploratory sandboxes as liminal environments in Chapter 12.

Exploratory sandboxes are liminal environments for experiencing alternatives to automation and algorithmic rules. In the book, we explore the genealogical roots of this ideal of prototyping as a material and political engagement that creates possibilities for exploratory and participatory futures resisting automation. The genealogy of prototyping for governance starts with the clock as an instrument enacting the early fantasies and anxieties of time control, including monopoly over the future through prediction (from Chapter 3). To challenge the ideal of automation and its teleology of time control, we then examine the histories of instrument-making in ancient Greece and the Renaissance (Chapters 6 and 7). Together with the ethnography of instruments made in hackerspaces (Chapter 8) and other liminal environments (Chapters 9 and 10), we offer example of prototypes that support public uses of time and agency over the futures. The combination of ethnography and genealogy then informs the proposal for sandboxes as participatory environments for exploratory governance of technological futures (Chapter 12).

Starting with anecdotes about sundials in Chapter 3, we will map the cautionary tales on how technology becomes a ritual and myth reducing governance to a matter of infrastructure that functions without political subjects and outside of history. The early clocks define the dream of governance as automation that disregards personal and social time, lived experience, history, and an open future. All emerging technologies are then modeled after the clocks. They act as devil's bridges and pacts with the devil that promise unrestricted and absolute power with a hidden clause about the future. Emerging technologies and infrastructures enforce automation without participation and agency over the future. No matter how democratic they claim to be, they will always become a tool of oppression and totalitarian rule that is based on the myth of automation. By monopolizing the future, clocks like the devil's bridges metaphorically take away our 'firstborn', our agency, and the possibility for change and transformation. Such governance machines and infrastructures always support surveillance, exacerbate inequalities, and create new vulnerabilities.

Before science instruments or infrastructures become governance machines embedded in technical standards, market expectations, and other bureaucratic structures (Chapters 3–5), they are prototypes that support personal and community commitments. It is in this liminal and open stage that we seek to extend participation. Liminal and experimental environments for prototyping in the hackerspaces described in Chapter 8 offer examples of such engagements outside the market forces, industry standards, patents, or other power structures. Together with the historical examples or early instruments in Chapter 6, these fringe prototypes demonstrate the alternatives to governance as automation. In Chapter 12, we will then extrapolate the genealogical lessons and examples into a proposal for an experimental sandbox that combines prototyping with governance and supports personal and social action or agency over the future.

Media Archeology as Exorcism

The discussion of time and the future as a problem of prototyping and automation pays homage to Siegfried Zielinski's project of 'time media' and 'time machines'. We have extended his central question 'Who owns time?' (Zielinski, 2006) into a challenge: How to make time a public resource that involves citizens in shaping the future? Rather than examining the forgotten and neglected futures of the past, we are focusing on the dominant instruments of time and future control described in Chapter 3 as governance machines. While, as governance machines, prototypes reduce governance to automation, as exploratory tools they have the potential to support public engagement and enact public interests. All prototypes have the potential to become a form of social action through which we can experience our personal and collective power over the future and time.

The genealogy of automation in Chapter 3 thus follows Zielinski's revision of media history, but not his goal of resurrecting the 'dead' and forgotten futures of the past through art and media archeology. We captured the dynamic of 'imagination and calculation' (Zielinski, 2006) as a question of action and structure (knowledge) to focus on how we can democratize future-making and prototyping. The early attempts to govern via prototypes (Chapter 3, especially Chapters 6 and 7) then serve as material for our genealogy that aims to 'exorcise' automation from governance (and prototypes) in the rest of the chapters (Chapters 3–8).

We call this process exorcism, because it uses genealogy to identify and defuse the arbitrary exercise of power in promissory infrastructures and new instruments that 'possess' our private and public lives. By identifying moments of resignation, in relation to politics, agency, and the future, we create an opportunity to rethink the role of prototyping in governance (Chapters 8 and 12).

The alternative history of instrument-making from the Renaissance period (Chapters 6 and 7) to today's hackerspaces, makerspaces, and citizen science labs (Chapter 8) then illustrates the importance of the alternative engagements with instruments and future-making.

To explore prototypes that support agency over the future rather than control, we propose exploratory sandboxes (Chapter 12) that will extend the practices identified in the forgotten history of instrument-making (Chapter 3) and observed in the liminal spaces (Chapters 8 and 9). Before instruments or algorithms become infrastructures owned and regulated by anyone, they are prototypes and explorations that express conflicting ideas, values, and visions for society. At this early, ambiguous, and experimental stage, we need to increase participation and redefine public interest. Rather than merely aligning and embedding values and political goals, or educating the public about hegemonic infrastructures, the liminal environments of hackerspaces and sandboxes support direct participation and agency.

Liminal and exploratory prototyping enables citizens to define their stakes in the future and prevent excesses of algorithmic rule and automation. As stakeholders in the future, citizens understand that time is a common good and a public resource that must be cared for and even fought for. Instead of being mere users of future infrastructures or media archeologists lamenting the loss of forgotten futures, citizens need to express their agency and visions through prototypes. They need to negotiate their future with others without closing it or claiming that one ideal would serve all.

The genealogy of automation in Chapter 3 thus shows the importance of prototyping in defining the agency over time and the future. Together with the ethnography of hackerspaces and liminal environments in Chapter 8, it positions prototyping as a problem of governance. Disrupted by every new tool and infrastructure that serves monopolies, our societies seem to resign upon politics reduced to the promises of automation. We are always prone to trade the uncertainty of social and personal agency for the certainty of cosmology or ontology (as we show in Chapter 5) that is promised by science and technology. To prevent politics and governance from abandoning the future as a political and social project and a matter of action (and outsourcing it to new machines and infrastructures), we need to rethink the different ways prototypes support our agency and define the future and time as goals of governance.

Time as a Condition of Automation

Time is a strategic resource for every infrastructure that promises automation and algorithmic control. What blockchain, the IoT, and various cloud services (SaaS, IaaS, PaaS, and CaaS software; infrastructure, platform, and containers as a service) do is simply synchronize nodes, processes, and data across networks. From satellite navigation to algorithmic trading, time is traded, measured, and quantified as a commodity through computers and atomic clocks. It is even 'minted' and 'stamped' on blockchain and decentralized blockchain ledgers, which define time as a literal medium of currency. As a resource, time quantifies and controls processes in the machines and networks, but as a personal or social experience, it is the opposite of control. It makes human life unique, unrepeatable, sacred, and 'autotelic', having a meaning and purpose in itself (Cassin, 2014). The purpose of this book is to rethink prototyping and design that uses the future and time as an autotelic medium of personal and social agency (Kairos), rather than reducing it to a resource and cosmology (Chronos).

To prevent the loss of agency over the future and time, we will start by 'uncover(ing) the dynamic moments... [that] revel in heterogeneity' and 'enter into a relationship of tension with various present-day moments, relativize them and render them more decisive' (Zielinski, 2006). Prototypes can help us recognize not only the missed opportunities in the past (Chapters 5 and 6) but also the present 'dynamic moments' of change and transformation. They define possibilities for action rather than ontological or cosmological certainty and resignation. To capture the experience of prototyping as a matter of agency over the future and time, we will use the dichotomy of Kairos and Chronos (Chapters 5, 6, and 8) and define time as a medium of action and politics rather than as a matter of ontology or cosmology. As political subjects and citizens, we use the future and time as Kairos, an opportunity for transformation. As users and consumers, we are controlled by the promises of the new infrastructures that represent time as control over the future based on the insights into Chronos and cosmology.

The genealogy in Chapter 3 is thus an 'excursion into the deep time' (Ibid.) of automation that reveals the tension between time as Kairos (experience of chance, uncertainty, and opportunity) and Chronos (cosmological phenomena). By 'expanding the present' and 'slowing down' (Ibid.) the original infrastructure of control, the clock, we will recognize the moments of loss of personal and social agency over the future and time. By following the genealogy of automation in Chapter 3 and then practices in hackerspaces in Chapter 9, we will question the demarcation of technology from governance, structure from agency, and time as Chronos from Kairos. We will highlight the hybrid practices and liminal environments that increase our agency over the future and time. Such practices driven by Kairos offer an alternative to the governance machines and their reduction of the future to algorithmic domination, automation, and Chronos.

In contrast to time as a means of automation, the concept of time in this book is a matter of personal and social agency that includes unpredictability and chance. Time as an opportunity for personal and social action is synonymous with being, meaning, and creation that include failures and falls, and resist the monopolization of the future by clocks, instruments, and infrastructures. The dichotomy between the quantified and controlled time of instruments and infrastructures (Chronos) and the unpredictable and experiential time of living (Kairos) defines the central questions in this book: How can we design instruments and infrastructures that support agency over time and the future rather than taking it away? How to support personal and social action in prototyping (Chapter 8)? How to develop infrastructures without becoming their victims, slaves, and parasites (Chapters 3 and 12)?

2   The Myth of Automation

Dreams and fears of automation emerge with every new instrument and infrastructure that promises a pervasive control of time through algorithms and associated bureaucratic structures, such as standards. They erode the experience of time as an agency to discover, decide, disrupt, or negotiate the future with others. To discuss this form of control as an ideal governance that imposes the myth of automation, we will start with a question: How do matters of public life become rituals and automated services that leave no room either for chance and improvisation or for agency and action? What are the metaphysical, political, and material conditions under which governance becomes a matter of automation and algorithms?

The reflections on algorithmic governance provide some guidance, but they often focus on the regulation and ownership of the algorithms and data responsible for the automation (Elkin-Koren, 2020; Larsson, 2018; Micheli et al., 2020; Saurwein et al., 2015; Shorey & Howard, 2016). Research on algorithmic governance often discusses broad epistemological questions of objectivity and accuracy, including the social, political, and economic implications of algorithms and data in critical data studies (Ananny & Crawford, 2018; Boyd & Crawford, 2012; Kitchin, 2017), even issues of energy and mineral consumption (Crawford, 2013; Parikka, 2015). These insights will inform our critique, but the focus will remain on the uses of time and the future as conditions of automation. We define automation as the control of time through rituals and prototypes of machines and infrastructures that close the future and impose a teleology with universal and final goals.

The discussion of automation in governance combines metaphysical questions of time and agency with political questions of power (Chapter 3): What defines good governance in an age of prototypes that disrupt and control citizens' public and even private lives, often without clear mandates? How do we ensure that algorithms' immense power over the future and time respects values that we hold dear in our institutions and political processes, such as human rights, the rule of law, the values of political pluralism, legitimacy, or accountability?

DOI: 10.4324/9781003189411-3

The dichotomies of agency and structure, or action and knowledge, experiences of time as Chronos and Kairos (timekeeping and timing), will help us understand how prototyping defines governance. Rather than reducing governance to automation (Chapter 3), we will be follow prototypes that democratize the power over the future and time (Chapters 8 and 12). Prototyping has the potential to open the future to public participation and define political and technological representation as a matter of practice. It thus defines attempts to 'save' time as a public good and reject the myth of automation with its disruptive infrastructures as modern-day devil's bridges (Chapter 12).

Design for Public Time and Open Future

There are many design and policy proposals that emphasize the public uses of space (Carmona 2015; Mitchell 1995; Crawford 2016; Jacobs 1962), but very few that claim similar need in the case of time and the future. How should we manage time as a public resource to prevent the excesses of monopolization that are common in the design of urban space? Critics of the excesses of urban design that commercializes cities and turns them into pseudo-public spaces (Mac Síthigh, 2012; Wang & Wang, 2019) provide a model for discussing the monopolization of future and time. When engaging with algorithmic rule over new infrastructures, we need to prevent the pseudo-public misuses of time and futures that lead to monopolies and commodification of private and public life.

Monopolization of the future with every prototype, platform, and infrastructure transforms lived experiences into algorithms and data over which we lose control individually and socially. While urban planning has historically urged developers to resist pseudo-public spaces, no one is asking IT developers to rethink their control over time. Automation, which dominates our private and public lives with its promises of innovation and progress, closes the future to technologies designed and owned by innovators and their investors. To challenge this, we must identify moments of resignation on time as a public resource (Chapter 3) and look for practices that support an open future and time as commons (Chapters 8 and 12). The blueprint for 'public' time and an open future in the sandboxes in Chapter 12 is then based on a genealogy of automation (Chapter 3) that defines the problem of time and the future commodified through prototyping (Chapter 8).

Once we identify the forgotten practices of time as a public resource and Kairos, including the liminal environments – hackerspaces (Chapter 8), we can define tools for designers, policymakers, and citizens for reclaiming time as a care for public infrastructure. The proposal for exploratory sandboxes (Chapter 12) supports personal and collaborative experiences on future-making that emphasize personal and social agency over time. The future(s) and time in liminal environments and sandboxes are like public squares or community gardens. They support messy individual, social, and public engagements that resist the pseudo-public rule of automation and algorithmic control.

The variety of practices discussed in Chapter 8 that shape the future over prototypes will help us identify the alternatives to disruption or strict regulations that come too late and do too little. Through the genealogy of early clocks, Renaissance instruments (Chapters 5 and 6), and bottom-up participatory experiments with design and prototyping in hackerspaces, makerspaces, and do-it-yourself (DIY) culture (Chapter 8), we will describe a forgotten history of prototyping that serves as a model for the sandboxes (Chapter 12). We need liminal and hybrid practices and environments that support interventions that are discursive as much as they are material, technological, or infrastructural. They make the future a personal and political challenge and define time as a philosophical, metaphysical, and practical question.

The examples of open science instruments in Chapters 8 and 9 that enact the agency over prototyping thus echo the mission of Renaissance artisans (Chapter 6). They represent the forgotten futures of science and technology that we claim define today's hackerspaces. The Renaissance artisans and their instruments offered precedents serving pluralistic and open futures outside the teleology of progress and innovation. The main function of the public and exploratory sandboxes discussed in Chapter 12 is to restore this and protect time and the future as a public and communal good.

Sandboxes safeguard society from the arbitrary excesses of every new prototype, technology, and 'demonic' infrastructure or devil's bridge. By supporting personal and social action over emerging technologies, they guard the open future and make it dependent on the participation of citizens as stakeholders. Rather than being mere users of future services or victims of algorithmic rules and automation, the liminal and hybrid interventions between governance and technology over sandboxes encourage citizens to become stakeholders in their future.

Clocks, Time Protocol, and Timestamping

Algorithmic governance is part of a long history of attempts to use instruments to control time and organize the social, private, and even biological lives of citizens. We call such tools governance machines because they reduce personal and social phenomena to automation on nonhuman scales. Whether these mechanisms and machines are calendars or clocks that use cosmological knowledge of astronomical cycles, predictive analytics and probabilistic and statistical analysis of data, or automated smart contracts on distributed ledgers, they all reduce governance to control of the future and time.

Governance machines optimize the actions, decisions, and behaviors of individuals and communities to serve predetermined goals of the inventors and investors. They transform the future from a medium of action into a means of control. Compared to older forms of time control via calendars, clocks, and rituals, today's governance machines use computing. The new tools of algorithmic control do not even measure time as an external cosmological phenomenon (movement of the Sun), but transform it into signals, patterns, and mathematical abstractions generated and interpreted by the machines. Computer clocks, time protocols, and time stamping techniques shifted the control over time to a circuit level patents owned by inventors and investors.

Whether as circuits, algorithms, rituals, or clocks, all governance machines reduce human action, history, and social institutions to a matter of cycles, patterns, signals, and data above and below the human scale. Technology as a problem of time control thus closes the future to the arbitrary rule of the inventors and the investors. It replaces the right of self-determination or the contingency of history with mathematical abstractions of natural and social phenomena on different scales. Instead of preserving time as a source of change, agency, and meaning, governance machines dominate the future and close it to one goal and control.

In order to capture how time became a resource for pervasive control, we will apply the classic dichotomy of time as Chronos and Kairos (Sipiora & Baumlin, 2002; Smith, 1969) on various instruments and prototypes from Chapter 4 to 8. Time as a linear, measurable, and external entity, or Chronos, is a mathematical abstraction defined by patterns and cycles in nature or society. As Kairos, it expresses opportunity – the personal and social agency and actions of people. Chronos is an abstract structure that eludes any personal or social action; it is a langue rather than an individual parole (Sanders, 2004), a strategy (institutions, power structures) rather than a tactic (individual use, adoption, or appropriation) (de Certeau, 2011).

Chronos is the core principle of all algorithms, rituals, and machines. It reduces individual life and social processes to predesigned systems that ignore commitment to a personal or collective project expressing Kairos (Kahn, 2019). In this book, we will use the classical Greek dichotomy of Chronos and Kairos (Sipiora & Baumlin, 2002; Smith, 1969) to summarize the tensions between structure and agency and the problem of legitimacy in algorithmic governance (Ananny, 2016; Kitchin, 2017; Ledford, 2010; Mittelstadt et al., 2016; Susskind, 2018). Governance as a matter of automation, algorithms, and Chronos brings a loss of personal and social agency over the future. In contrast to the measured and controlled time of Chronos that leads to governance machines and automation, the goal of public prototyping in liminal environments and sandboxes (Chapters 8 and 12) is to support Kairos.

We view Kairos as practices and tools that use time as a public good and medium of active, political life, or vita active (Arendt, 2013), which includes innovation and discovery. Time as a medium of agency is means tactical interventions, political and personal projects that use prototyping to explore both governance and technology (Chapters 12–15). Rather than outsourcing every decision to ontology or cosmology, prototyping for governance becomes a matter of Kairos. It is synonymous with taking responsibility for the future, risking, even failing, but making choices as individuals and communities without outsourcing them to cosmological forces. While time as Chronos results in systems and models imposed upon society that claim a superior knowledge of cycles and phenomena outside the history and lives of the citizens, as Kairos time supports personal and social agency and what Paul W. Kahn discusses in his origins of the legal order as a 'project' (Kahn, 2019) – political and social commitment, stakes in the future.

History and the Future Written by Victors

The origin story of Western philosophy – the prediction of olive harvest by Thales of Miletus (Mansfeld, 1985) – will serve as the starting point for our genealogy (Chapter 4). It shows how Chronos became an instrument of governance, promising predictions and control. Thales' 6th century BCE 'predictive analytics' over olive presses created the myth of automation that glorifies governance as a control over the future. However, it also offered the first critique of the myth of automation, later echoed in 4th century BCE passages in Demosthenes and Isocrates complaining about the time measurement over the water clock (clepsydra) (Landels, 1979) and the famous lament about sundials in Plautus (Gratwick, 1979; Landels, 1979; Henderson, n.d -b), discussed in Chapters 5–7.

Anecdotes and stories about the early clocks thus summarize the problems with bias, precarity, and lack of agency under algorithmic rule. They allude to the importance of democratizing innovation, discovery, and future-making to resist monopoly over governance machines and new infrastructures. Governance machines outsource human action, deliberation, and decision-making to clocks, calendars, or today's blockchain consensus mechanisms, machine learning algorithms, and other technologies. Negotiation, protest, and politics, as expressions of Kairos, become impossible under the automated governance over these new infrastructures.

Governance machines always claim higher ontological and cosmological truths as ideals for society while reducing politics to the metaphysics of data, patterns, and code – all modern expressions of Chronos. They impose predetermined goals automatically, rather than by seeking agreements among free citizens who deliberate and act together. Algorithmic governance in this sense is nothing more than a modern ritual that uses automation to control the future defined by stakeholders with power over new infrastructures. This ideal of automation then dominates current technocratic visions of 'government policies guided and informed by prediction markets' (Buterin, 2014), 'high powered cognitive technologies' in government' (Cummings, 2019) inspired by security assessments and penetration testing, or ideal of government operating like a 'lean startup' as envisioned by Tim O'Reilly, founder and CEO of O'Reilly Media (Brantley, 2014).

Similar visions of automated governance reduce political decision-making to a matter of control over the future and time, and they transform social and political processes into algorithms mocking the democratic rule. Instead of a historic opportunity to transform society via political action as a matter of time as Kairos, politics becomes a matter of ontology, cycles, and Chronos – a prediction market driven by investment in one predefined vision of the future, a penetration testing method that improves predefined requirements, or a lean start-up serving investors.

Technocratic governance thus enables the 'victors' to not only write history but also 'program' the future. Instead of Kairos as an opportunity for action by individuals and communities, governance and technology become a matter of Chronos, a measurable and programmable time with predefined future controlled by algorithms. The Chronos thus represents a political abdication that embraces cosmological certainty as a model for governance guaranteeing stability and profits to a small group of innovators and investors.

The ideal of governance as a well-designed, predefined, and automated system is at the core of Hobbes' social contract theory and the metaphor of the Leviathan or the ship without a rudder (Schmitt, 1996). In Chapter 8, we will discuss Hobbes' image of an ideal government as an artificial and super-human mechanism designed by humans to function independently of them while demanding unconditional obedience. Carl Schmitt's 1938 interpretation explains Leviathan's affinity with technology, since both enact the cosmological and religious promises of the ideal of an absolute (godlike) authority:

> Technically completed, man-made magnum-artificium, a machine that realizes 'right' and 'truth' only in itself – namely, in its performance and function – was first grasped by Hobbes and systematically constructed by him into a clear concept. The connection between the highest degree of technical neutrality and the highest authority is, as a matter of fact, not alien to the ingenious thinkers of the 17th century. At the end of Campanella's vision of the 'Sun state', there appears a large ship without a rudder and a sail but driven by a mechanism that is commanded and guided by the possessor of 'absolute authority'.
>
> (Schmitt, 1996)

Although the early anecdotes about clocks in Chapters 3 and 4 capture the technocratic dreams of algorithmic rule, it was Leviathan who imposed the technocratic rule as a universal and desirable goal. After Hobbes, automated 'contracts' became the only hope for society threatened by the uncertainty of Kairos as a 'state of nature' and 'war of all against all'. To understand how Chronos and cosmology became the ideals for governance, we need to revisit these tropes, metaphors, and anecdotes about innovation. They capture the origin of the technocratic reductions of governance to present-day prediction markets, lean start-ups, and RegTech attempts to integrate social norms into codes, guidelines, and constraints of various 'privacy, value, policy-by-design' (Cavoukian, 2009; Friedman & Kahn, 2002) and 'society-in-the-loop' (Rahwan, 2018) projects. The present governance machines only extend the control over the future and time from clocks to the automated social contracts and infrastructures that disrupt every aspect of personal and social life. To regain control over the future and time, we need to understand how prototyping became a form of teleology and then revive the forgotten histories of prototyping as a form of social and personal agency.

Chronos of Algorithms and Kairos of Prototyping

Governance machines that promise automated, blockchain, or AI-driven futures reduce the experience of time to impersonal and cosmological measurements (Chronos) that serve as models for society. Instead of personal or collective action, aspiration, and vision, rules become formalized, translated, and embedded into the code or design processes. Governance as a ritual, automated machine, and Leviathan makes time as Chronos the default. It reduces history and future to one goal-restoration (Instauratio) and progress in Chapters 5–7.

Chronos dominates society by imposing ahistorical and universal ideals that neither a person nor a community can question. The ideals become 'neutral' infrastructures – objective, impersonal, and 'just' machines that use models, algorithms, and data developed by experts and obeyed by everyone. Time as an opportunity (Kairos) for change becomes a resource for the new infrastructure as innovation. Someone has to design and maintain the supposedly 'neutral' rules of Chronos such as a ledger, a computer clock, a time log, or patterns in data. To reclaim the future as a commons and public resource, we must reject the ahistorical narrative of automated systems that embed deep structures of time, human nature, social behavior, or politics (Awad et al., 2018).

Algorithms are not mysterious entities at the end of history that we must obey like ancient gods through new automated rituals promising singularity or other absolute goals (telos) for technology, society, and history. They are the result of human action and knowledge, hybrids of Chronos and Kairos, combinations of insights, ideas and prototypes, agency, and structure. To save governance and politics as a matter of social and personal opportunity (Kairos), we must democratize prototyping and power over the future and time. The common future should be as much a matter of political choice as of design and innovation. While the genealogy of algorithmic governance addresses the ahistorical narrative of emerging technologies that embrace Chronos as the ideal for society (Chapters 4–7), the ethnographic accounts in Chapters 8–11 will capture Kairos as practice in hackerspaces and makerspaces that serve different visions of the future.

Prototyping, which supports Kairos in technology and governance, bridges the democratic deficits in shaping the future. It refuses to let innovators and their investors control time and the future. Instead of Chronos defined by corporate algorithms and data, we will propose sandboxes as places where time can be experienced as Kairos to engage citizens in shaping the future and insisting on time as a public resource (Chapters 12–15). Participatory proto-typing of algorithmic futures in sandboxes thus reclaims the control over the future and time as Kairos; it defines it as an opportunity to transform both technology and governance. Rather than imposing a future defined by a new infrastructure and its teleology, prototyping in the sandboxes supports exper-imentation and negotiations of preferred future(s).

Exorcism of Algorithms in Public Sandboxes

Inspired by the critiques of ahistorical narratives of technnological progress and automation in media archeology (Oliver. (Editor) Grau, 2007; Kluitenberg, 2006; Parikka, 2012; Zielinski, 2006), we will use the early time machines, the sundial and the klepsydra (water clock), to discuss collisions between the impersonal time of the universe (Chronos) and the very personal time (Kairos) defined by life, history, and politics. In the next chapters, we will show how prototyping of instruments became a design of governance machines that reduce politics to ontology and cosmology.

The dichotomies of Kairos and Chronos, agency and structure, parole and langue, project and system from Chapter 3 to 7 summarize the political scan-dal of automation. Automation promises efficiency and structure, but robs citizens of their agency over their time and future. When infrastructure becomes an instrument of governance, citizens resign upon personal and col-lective agency and time as Kairos. Their private and public lives become quantified and automated as serving the concept of time as Chronos. The genealogy of automation nevertheless also reveals forgotten and overlooked alternatives of time as Kairos that lead to the present engagements with pro-totypes in the liminal environments (Chapters 8–11) and sandboxes (Chapters 12–15).

The exploratory sandboxes challenge the genealogy of governance machines that control the future as a matter of automation. Rather than reducing decision-making to an ontology of mathematical models and natu-ral laws identified at a nonhuman scale and measured with scientific instru-ments or formalized as algorithms, the genealogy explores the meaning of action and prototyping as experiences of Kairos. These experiences are messy, hybrid, and liminal and stand above the certainty and stability of orbits, patterns, and various forms of Chronos. The genealogy of automation thus reveals the importance of time as Kairos, enabling human agency and action.

Prototyping governance means rethinking the individual and societal uses of time as Kairos in discovery and innovation. It means resisting the undem-ocratic and arbitrary rule of designers and their patrons and insisting on public engagement in the early stages of prototyping. The more automated and autonomous algorithms become, with their promises of regulated and controlled futures, the more we lose autonomy and agency as citizens and communities. Inspired by the forgotten history of instrument-making by artisans and natural philosophers in Chapters 6 and 7, we will identify alternatives to automation that defies the time as Chronos with its teleology of progress, restoration, or singularity.

In the current hackerspaces and liminal environments (Chapter 8), we see a model of prototyping that supports Kairos as experience of improvisation and ad hoc engagements that serve various needs, goals, and values. We will extend this model in the proposal for public and exploratory sandboxes in Chapter 12. Instead of enforcing the status quo of every new infrastructure that divides society into early adopters (developers and investors) and users (patrons and parasites), prototyping in the sandboxes is a struggle to define a common and public good. It is an ongoing struggle to preserve time as an open and shared resource that can serve various normative ideals embedded in the infrastructures for governance.

To preserve social and personal agency over the future, we must pay attention to time as Kairos in governance, as we do in technology. This means challenging the convergence of politics with technological infrastructures that reduce time to cosmological patterns, data, natural laws, or ontology expressing time as Chronos. To democratize future-making in the sandboxes, we have to insist on engaging the citizens in their futures as a matter of Kairos, an opportunity to change rather than obey predefined structures and commands. In the age of prototypes, citizens are stakeholders in their future, rather than mere users of future infrastructures.

Part II

Governance over Rituals and Machines

3 Genealogy of Algorithmic Rule

The origins of the myth of automation go back to the anecdotes about Thales of Miletus from the 6th century BCE. They capture ambiguous accounts of Thales' astronomical observations worthy not only of praise but also of condemnation. Thales, according to one of the anecdotes, became a millionaire who turned his knowledge of astronomy and meteorology into a prediction of olive harvest. According to another, he was a loser whose interest in the heavens caused a fall into a ditch. In one of the accounts, his knowledge of time as Chronos, measurable cycles and patterns in nature, leads to a prediction and good fortune. In another, it leads Thales to denounce a society dominated by such predictions that support the rule of merchants and aristocrats who mock his fall.

The origin story of Western philosophy in these two accounts of Thales by Plato and Aristotle captures the paradox of stargazing leading to a prediction as well as fall. It connects Thales' knowledge of astronomical cycles and time as Chronos to his free time, which we will interpret as Kairos. Kairos means time as an opportunity to discover, challenge, and act without certainty of expected outcomes and predictable future. It is time synonymous with freedom to act and agency to discover, innovate, and transform. A successful prediction as well as a fall into a ditch are legitimate outcomes of the freedom and time to explore, prototype, and question everything. Thales' prediction and fall capture the experience of time as Kairos, an opportunity for success and failure, or, as we will see later, discovery and leisure.

The anecdotes about Thales capture an essential attribute of a free Athenian citizen – his agency over time that uses cosmological insights to impact society. Thales is free to develop a new forecasting tool and challenge the power structures in society based on the insights into the structure of time (and space) – cosmology. In both cases, he uses his free time (Kairos) to discover and use the knowledge of time (Chronos) by either monetizing it as a business opportunity or criticizing the society that ignores the conditions which make such knowledge possible (free time and autonomy). Thales' insight into cosmology and ontology of cycles, patterns, and data (Chronos)

DOI: 10.4324/9781003189411-5

goes hand in hand with his agency and freedom of action (Kairos), described as freedom to explore and fail (care about things that no one cares about).

Thales' prediction, fall, and critique frame the problem of science, technology, and society (governance) as a question of control over time and the future. Since the sundial and the water clock (discussed further in Chapter 4), every new tool, instrument, and infrastructure promises control over the future while obscuring the source of that control – time as Kairos. The power of the new tools and instruments over the future conceals and makes us forget the aspirations that made them possible (Thales' critique of society that mocks his fall). Instruments and tools that take advantage of the insights into Chronos often reduce politics to a cosmology and ontology of cycles, patterns, and data. They support the fantasy of automation and algorithmic rule (Chapter 5). Yet, they also hold the potential for a critique that reveals unexpected origins, aspirations, and applications of Chronos and cosmology in politics (Chapter 6) or technology in governance.

Thales' forecasting tool as well as the early descriptions of clocks (Chapter 4) define the possibilities, contradictions, and excesses of time as Kairos and Chronos. They reveal the tension between knowledge of time as Chronos, constraining the future to predictable and even predefined goals, and the experience of time as Kairos, the freedom to act, discover, and open the future to new ventures. When technologies become infrastructures, they embody the control of time as Chronos, but as prototypes (Chapter 6) they support the experience of time as Kairos. Rather than closing the future to monopolies, the early prototypes of instruments (Chapter 6) and institutions (Chapter 7) open the future to personal and social projects. By using the accounts of Thales' stargazing, early clocks, and Renaissance instrument-making (Chapter 5), we will reflect upon the forgotten history of discovery and innovation that express Kairos in technology as well as governance and explore themes beyond the teleological promises of progress (genealogically linked to Francis Bacon's project of restoration – Instauratio – Chapters 5–7).

The genealogy of the early instruments will help us rethink the relationship between technology and governance as a problem of control over the future. Time as Kairos in the early prototypes is an experimental engagement with technology and governance that defines the future as a public good and a project open to personal and social action. To analyze the future as a public good, we will explore the forgotten history of Renaissance instruments (Chapters 6 and 7) and linked them to present prototyping in the hackerspaces in Chapter 8. The history of prototyping as an expression of Kairos and agency in Chapters 2 and 3 will then support a proposal for exploratory and public sandboxes in Chapter 12. The early Renaissance prototypes and experiments with technology and governance reinforce personal and social power over the future and time. They show how we can prevent political apathy that reduces social agency to algorithms, models, and other expressions of Chronos.

Algorithmic Rule over Olive Presses

Thales, according to Aristotle, created the first disruptive prototype or a 'device for the business of getting wealth (κατανόημά χρηματιστικόν – money making tool)', described also literally as a 'device to secure a monopoly (μονοπωλία)' (Aristotle, Politics, Book 1, Section 1259a, 1944a). The 'cunningly designed' (ἐτέχνασαν) tool was one of the first tools of predictive analytics and example of disruptive innovation (Johnson et al., 2008). It used the knowledge of cosmological 'Big Data' (Chronos) to monopolize the future while demonstrating the value of free time to do research and design (Kairos).

In Thales' anecdotes, knowledge of Chronos is a way to monetize signals, patterns, and data and challenge society. Thales controls the future and time by designing a tool for monopoly that disrupts society. He also 'controls' the future by exercising his personal autonomy and sovereignty as Kairos, by having time to explore, discover, fall, and even challenge society. Therefore, the relationship between action and knowledge in Aristotle's version of the story leads to the monopoly on olive presses so 'when the season arrived, there was a sudden demand for several presses at the same time, and by letting them out on what terms he (Thales) liked, he realized a large sum of money' (Ibid.).

Thales becomes an accidental millionaire whose goal is to show how easy it is for philosophers to become rich if they choose (βούλωνται – if they wish)' and that 'this is not what they care about (σπουδάζουσιν – in the sense of diligence, to be busy, eager to do something, dedicated and zealous about something, to examine or study seriously)'. Rather than making someone rich and powerful, the purpose of the disruptive innovation monetizing new knowledge is to perform the agency and interests of a free Athenian citizen and philosopher. 'Care' as spudazusin (σπουδάζουσιν) expresses the agency of the philosopher – it is an ability to influence the future by connecting cosmological insights with political action or social impact.

The insight into time as Chronos enables prediction and automation, but it does not dictate the decisions of a philosopher and free Athenian citizen. Thales' choices express his agency to explore, to instigate political change, or even fail by indulging in stargazing and leisure. His personal time is an experience of Kairos; it is action and freedom to explore and intervene into technology as much as society. In both Plato and Aristotle, the value of free and unstructured time as Kairos, an opportunity for success and failure, for serious research and leisure, is the prerequisite for knowledge of Chronos.

Thales' agency over his time overrides the knowledge of time, astronomical and weather data, patterns, and algorithms, leading to a monopoly and wealth. The monetization of time as Chronos is thus only one effect of being a free Athenian citizen with time to watch the stars, design predictive analytics tools, monopolize olive presses, or fall into a ditch. Insights into the cosmological (astronomical and weather) data and other phenomena of Chronos remain as important as the experience of time as Kairos, which defines Thales' personal agency.

Mocking the Rich with Big Data

Aristotle's passage on Thales captured how his time as Kairos enabled the knowledge of Chronos – the discovery of cosmological patterns and cycles serving predictions and monopoly. Free, unstructured time for stargazing also defines Thales' autonomy and agency in Plato's version of Thales in Theaetetus (Plato, Theaetetus, Section 174a, n.d.). Thales in Plato refuses to impress the wealthy and powerful citizens of Athens with his monopoly tool. Instead, he uses his insights into Chronos to mock the political, social, and economic elites and redefine the relationship between governance and innovation (discovery).

The Athenian elites in Plato's version of the anecdote laugh at Thales' stargazing and fall into a ditch. This provokes Socrates to make an important speech about the relationship between our values and knowledge, or governance (politics) and discovery (innovation), providing an early example of what we will discuss here as the use of technology to govern the future and society. The tensions between knowledge and action, Chronos and Kairos, in Socrates' speech on Thales, illustrate the theme of prototyping as an expression of Kairos. It expresses the agency over time and the future that leads to knowledge and insights about time as Chronos without being reduced to it.

Most commentators interpret Thales' passage in Theaetetus (from 174a) as a polemic against Protagoras' dictum that 'man is the measure of all things'. They view it as a defense of expert knowledge and science against rhetoric. While these readings of Theaetetus support Aristotle's image of Thales as an expert on celestial cycles and a designer of powerful tools, they ignore the more radical side of Thales' disobedience and agency. Thales' fall inspires Socrates to explicitly assert that governance is an experience of future-making and agency. He describes Thales as an 'expert' on the future due to his unique insights and critique of the existing status quo.

Thales is so distracted by his astronomical observations that he falls into a ditch before the eyes of 'a neat and witty Thracian servant girl' (Ibid.). The passage describes his 'distractions' as a type of leisure and indulgence in obscure interests in celestial phenomena that no one cares about: 'he was so eager to know the things in the sky that he could not see what was there before him at his feet' (Ibid.). Astronomy, as knowledge of Chronos, patterns, and data occurring on a nonhuman plane, makes the philosopher ill-equipped for mundane activities such as walking and making money, yet gives him a unique perspective on time. He becomes prone to accidents and phenomena of Kairos, also eager to criticize the political and social status quo mentioned in the following part (174e to 175b). There, Socrates uses the fall of Thales to explain how knowledge of cosmology challenges the illusions of the contemporaries about their wealth and ancestry.

Socrates performs a 'philosophical' use of Big Data, Chronos, and cosmology in this version of Thales. What Thales insights into Chronos reveal is that merchants and aristocrats hold naive views of their social and economic importance in the universe, which the philosopher unmasked. Wealth and ancestry are insignificant when compared to the large-scale phenomena in time and space that Thales studies: '… when he (Thales) hears that someone is amazingly rich, because he owns ten thousand acres of land or more, to him, accustomed as he is to think of the whole earth, this seems very little' (Ibid.). Rather than impressing merchants with a monopoly tool that preserves the importance of wealth, Plato's Thales uses his knowledge to mock the merchants.

The passage continues with a similar critique of the aristocracy. Thales mocks the inability of aristocrats to calculate the sheer number of ancestors and to comprehend the scale of time. To praise someone's noble lineage 'because he can show seven wealthy ancestors' is a 'dull and narrow vision'. It is a sign of a 'silly mind' and 'vanity'-or, worse, of a lack of education, for 'they cannot keep their eyes fixed upon the whole and are unable to calculate that every man has had countless thousands of ancestors and progenitors, among whom have in any instance rich and poor, kings and slaves, barbarians and Greeks' (Ibid.). Rather than supporting the status quo, Thales' knowledge of ontology and cosmology challenges the rule of merchants and aristocrats and inspires a critique of social norms.

Thales' cosmological insight into time as Chronos is part of what Plato describes as an insight into the whole (ὅλον-holon). It is an insight that is both politically and ontologically radical and reveals an exponential growth of generations over time or the immense size of the Earth exceeding human imagination and norms. With knowledge of the 'whole', Thales crosses the divide between politics and cosmology (or ontology). Instead of introducing a new infrastructure to maintain the monopoly and wealth, knowledge of Chronos mocks the wealth and lineage as values that determine power.

In Plato, Thales demonstrates cosmology and ontology (Chronos) that undermine the social and political order in Athens (experience of Kairos). The wealth of merchants or the noble lineage of the aristocrats are insignificant parts of the whole, the holon (ὅλον) that the new class of philosophers can 'calculate'. As a representative of this new class, Thales demands that lawmaking and governance become part of future decisions based on insight into the 'whole' of time (and space). The insight into the whole, the holon (ὅλον) – remains a result of free time to contemplate the stars and question the social and political order in Athens.

Thales uses his knowledge of the Chronos (scientific facts about the size of the Earth or the progression of time) to exercise his agency as a radical use of the future for governance. His insights into cosmology and ontology enable him to envision a future beyond the status quo of merchants and aristocrats. It is a future described as mellos (μέλλωis) – a care for 'whole' beyond the status quo. His insights into cosmology and ontology confirm the importance of the philosopher as a free citizen. It is someone with a power over time and the future as Kairos, an opportunity to research, predict, create a monopoly, or simply indulge in activities that may seem useless, ridiculous, or dangerous to the contemporaries.

Future between Control, Care, and Critique

In the famous passage from Theaetetus (177d–178a), the insight into the universe as a whole, the holon (ὅλον), gives Thales the autonomy to think and act like a god (176b) with respect to the future. Instead of an immediate advantage – future as ophemilos (ὠφέλιμος) that includes monopoly and prediction in Aristotle, Thales' future in Plato is about 'care' – mello (μέλλω, μέλλοντα χρόνον). It is a type of 'care' that also Aristotle mentions in the second part of his passage on Thales as spoudazo (σπουδάζω) – diligence, zeal, respect, eagerness (Thales studies and cares for things that no one else cares about).

In Plato, Thales' control over the future also implies nomos (νόμος), lawmaking, and governance, that try to achieve something permanent and binding even 'after time' (ἔπειτα χρόνον):

> If the question asked concerning the whole class to which the advantageous belongs; and that whole class, it would seem, pertains to the future. For when we make laws, we make them with the idea that they will be advantageous in after time; and this is rightly called the future.
>
> (Plat. Theaet. 178)

Plato uses the anecdote about Thales to contrast the merely 'advantageous' (ὠφέλιμος) future with the radical idea of a future as care and concern (μέλλω).

Future as matter of care then implies lawmaking and action, that is, 'advantageous' after time' (Ibid.), synonymous with the idea of the 'whole'. While 'advantageous' knowledge of cosmological cycles (Chronos) leads to monopoly or predictive analytics, when it includes care for the whole and for what will come 'after time', it brings a critique of the present. It implies a future that challenges the status quo and the bias of ancestry and wealth in society. Rather than confirming any status quo that claims to reflect cosmology, Thales' knowledge mocks the values of merchants and aristocrats in Athens as ignorance and incorrect application of the knowledge of cosmology.

Thales criticizes the 'predictable' and 'advantageous' futures and expresses his care for the future as a problem of governance and agency interpreted here as a matter of Kairos. The 'advantageous' (represented by the sophists in Theaetetus) simply signifies political apathy and resignation upon the search for better governance. It makes the future a matter of prediction, monopoly, or what we call a myth of automation. Plato, through Thales, looks for a different use of the future that implies care for governance, law-making, and politics as an open project (178c-e) or mello (μέλλω). Such a 'political' future engages citizens in parallel with knowledge of the universe and values in society, with time as Chronos and Kairos, with cycles and patterns in nature, as well as actions, values, and agency.

To illustrate the idea of the future as lawmaking (opposed to the control over monopoly and predictions), Plato then uses two surprising metaphors. One compares the care for the future (mello) with the 'connoisseurship' of wine and banquet food, while the other equates it to the art of 'making music that has never been played' (Ibid.). Connoisseurship and artistic creation define the care for the future as the ability to combine knowledge of the universal (food, sounds) with appreciation of the unique (new music or special tastes that only an expert can recognize), Chronos and Kairos, a celebration of friendship and life.

'Future makers' or 'lawmakers' like Thales balance the knowledge of ontology and cosmology (Chronos) with action (Kairos) described as expertise, connoisseurship, and artistic creation. To 'control' the future means, on the one hand, new prototypes and even predictions (monopoly). On the other hand, it means to care and create unexpected insights and visions about society like an artist or a connoisseur. Instead of a monopoly that rules over all, caring about the future is more like a banquet and symposium with friends, an authentic experience of friendship and a search for the common good.

The dichotomies of time as control and care (including connoisseurship and creation), Chronos and Kairos, monopoly and banquet, can help us explain the origins of the myth of automation. Its origins include the problem of prototyping, discovery, and creation of something new, a care for something that no one has cared about before. We argue that prototyping is a practice that either controls the future and closes it off to prediction or liberates the future as something public and open that embraces our agency as such radical interest in what might exist.

In the following chapters, we will use the examples of the early clocks and instruments (Chapter 5) to elaborate further upon the dichotomies that originated in Thales' anecdotes. In contrast to the monopoly tools and governance machines that reduced the future to the control of Chronos, we will examine Kairos as a radical engagement with the future (often leading to a critique). While the future as a matter of expert knowledge (Chronos) leads to predictive analytics (monopoly tools and governance machines), as an experience of connoisseurship and creation (Kairos), it supports personal and social agency.

Advantageous Contraption

Thales' anecdotes define the origins of Western philosophy as the problem of future and time control through science and technology. While Aristotle's version described the first monopoly tool that 'privatized' the future and time, leading to today's algorithmic rule, Plato's account introduced the concept of the future as care for governance and lawmaking. In Plato, Thales is neither a prophet nor an entrepreneur, but a philosopher and free citizen concerned with the future, which is described as a banquet or an art.

Thales exercises his epistemic and political autonomy as knowledge (of Chronos) that controls the future and time in two ways. He uses his free time as an opportunity (Kairos) to develop a monopoly tool that controls the future through a prediction (Chronos). At the same time, he insists on the future as a problem of lawmaking and a critique of the present (Kairos).

Governance as a problem of control over the future in Aristotle and Plato's anecdotes remains a challenge. Although the future under the rule of Chronos is defined by ontological and cosmological commitments, as a matter of Kairos, it becomes a medium of political agency. In both cases, Thales remains the ultimate lawmaker and 'modeler', insisting that his power over his time (Kairos) is as important as his knowledge of time and the 'big' cosmological data (Chronos). While his monopoly tool over olive presses strengthened the existing power structures in society, his critique challenged the ideal of a society, in which olive presses become the only value.

Thales' monopoly over olive presses hints at the possibility of algorithmic rule as a control over time, reducing politics to the ontology of patterns and data. However, the same insight into Chronos also challenges the logic of the quick fixes that define the future as an advantage and possible monopoly. In Plato, Thales defines the authentic experience of the future as an issue of good governance beyond the 'advantageous' monopoly:

> ...if he had not made his pupils believe that neither a prophet nor anyone else could judge better than himself what the future to be and seem... Both lawmaking, then, and advantageous are concerned with the future, and everyone would agree that a state in making laws must often fail to attain the greatest advantage?
>
> (Plat. Theaet. 179a-c)

Rather than being a reflection of the cosmological order of the universe, the future becomes an act of judgment and decision-making that challenges the balance and status quo in society. It is a future defined by attempts to regulate algorithms and invoke law that will shape the interests of various 'stakeholders', present merchants, and aristocrats. Thales' anecdotes, in this sense, show the central role of automation and time in our understanding of governance. Against the reduction of governance to a problem of automation and Chronos, we emphasize the forgotten, alternative, and little-researched accounts of governance as the experience of Kairos. Instead of the rule of governance machines that reduce politics to cosmology, we will explore the possibility of governing through prototypes that preserve politics as a matter of open futures and time defined as a commons.

The origin story of Western philosophy thus predicts politics as automation and algorithmic rule, but it is also a story of stargazing, agency, and the freedom to explore and question everything. Since Thales' monopoly contraption and his famous fall, knowledge of time as Chronos challenges our agency over time as Kairos. On the one hand, knowledge of time reduces the experience of opportunity (Kairos) to disruption and innovation, and to knowledge that privatizes the control over the future through various monopolies, computer clocks and algorithms, the modern-day olive presses, and governance machines. On the other hand, time as Kairos remains an opportunity to prototype and decide how to apply the knowledge to society. By using discovery and innovation to criticize and transform society, as Thales did in Plato's anecdote, we can explore the future beyond the promises of a monopoly.

In the next chapters, we will use examples of the early clocks and Renaissance instruments to explain how future-making and prototyping both reduce and preserve the experience of agency and Kairos (Chapters 6 and 7). We will discuss the relationship between Chronos and Kairos, timekeeping and timing, or infrastructure and governance, as a problem of prototyping and control over the future and time.

Hungry Parasites as the First Victims of Algorithmic Rule

> We've reached the point where this town's stuffed with sundials – while most of its citizens creep about all shriveled up with emptiness. Plautus, Lady from Boeotia
>
> (Jacobus, 2014)

While Thales' anecdotes discuss the cosmological cycles that govern society, the next fragment identifies an actual instrument of time and society control, the sundial. It is a fragment of a Roman playwright attributed to Plautus and quoted in Aulus Gellius (c. 125 – after AD 180) Latin 'commonplace' book *Attic Nights*, which consists of encyclopedic entries about famous authors and their tropes (Ibid.). The quote begins with a curse on Palamedes, the mythical inventor of the sundial in Athens, and ends with laments about a city full of sundials that turned its citizens into 'hungry parasites'.

The fragment is an explicit condemnation of the arbitrary 'algorithmic' rule of an instrument, the clock. It curses the instrument for reducing time to timekeeping and establishing the rule of an infrastructure as a cult of an old-new sun god. Whereas the early accounts of Thales' monopoly contraption ('model' based on astronomical data) remained ambiguous, the laments of the victims of the sundial are explicit and cautionary. The 3rd century BCE 'hungry parasites' accuse the clock and the rule of cycles and patterns (to which we could add data and algorithms) of injustice and control.

The complaints about automation as an arbitrary rule repeat with every infrastructure that claims to become a tool for better governance. We will call such infrastructures governance machines because they not only measure time or other patterns in nature (Chronos) but also enforce them as ideals for governance. Governance machines conceal the importance of time as Kairos in discovery and innovation and enforce the rule of cycles, patterns, and data (Chronos). They give an advantage to patrons, investors, and early adopters, while condemning the rest to become 'hungry parasites' whose plea Plautus captured.

The first victims of Chronos' rule are citizens deprived of the freedom to act (eat when hungry) and forced to obey the rule of an impersonal instrument of time control, the clock. Their empty stomachs in a city full of sundials recall a familiar trope repeated in current critiques of 'smart city' governance (Karvonen et al., 2018). New infrastructures that promise transparency and efficiency worsen the precarious lives of city residents. While governance machines claim universal and equal control over everyone and everything, they hide the power they bring to the few. Under the new infrastructure, most citizens become 'parasites' who have no role in the future automated society.

The 'parasites' in Athens and Rome are surplus class of citizens who have lost their purpose and agency in a society ruled by sundials and new infrastructures. Literary sources describe them as 'idle poor' while free citizens who have neither income nor work (Barbiero, 2018). They are forced to hang out in public places to seduce and entertain wealthy patrons to get a free dinner at their tables. This loitering earned them their name, parasitos, which literally means someone eating at someone else's table (Greek para-, meaning 'next to', and sitos, meaning 'food'). As a social and economic underclass, parasites predicted the future 'precariat' (Standing, 2019) and its loss of agency in an automated world of obsolete humans.

The original meaning of the term 'parasite' (someone seeking free dinner) precedes its biological use, which refers to an organism that leeches on another. In its original meaning, the parasite expresses a lack of relationship with the host, a degrading, and even dehumanizing condition. The parasite is not part of a functional unit, a society, or a body-politic, but merely a surplus prone to transgressions. There is neither a relationship nor a struggle between the parasite and its 'host' (patron), only occasional and arbitrarily arranged dinners controlled by the precise new clock.

The victims and patrons of automation thus do not form any politics or future together. Parasites' loss of agency over the future and time only anticipates future unemployment and general loss of rights and agency in a fully automated society. Like the parasites in the public squares of Rome or Athens, today's social media users waste their time on the semipublic platforms that monopolize their attention and time. They wait for their social media patrons to decide what and when they will 'consume' on the 'tables' that manipulate their emotional states and needs.

The 'hungry parasites' trope describes neither heroic nor tragic figures, but jesters. As victims of Roman globalization and economic inequality, the parasites faced similar challenges of redundancy as the modern precariat under the present automation and AI optimization. The only way for a parasite to express agency is to seek luxury, entirely dependent on the benevolence of the patrons. Parasites as transgressive subjects under the algorithmic rule then mark the resignation on politics and the common future (which we discuss as 'future making').

Transgressive Subjects under Automated Body Politic

The surplus citizens under the sundials or today's algorithms are neither political subjects seeking justice nor slaves devoid of any agency. They are 'bellies' who muddle through, survive, and even mock the system, as we read in another classic critique of timekeeping, Alciphron's book III, 'Letters of Parasites' (Henderson, n.d.-a). The passage satirizes the classical unity of the 'body politic' and presents hungry bellies that do not form a social and political unity or bond (body politics). The passage also alludes to the reign of false scarcity, urgency, and hidden slavery present in every governance machine since the clock, including today's algorithmic services.

Parasites' bellies do not coordinate as equal members of a society (public 'body'), nor do they respect any hierarchy (i.e., the head is above the belly). Instead of enacting the classic fable about society as coordination between the belly and its 'members' (Harvey, 2007; Jagendorf, 1990), these bellies serve no purpose. They are a surplus in a globalized and efficient society controlled by sundials that prohibit citizens from eating when hungry, even when food is abundant. Once introduced, artificial scarcity by sundials becomes a standard form of control, leading to the present algorithmic systems and infrastructures.

Timekeeping has automated and globalized society, turning citizens into parasites who do not control their own metabolism. Their only option is to be tolerated as guests on tables and platforms. In the past as much as in the present, automation reduces citizens to a surplus, a precariat, parasites, and jesters managed by patrons and their tables, platforms, and sundials. These victims of artificial scarcity and arbitrary control over new instruments that promise objectivity, transparency, and equality summarize what is the problem with the rule of governance machines.

Whereas in the past, as bellies under the clocks, the parasites lost their agency over their lunches and dinners, in the present, as aggregated data patterns, they have no power over any aspect of their lives. They serve the platform owners who offer them free services and 'meals' on the new tables and tablets of 'surveillance capitalism' (Zuboff, 2018). Like the 'freeloaders' of the past (which seems to be the most appropriate translation of the word 'parasite'), they are still idle poor that will never become members of any society or future.

Today's parasites are dehumanized 'infra-individual data and supra-individual patterns' of algorithmic systems (Rouvroy, n.d.). They are hosted by new algo (data) patrons who control and monetize their every click (infra-individual data) and profit from their aggregated data (supra-individual patterns). The story of the sundial and its parasites is a forgotten history of the future. It describes the early 'subjects' under the algorithmic rule (timekeeping) as permanently hungry, nihilistic, and cynical victims of the arbitrary rule of an instrument and its patrons.

The clock deprived the parasites of control over their own metabolism and needs, not to mention any prospects and future. It forced them to wait for the time to eat or to be fed on someone's table. In the context of automated body politics supported by timekeeping and other future algorithmic infrastructures, the numerous 'bellies' compete for an artificially scarce resource. Rather than seeking a common future or political unity, matters of 'governance' become matters of metabolism and management of scarcity. They metaphorically summarize the problem of optimization and control of the future: time becomes a resource of a system outside history or society, without a possibility for action, unity, solidarity, or community.

How to discuss this extreme loss of agency over the future and time that comes with every new instrument and infrastructure? What are the prospects for the surplus citizens as infra- and super-subjects of future blockchain, AI, and machine learning algorithms that claim better governance? What fables will capture their struggles? Is there any alternative to the reduction of citizens and political subjects to a surplus, precarious, obsolete, and transgressive parasites of the algorithmic platforms and tables?

To capture the reign of Chronos that enables algorithmic governance and leads to parasitism, we will take a closer look at the process of how instruments become tools of governance. We will discuss the convergence between ontology, cosmology, and politics that led to the ideal of automated governance and to the emergence of governance machines. While previous sections have described how sundials introduced control over the private lives and metabolism of citizens as parasites, the next chapter will focus on the water clock (clepsydra) and the theme of universal slavery. The clepsydra expanded the time control from private life to public institutions, further weakening citizens' power over their future and time.

To prevent the rule of the governance machine and Chronos, we must capture the genealogy of this resignation upon agency and the possibility of personal and social action (described as Kairos in governance as well as in technology in the next chapters). The ontological and cosmological search for cycles in nature and patterns in data prepared the stage for the pervasive control of society by Chronos, data, and algorithms. After discussing the persistence of the myth of automation and the rule of governance machines (Chapters 5 and 6), we will look at forgotten examples of instruments that introduce the idea of prototypes in governance beyond 'advantageous' monopolies and Chronos. We will use examples of Renaissance instruments (Chapters 6 and 7) and later open-science hardware (Chapter 8) to capture alternatives to the pervasive control over the machines of governance. As an experimental practice that connects questions of technology and governance, prototyping in the service of Kairos will define a model of experimental governance of technological futures in the exploratory sandboxes in Chapter 12.

4 From Rituals to Instruments

Since olive presses and sundials, the myth of automation defines ideal governance as the rule of Chronos. It is a rule of patterns, cycles, and insights from the nonhuman scale applied to society. Control over instruments that measure Chronos sidelined the political issues of unity, distribution, and hierarchy among the 'parts' in the 'body politic' and defined governance as a design problem. Rather than being a matter of opportunity and the 'right' timing (Kairos) for negotiation and deliberation, politics becomes a matter of pervasive time measurement and 'timekeeping' (Chronos), leading to control over the new instruments. Although the instruments promised to optimize the private and public lives of citizens, they only divided them into parasites and patrons of the new infrastructures.

The anecdotes about sundial and clepsydra (water clock) show how measured and predictable phenomena of nature, such as the solar cycle, become superior models for society. The cycles and patterns promise neutrality, stability, and predictability from a nonhuman scale as a solution to the arbitrary exercise of power and other excesses in politics. Under the various clocks and automated infrastructures that leverage AI, blockchain, and the Internet of Things technologies, the possibility of change and transformation (Kairos) becomes limited to science and technology. Kairos remains an experience of discovery and innovation, but not of social or political change or decision-making. Instead of deciding upon their lives, citizens under the rule of Chronos become a surplus in systems that monopolize their time and deprive them of agency or possibility to act and influence their future.

The transformation of instruments into governance machines marks the birth of algorithmic governance defined here as the rule of Chronos and the myth of automation. The persistent myth reduces politics to ontology and cosmology and defines governance as a matter of prototyping new infrastructures. While innovation and discovery express the experience of time as Kairos, human action and governance become effects of the new infrastructure and Chronos. Time as Kairos ceases to include social practice, political process, or decision-making. Instead, the examples of Kairos as political and social agency and opportunity for critique of the society become effects of the

DOI: 10.4324/9781003189411-6

arbitrary power of cycles, patterns, and Chronos that very few could question, resist, or change.

By transforming instruments into governance machines, we secularized the power of the archaic gods of Olympus and their celestial 'automation'. We applied the knowledge of cosmology and ontology to regulate human behavior and maintain the political status quo of those who design the instruments and the rest who become parasites. The transformation of rituals into machines of governance then reinforces the myth of automation and further reduces governance to a matter of insights, expert knowledge, or technology ensuring control.

While in the past it was myths, legends, and rituals that exercised such absolute power over society, after Thales it was the clocks and emerging infrastructures, including today's algorithmic services. Whereas in the past, capricious gods would occasionally commit transgressions and step out of line, the instruments exercise absolute control. They fulfill the promise of the myth of automation, which is absolute control of something claiming to be natural and necessary. While the gods made impulsive decisions or failed in their ventures (all examples of Kairos), no human or nonhuman can escape the power of the machines and algorithms as a means of control.

The sundial as an example of a governance machine is stricter than any sun god, including Helios, who often betrayed the other gods or mortals. By its design, the sundial as a governance machine is inherently incapable of making unpredictable decisions, having tragic and scandalous affairs, or fathering illegitimate children. With its cyclical and predictable patterns, it controls the behavior of the rich and poor, of mortals and gods, and even the entire universe. While concealing the arbitrariness of its first act, namely the discovery of cycles and patterns in nature, the instruments redefine the ideals of governance. Instead of the rule of opportunity and Kairos, governance becomes an opportunity to enforce the ideal of Chronos with its instruments, designed by the developers and engineers who serve as the priests of automation.

Governance machines reduce politics to new rituals through which designers, modelers, developers, and innovators rule and enforce Chronos as a universal dominion over nature and society. Clocks, as the early examples of algorithmic rule, define time as a matter of monopoly and control, imposing the myth of automation and its logic of an ancient cult. Thanks to Chronos, politics became a ritual and a worship of algorithms, models, patterns, and rules observed at a nonhuman level (e.g., the movements of the Sun, the behavior of users on social networks, and other aggregated data), even though neither Chronos nor its instruments were originally intended to become governance machines.

If we look at the early anecdotes about Thales' contraption (Chapter 3), they demonstrate the possibility of a monopoly as a reason to criticize and challenge the status quo in society. Rather than dreaming of a trustless and decentralized blockchain algorithm that synchronizes data in the ledger, or an AI algorithm that knows and predicts everything about everyone, governance was always an experience of agency that does not guarantee epistemic, ontological, or political certainty. To capture the lost experience of Kairos in governance reduced to technology, we have to look at the early critiques of timekeeping that highlighted the problem with the arbitrary rule of Chronos leading to present algorithms further enforcing precarity and slavery.

Arbitrary Power of the Sundial

When Plautus' parasite accuses timekeeping of 'breaking up' and quantifying (comminuit misero articulatim diem) the day into small parts (horas) full of misery (Henderson, n.d.-b; Jacobus, 2014), he expresses a very modern sentiment. He described a surveillance infrastructure that deprives citizens of the pleasure of eating when they are hungry. The infrastructure creates a false scarcity so that even when there is food, no one is allowed to eat:

> When I was a boy, my only sundial (solarium) was my belly, and it was easily the best and most reliable timepiece of all. On its giving you notice, you eat, except when there was no food; now, if there is it isn't eaten, unless it suits old Sol.
>
> (Henderson, n.d.-b)

By dividing the day into arbitrary parts (hours), the clock created the conditions for today's algorithms to extend artificial scarcity and indiscriminate control to every aspect of our lives and society.

The rule of arbitrary divisions and measurements through Chronos or later algorithms has the same effect as any other arbitrary exercise of power. It serves the interests of the few who benefit from the new tool, while depriving most of their ability to challenge and limit the new power. Chronos is an arbitrarily defined, predictable, and linear time that controls everyone and everything. Rich or poor, bellies, planets, or stars, all have to obey the rules of the clock as governance infrastructure. Designed by the accursed inventor (ut ilium di perdant, primus qui horas repperit quique adeo primus statuit hie solarium) (Ibid.), an ancient Mark Zuckerberg, the clock synchronizes the behavior of the masses at mealtimes. It subjects all citizens to scarcity under an arbitrary but universal rule of the Sun and its cycles.

Under the sundial, most citizens cease to be subjects of an existing or future political unity and society. They become bellies controlled by their metabolism, over which they have no power. This loss of freedom to eat when they are hungry predicts the future loss of agency under emerging infrastructures. The sundial as the origin of algorithmic governance demonstrates how time as Chronos deprives citizens of agency over their time as an experience of Kairos. Based on cosmological observation of the Sun's orbit or later patterns in the data, Chronos rules over private and public life and even biological needs such as hunger. It defines governance without political unity, without purpose, and even without subjects. Politics becomes a pure process outside history or any social context, a worship of the rule of the Sun or other phenomena of Chronos with new rituals and instruments.

The anecdotes about the sundial, clepsydra, and Thales' contraption describe the various forms of control over society by instruments as governance machines. As effects of Kairos, all instruments are prototypes that promise a better, more accountable, and more transparent future. It is a future based on independent measurements, avoiding error-prone and corrupt humans and institutions. The dream of governance by design promises security, predictability, and optimization based on instruments, but obscures the arbitrary moment of its invention that affirms the importance of action, agency, and time, such as Kairos.

The experience of Kairos as discovery and innovation is responsible for the clocks and future infrastructures that divided citizens into winners and losers, inventors on one side, and victims, jesters, and hungry parasites on the other. As parasites, citizens have to obey the false scarcity and quantification of time that define them as surplus bellies and later also manipulated patterns and data and subjects without influence over their future. Instead of negotiating power relations and responding to opportunities and risks (all phenomena of Kairos), politics becomes an effect of scientific and technological disruption. It is a disruption that establishes a rule of powerful inventors and entrepreneurs with their protocols and instruments that further expand the myth of automation with new rituals.

Automated Injustice with Clepsydra

Anecdotes of Thales' olive presses, Plautus' curse of the sundial, or the lamentations of the hungry parasites, all describe how Kairos capitulates to Chronos. Politics becomes a domain of designed precarity and false scarcity over instruments whose original purpose was exploration. The sundial as a technology that obliterated the autonomy and agency of the parasite belly, this 'hollow-surfaced shadow-receiving device' (Gratwick, 1979) was originally a scientific toy that supported the experience of Kairos – play, exploration, and engagement. Even in the 5th century BCE, it served as a popular entertainment for Greek aristocrats to discuss cosmology and philosophy, and only in the late 4th century BCE it became a 'clock' - an instrument that regulates mealtimes.

Control was further strengthened by the water clock (clepsydra), which influenced not only the private lives of citizens (meal times) but also public institutions by measuring the length of speeches at court hearings (MacDowell, 1985) or sessions in the brothels (Rosenzweig 2004). The linear, measurable, and impersonal time of natural phenomena and Chronos becomes a dominant model of how to manage public and private affairs, further undermining the experience of Kairos as an opportunity, chance, and complexity. While the sundial established false scarcity as a means of control, the clepsydra provides an early example of a tool that supports biases intrinsic in today's aggregation of data serving predictive analytics.

Clepsydra introduced timekeeping of speeches and quantification that brought similar effects as today's statistical analyses of social phenomena – bias and lack of justice: 'even double the amount of water (in the clock)... would be insufficient' (Demosthenes, 53.4, n.d.) to prevent the injustices of this new infrastructure for automation. Automatization and standardization of the length of speeches in the 4th century BCE triggered familiar complaints against bias in the quantification of social phenomena (Mennicken & Espeland, 2019). While the new infrastructure promised efficiency and transparency, it enforced its own agenda, which in the case of clepsydra meant shorter prewritten speeches doing injustice to the content. The short 'automated' speeches overtook the improvised ones, giving the early adopters – the sophists – an advantage of crushing the unprepared, often old claimants and political opponents.

In his play 'Acharnias', Aristophanes captures the 'algorithmic' scandal, which took place in Greece of the 5th century BCE. He accused clepsydra of tarnishing the dignity of a pacifist and opponent of the Peloponnesian War, who could not defend himself because of the measured speeches:

> 'Is this not a scandal?' What! the clepsydra is to kill the white-haired veteran, who, in fierce fighting, has so oft covered himself with glorious sweat, whose valour at Marathon saved the country!'
>
> (Aristophanes, Acharnians, Line 692, n.d.)

Instead of supporting justice, the clepsydra made justice 'mechanical'. It reduced justice to a controllable and automated 'algorithm' (defining the length of speeches) that served the new class of professional orators described by Plato as sophists.

The prewritten speeches for clepsydra laid the foundation for today's 'prewritten' smart contracts that automate not only the decision-making process but also the execution of the 'judgment', leaving no room for doubt, error, or ambiguity. Blockchain smart contracts or prewritten clepsydra speeches thus transform the individual cases into patterns analyzed by the algorithms to support efficient and 'fast' justice. Both serve the interests of the early adopters and designers but undermine citizens' expectations of justice, better governance, or nonarbitrary procedures. In Plato's dialog 'Theaetetus', Socrates further describes this 'mechanical' justice that sets out to execute rather than 'attain the truth' as slavery (Plat. Theaet. 174a).

In this famous passage, Socrates accuses the klepsydra of depriving the citizens of freedom, agency, and even leisure that we describe here as phenomena of time and life as Kairos. The klepsydra becomes the enemy of the philosopher, who is an exemplary free citizen like Thales, and whose agency and autonomy are synonymous with Kairos. Under the rule of klepsydra, citizens lose their freedom of action and agency over time (including leisure), and they resign upon experiments with the length and subject of their speeches.

The worship of Chronos leads to monopoly contraption, automatic (in) justice, and even censorship. It establishes the rule of the sophists, or the developers and designers who define the new rituals and protocols, acting as the priests of the new gods. Therefore, the rule of infrastructures is neither reflected nor negotiated, but enforced by 'accursed inventors'. With standardized and measured speeches in the trials, a precedent was for today's algorithms that produce a pathological society in which citizens act as what Socrates calls 'servants in breeding' (Ibid. 172d).

Sophists willingly submitted themselves to the extreme quantification of their speeches, which leads them to care only 'whether your speech is long or short' rather than seeking truth or insight into the whole (holon):

> The latter (freemen, philosophers) always have that which you just spoke of, leisure and they talk at their leisure in peace; just as we are now taking up argument after argument, already beginning a third, so can they, if as in our case, the new one pleases them better than that in which they are engaged; and they do not care at all whether their talk is long or short, if only they attain the truth.
>
> (Plat. Theaet. 172a)

When algorithms and time measurements dictate the actions of the citizens, the politics as Kairos becomes a forgotten practice. The Chronos reduces politics to a matter of designing new instruments, infrastructures, and platforms where, as the cliché goes, 'if you are not invited to the table, you are on the menu'. Before an instrument or infrastructure becomes an oppressive governance machine that controls time as Chronos, there is always an ambiguous effect of Kairos in technology as much as in governance. It is discovery and innovation, even disruption, that can serve different visions of the future and society. It is at this early phase of prototyping that we have to restore the importance of political agency and Kairos and democratize future-making.

Slaves of the Clepsydra

While the sundial ruled with false scarcity, clepsydra introduced false urgency and slavery, leveling everything to a matter of survival undermining the human agency and freedom. The sundial created parasites and patrons, but clepsydra turned all citizens into slaves 'racing' to save their lives:

> But the men of the other sort are always in a hurry – for the water flowing through the water-clock urges them on and the other party in the suit does not permit them to talk about anything they please, but stands over them exercising the law's compulsion by reading the brief,

from which no deviation is allowed (this is called the affidavit); and their discourse is always about a fellow slave and is addressed to a master who sits there holding some case or other in his hands; and the contests never run an indefinite course, but are always directed to the point at issue and often the race is for the defendant's life.

(Plat. Theaet. 172d)

The instruments of timekeeping, as predecessors to algorithmic governance, reduced all public life to a matter of survival, to trials and result-oriented activities that Socrates calls slavery. Rather than improving knowledge or governance, the instruments created an automated society that deprives everyone of the ability to make decisions about their future. Even sophists, as friends of clepsydra, end up becoming slaves to their own invention and 'servants of their arguments' in the passage of Theaetetus discussing the invention of clepsydra:

I like your saying that we who belong to this band (philosophers) are not the servants of our arguments, but the arguments are, as it were, our servants and each of them must await our pleasure to be finished; for we have neither judge nor, as the poets have, any spectator set over us to censure and rule us.

(Plat. Theaet. 173c)

To save autonomy and agency as the experience of Kairos, possibility of acting and changing the future, Plato (via Socrates and Thales) rejects the clepsydra and explores more radical uses of Chronos. Instead of a contraption that produces more sophists and slaves, he shows how Chronos could empower the citizen to discuss different values in society (Chapter 3). He draws on the anecdote of Thales' fall into a ditch to argue that knowledge of Chronos is means of a critique. In Plato's account, Thales uses his cosmological knowledge as a power to challenge existing stereotypes and injustices in society and inspire citizens to rethink and redefine the future as something beyond the immediate interests and benefits of different groups (merchants and aristocrats).

Future becomes an insight, but also action that challenges the status quo: 'studying the stars and investigating the universal nature of everything that is, each in its entirety, never lowering itself to anything close at hand' (Plat. Theaet. 174a). Plato's 'universal nature' and insight into the 'whole' thus support both the infatuation with Chronos (quantification and patterns in nature and the universe) and the insistence on Kairos as an agency. Both experiences and uses of time define agency and autonomy as the ability to use the insight into the whole (holon) to decide upon the future as free citizens and even lawmakers. Rather than resigning upon the future and reducing it to automation, monopolies, or algorithmic rule, philosophers like Thales use their insights into time and the future to improve governance.

Rituals, Science Instruments, and Governance Machines

Sundials and clepsydra, as the original governance machines, transformed personal and social life into predictable and controllable patterns that determine the right time to eat or the duration of sessions in courts. Today's infrastructures go further in this control of citizens' private and public lives through machine learning algorithms and consensus mechanisms. As instruments of Chronos, they model all social interactions, decisions, aspirations, and opportunities (Kairos) according to the nonhuman scale of data. To the extent that arbitrary models become 'factual' and 'evidence-based' policies, they further reduce citizens to controllable patterns, parasites, bellies, and slaves of systems that function perfectly well without them.

To discuss the transformation of instruments into machines of governance, we have traced the genealogy of the ideal of 'automated body politics', beginning with ancient rituals and clocks and leading to current attempts to 'code' governance. While this answered the question of when this change occurred, it remains unclear why we have reduced decision-making and agency to the inevitable but arbitrarily constructed Chronos? Why has politics become a matter of cycles, patterns, models, and data? The belief in structures superior to human agency is part of an old belief in rituals that leads directly to current fantasies of incorruptible algorithmic governance: 'For the evangelist, blockchain is not only a tool that facilitates decision-making processes but comes to stand in for the political process itself. This is "governance by design", where cryptographic protocols not only have politics, but are politics in the age of algorithmic governance' (O'Dwyer, n.d.). As Rachel O'Dwyer noted in her work on blockchain governmentality (Ibid.), the idea of certainty of the algorithms and data patterns promotes the ideal of political control.

Algorithms reduce political processes (Kairos) to logical conclusions described as chains of events (Chronos) that enforce an arbitrary epistemic certainty beyond human control. They become a model for governance, which O'Dwyer describes as 'algorithmic production' rather than the description of 'the real' leaving no 'contingency or space for disruption, critique or recourse' (Ibid.), discussed in this book as the experience of time as Kairos. Governance machines disguise the loss of agency to impose the myth of automation as an incorruptible and nonarbitrary control. Instruments enforce a magical belief in patterns and structures that are inescapable and 'true' because an algorithm 'decrees them' (Ibid.). They replace the experience of time as Kairos in governance with automation via Chronos defined by cosmology captured by instruments. The myth of automation then transforms all instruments into means of rituals and worship of the Chronos as predictable, predefined, and logical structures standing above the personal and social life.

In the anecdotes about clepsydra, sundial, and Thales' contraption, we can read the early warnings of precarity, false scarcity, and slavery that automated systems bring. They capture resignation upon agency, autonomy, and self-determination which precede the loss of governance and politics, described here as the rule of Chronos. The reduction of the social and individual experience of time (Kairos) to cosmology and ontology (Chronos) preserves the status quo of the various patrons with their clocks and tables. Whereas the history of the sundial and clepsydra captures the moments when instruments become governance machines, there is also a forgotten history of instrument-making as a practice that preserves time as Kairos in personal and public matters.

Renaissance artisan instruments took up the critical aspect of Thales' project, which emphasized open-ended views of governance as future-making and lawmaking discussed in Plato's anecdote. Thales' contraption and knowledge of Chronos enabled algorithmic rule, but they also emphasized the gap between theory and practice, or insight (into holon or Chronos) and action (Kairos), technology, and governance. Time as insight into Chronos and experience of Kairos in Thales not only leads to the monopolies and predictions but also remains an opportunity to fall, fail, and reconsider the values of society.

The same knowledge and data that produced the monopoly over olive presses supported Thales' critique of the society. While Aristotle admired Thales' prediction that controls the future, Plato warned us against such power that reduces the future to existing prejudices in society (wealth and ancestry). Plato's passages on Thales in Theaetetus introduced the idea of future as a matter of governance and lawmaking that preserve agency and the experience of time as Kairos. Plato defines governance as a search for an authentic experience of time, future, and agency closer to banquets with peers or composing new music rather than monopolizing existing political and economic power or asserting absolute control.

Renaissance artisans (Chapters 6 and 7), like today's open science hardware developers (Chapter 9), continue in the tradition of Thales' ambiguous 'contraption' and knowledge. They demonstrate the importance of personal and social action through prototyping that supports Kairos in technology and governance. The genealogy of prototyping in Chapter 3 and the ethnography of direct engagement with science and technology in open and citizen science projects in Chapter 9 will show how prototyping saves the experience of time as Kairos. It will help us to define a proposal for an experimental governance of technological futures in the exploratory sandboxes that explicitly link the work on the technology with governance in Chapter 12.

5 From Instruments to Governance Machines

Cosmology, Ontology, and Politics

Resignation upon Kairos in governance repeats with every instrument and technology. Superior knowledge of data, patterns, and cycles promises to automate governance over machines but conceals the divisions that it creates between hungry parasites and patrons. In a recent critique of algorithmic governance, Evgeny Morozov captured the enslavement over new (algorithmic) infrastructures with familiar tropes of scarcity and urgency. He accused Silicon Valley 'sophists' and 'patrons' of securing their profits over the new infrastructure for governance while imposing austerity on parasites deprived of agency:

> Algorithmic regulation is perfect for enforcing the austerity agenda while leaving those responsible for the fiscal crisis off the hook. To understand whether such systems are working as expected, we need to modify O'Reilly's question: for whom are they working? If it's just the tax-evading plutocrats, the global financial institutions interested in balanced national budgets and the companies developing income-tracking software, then it's hardly a democratic success ... Algorithmic regulation, whatever its immediate benefits, will give us a political regime where technology corporations and government bureaucrats call all the shots.
>
> (Morozov, 2014a)

According to Morozov, attempts to 'automate' regulations lead to enslavement 'by design' that prevents political deliberation and transformation. These interventions prevent discussions about the causes of the crisis, or reflections upon the context, values, and aspirations. Algorithmic regulations simply impose decisions and values that claim to be universal, while further diminishing the importance of personal agency and social action. In Morozov's example, algorithmic regulation as a solution to the financial crisis ignores the causes of the crisis. It imposed 'automatic' austerity that benefits only those who designed the systems and rules. Such a critique echoes Plato's theme of hidden slavery and Aristotle's monopolization of the future, including the control over urgency and scarcity (Chapter 4), responsible for the division of society into patrons and parasites.

DOI: 10.4324/9781003189411-7

When we apply algorithms to governance, we reduce the questions of politics to a cosmology and ontology of data, patterns, and Chronos that promise an ideal, transparent, and universal rule benefiting the early adopters, designers, and investors. We tell a modern story about a magic infrastructure that works like a devil's bridge. It promises omnipotence, but hides the caveat about the future, the need to sacrifice our 'firstborns', our ability to act and define the future. Legends about devil bridges always include a human sacrifice that metaphorically depicts the loss of agency. Enchanted by the new infrastructure, we surrender our personal autonomy to automation. Instead of being citizens who experience time as Kairos, an opportunity to question, negotiate, and decide on the future, we become slaves to Chronos and its monopoly infrastructure.

Algorithms claim universal patterns in nature and society, but their use in politics is neither universal nor just; it is arbitrary and without a clear mandate. From clepsydra and sundials to blockchain technologies, all algorithms, patterns, and cycles create predictable and profitable futures for the few while foreclosing the opportunities for the many. Instead of enabling citizens to negotiate agonistic interests and futures, algorithms lead to a resignation upon shared future(s). Chronos outsources decision-making and deliberation to blockchain consensus mechanisms, machine learning (ML) algorithms, and other magical infrastructures, depriving everyone of agency. It generates parasites dependent on new infrastructure, sacrificing their agency and open future for the ideals of progress or restoration (Instauratio discussed in the next chapter).

Governance machines bring automated biases, hidden slavery, mechanical injustice, and time control by new patrons and innovators. Instead of reconciling the ontology and cosmology of Chronos with politics and governance serving Kairos (discussed as a dichotomy of structure and action, or timekeeping and timing), the instruments impose one future that will rule all. To resist control of time and the future, we emphasize the acts of 'creating', designing, and making decisions about technology as much as governance. Instead of becoming parasites, we should strive to be like Plato's connoisseurs and artists who indulge in the uniqueness of their experience rather than promises of universal control. Instead of excessive control and automation, the prototypes that we will describe in the next chapters, support the efforts to create a shared public future.

Kairos and Chronos, Timing and Timekeeping

The reduction of politics to cosmology and ontology is based on the discovery of time as Chronos, concealing the importance of time as Kairos. Chronos provides insights into patterns and phenomena that transcend human life and society and imposes them as an ideal of governance as automation. The anecdotes about Thales in Aristotle and Plato capture the origins of this admiration of Chronos leading to prediction and control of the future. In Aristotle,

Thales predicted the future based on observable cycles and patterns in nature to perform the philosopher's ability to use time for creative endeavors and research. In Plato, Thales uses the same insight to openly reject the status quo in society, dominated by the values of wealth and lineage.

Timekeeping instruments, starting with Thales's contraption and various clocks, quantify and stabilize the phenomena in nature., By proxy, clocks then stabilize society by dictating citizens' behavior, such as when to eat or how long to speak in court (Chapter 5). Governance under the rule of Chronos becomes a matter of a design of an infrastructure that promises further automation and control over the future through algorithms, such as consensus mechanisms or ML. To save the personal and social agency that guarantees an open and public future, we need to make visible Kairos and actions associated with discovery, innovation, negotiation, and decision-making. Opportunities, insights, and the right timing are as important for governance as they are crucial for innovation and technology (and in both cases they come with risks and uncertainties).

The tensions between the two concepts of time, Kairos and Chronos, timing and timekeeping, define the central challenge in prototyping for governance. On the one hand, time is about opportunity, the right timing, and action that take place in both technology and politics. On the other hand, time is a chronological process determined by the patterns in nature and universe that we impose on society. To save public time and the future as Kairos in politics and not just in technology, we need to increase the participation in innovation and discovery and prevent the reduction of citizens to a surplus in a system.

The dichotomy of Chronos and Kairos is an ambiguous one; it is fluid and complementary. It expresses a tension between natural systems and political projects, between langue and parole, or between structure and action. Initially, the two concepts of time were interchangeable, so Kairos meant right timing but also 'due measure' or 'proper proportion' referring to the immutable laws of the universe, such as the seasons in Hesiod's works or the days and numbers in Pythagoras (Sipiora & Baumlin, 2002). As an opportune moment to act, express vulnerability, or even mortality (e.g., in the Iliad), Kairos gradually contrasted with Chronos, which became an external structure that describes ontology or cosmology (Ibid.). Kairos became a matter of context, chance, and action, and as we claim agency as the ability to transform, challenge, disobey, explore, and experiment.

While in science and technology, we embrace Kairos as a matter of discovery and innovation, in governance we seem to resign upon time as Kairos. Time as an opportunity for transformation (Kairos) in science and technology brings new knowledge, prototypes, and infrastructures. In governance, it is the essence of the political process that includes disobedience, protest, deliberation, and negotiation. Imposing science and technology insights as Chronos on governance is a decision that embraces automation, immutability, and predictability as ideals for society. It embraces governance machines that promise to regulate society 'by design' without a political consensus or even representation in the processes of designing such futures.

Time as Chronos promises to control, model, and predict phenomena in nature as well as in society. It diminishes the importance of social and political agency and action as matters of opportunity or chance (phenomena of Kairos). Instead of supporting citizens in making decisions about their future, it emphasizes the control of human behavior guided by hidden patterns. Governance under the rule of Chronos regresses into myths, magic, and devil's bridges that promise universal rules expressed in code or RegTech solutions (Maupin, 2017). The ontological and cosmological certainties of Chronos obscure the benefits and interests of the new patrons in the platforms, infrastructures, and tables that transform the rest into hungry parasites.

Governance over Technological Myths and Rituals

Many philosophers in the past accused science and its instruments of weakening or even destroying public life and politics (Arendt, 2013), the basic structure of human experience and consciousness (Husserl, 1970), or even being (Heidegger, 1977). They blamed instruments for introducing a nonhuman perspective and scale of planets and atoms into human affairs that relativize the personal and social struggles on the planet or in society. Automation through instruments and infrastructures further exacerbated the problem with outsourcing politics to an ontology and cosmology ignorant of the 'being' (Patočka, 1996) or actions that change history and politics (Arendt, 2013).

When the predictability of orbits, patterns, or data becomes a model for society, we resign upon Kairos in our actions and decisions. Knowledge of Chronos in nature and universe becomes the ideal that promises to turn contingent phenomena in society into something stable, predictable, and natural. Like rituals and magic before, new instruments and infrastructures suppress any dissent and even punish political action, agency, vision, or values that question the 'natural' and necessary order.

Roland Barthes described this 'naturalization' of political phenomena as a myth inherent in all modern media and technologies. Myths and rituals decontextualize and depoliticize human actions and speech. They reduce them to the innocence and security of an absolute truth and certainty that are based on a nonhuman scale:

> Myth does not deny things; on the contrary, its function is to talk about them; simply, it purifies them, it makes them innocent, it gives them a natural and eternal justification, it gives them a clarity which is not that of an explanation, but that of a statement of fact.
>
> (Barthes, 1993)

In a world where AI, blockchains, and various forms of automation predict and control every feeling, action, and idea by providing the 'natural and eternal justification (and) clarity' (Ibid.), we are governed by myths and ritu-als. Neither individuals nor the communities can question or change the absolute control and authority of the hidden patterns claiming to represent the natural and universal order:

> In passing from history to nature, myth [and we can add code] acts economically: it abolishes the complexity of human acts, it gives them the simplicity of essences, it eliminates all dialectics, with any going back beyond what is immediately visible, it organizes a world without contradictions because it is without depth, a worldwide open and wal-lowing in the evident, it establishes blissful clarity: things appear to mean something by themselves.
>
> (Ibid.)

When we reduce governance to rituals based on Chronos (natural cycles, algorithms, data), we neglect 'the complexity of human actions' (or what we call Kairos) and impose the rule of the myth of automation. Algorithms become something of a technological folklore for which no one is responsible but which everyone obeys and reproduces since it represents the hidden order in society and nature. Like folklore and myths in the past, algorithms in the present pretend to be something that has existed since the beginning of time in a world that is 'without contradictions...' without depth, a worldwide open and wallowing in the evident, it establishes blissful clarity' (Ibid.)

Chronos, as the essence of the myth of automation and algorithmic rule, transforms governance into a technological ritual that divides society into patrons and hungry parasites. Chronos defines the quantification of time that abolishes history but also the 'complexity of human action' (Kairos) and enforces the 'blissful clarity' and slavery of 'Big Data' patterns, powerful consensus algorithms and hidden ML insights. It makes impossible to resist the rule of the new cursed inventors, patrons, and their governance machines that deprive everyone of agency. By recognizing how Kairos enables proto-types and knowledge, we can restore political agency and define alternatives to governance machines. Prototypes as tools of governance make visible and contestable the choices that individuals and communities make in response to the opportunities and challenges in both technology and governance.

To save democratic governance, we must preserve the importance of Kairos, time as an opportunity for action and decision-making. Prototyping for public and open futures, explored in Part III, opposes the automation and algorithmic rule as myths and rituals that turn citizens into hungry parasites dependent on the tables and platforms of their patrons. Against enslavement by Chronos imposing patterns and cycles from the micro and macro scales upon society, time as Kairos supports the experience of participation, reflec-tion, social, and personal interaction. By rejecting the myth of automation, prototyping embraces the paradoxes of Chronos and Kairos in technology and governance and saves the future as open and public good.

Dissenting or Bending the Sundial Pointer

The technocratic attempts to reduce politics and governance to automation and cybernetic control make prototyping a central concern for saving democracy. Prototyping restores Kairos in governance as a matter of agency against the rule of Chronos as the certainty and predictability of patterns and cycles. Instead of reducing values, visions, and governance to predetermined patterns expressed in code, prototyping 'translates' them into material engagements with 'future making'. It supports the negotiation, exploration, and testing of both values and code. Thus, prototyping restores the future as a matter of personal and social agency or Kairos, described by Hannah Arendt as 'active life' (vita active) and the ability to 'begin something new and of not be able to control or even foretell its consequences' (Arendt, 2013).

The open future is an effect of personal and social agency over time that defines the conditions for democratic rule as an experience of time as Kairos. When we renounce Kairos in governance, we accept the fate of the Greek or Roman parasites under the rule of the clocks. Like characters in book III of Alciphron's 'Letters of the Parasites' (Barbiero, 2018), Trechedeipnus and Lopadecthambusa (Dinner Chaser and Dish-crazy), we stop questioning the rule of the sundial and try to trick the pointer of the 'hateful clock' to deceive the patron's slaves who announce mealtimes.

The parasites under Alciphron's clock resigned upon their agency to such a degree that they even joke about suicide by attaching themselves to the sundial and bending the pointer of the clock to run faster. Instead of cursing the clock and its inventor, as the parasites do in Plautus' story (Chapter 5), in Alciphron they regress into caricatures and parodic attempts to hack the instrument that is softly killing them.

Sundials are infrastructures that claim to embody cosmological truths and laws while reinforcing the patron's power, rigidity, and fixation on the absolute and universal rule (and truth) of Chronos in society. Consumption of food in the right time represents the submission of the parasites that becomes a blueprint for all future surveillance and control. The new rituals of consumption and behavior signal an 'elite conception of time as an immovable barrier to the satisfaction of physical hunger as the sundial itself. The clash enhances the impression of the vast difference between the parasites and their masters' (Barbiero, 2018).

The insistence on clocks as public infrastructure or even a public good serving everyone equally only strengthens the rule of the patrons. While the visible and 'transparent' pointer of the sundial expresses the higher truths about nature, cosmology, and mathematics, it also preserves the power of the patrons over the parasites. The patron, sundial, and sun perform together the power over time and the future that connects ancient rituals and myths with present technologies.

Myths and rituals are the origins of automation that show how the certainty and stability of the solar cycle or similar patterns in nature serve as a preferred model for governance for the elites. The universal power of time as Chronos rules over the individual uses and experiences of time as Kairos. Time becomes a 'public' infrastructure for governance that claims to organize and protect citizens against chance and arbitrary phenomena of Kairos. Nevertheless, time as Chronos also imposes arbitrary defined cycles and patterns mediated by instruments that serve the interests of patrons.

Instruments as governance machines embrace the narrative about an infrastructure for the public good. They worship the 'objective' measurements and algorithms that nonetheless serve the private interests of the patrons, for example as Decentralized Autonomous Organizations (DAOs) proposed by their Silicon Valley patron, Ethereum inventor Vitalik Buterin, as the future of governance. Buterin describes this new 'clock' as something visible and transparent for all, an infrastructure that makes it structurally impossible to cheat. The pointer of this new 'clock' – the decentralized public ledger whose code and transactions are visible to all – not only 'makes it obvious to everyone if they start to cheat, but rather it is not even possible for the organization mind (set of smart contracts) to cheat' (Buterin, 2015).

The 'unbendable' pointer of the Ethereum machine, like the sundial pointer in the Alciphrone passage, represents the power of patrons over parasites. In the case of Ethereum, the patrons are the developers with the power to bend and make decisions about the public (open source) algorithms that synchronize the nodes in the new 'clock'. The arbitrary power of these developers to alter and even fork the 'public' infrastructure and bend the new pointer became visible only after the 2016 attack on DAO. What it revealed was that all clocks, computers, networks, and infrastructures, including blockchain ledgers, exaggerate their public good function of "resistance" to 'bending' and hacking. Although the 'pointers' perform timekeeping and Chronos, time for data synchronization in networks and ledgers, their design is neither universal and transparent nor truly public and unbendable or unhackable.

Instruments and prototypes often obscure their vulnerabilities and arbitrary origins (Kairos). They impose themselves as infrastructures that represent the public good. They use universal patterns in nature or measurable states of the networks to define new governance machines. As ideas, opportunities, and examples of innovation (Kairos), they claim to represent something universal, certain, and measurable (Chronos). However, their design is neither universal nor natural or necessary. It is an arbitrary result of prototyping, knowledge, and Kairos that expresses the agency of inventors and patrons to close the future for the parasites.

Time as Chronos, controlling dinners, transactions, and other social interactions via clocks and decentralized ledgers, obscures the actions as Kairos, design and governance decisions responsible for the new infrastructures. There is always someone with a power to bend the pointer or fork the ledger and define how data are synchronized or resources shared. Another issue is the dependence of most emerging technologies on infrastructures that precede them and enable them to work. Even if we continue to decentralize the processes on the ledgers with different consensus mechanisms, we will never fully decentralize the actual computer clocks.

The design of the clocks determines the ledger synchronization no matter how democratized the new infrastructure claims to be:

> Time is essentially a representation of the universe current global state. This means that for any given moment, every single entity must share the exact same value. This is obviously a huge problem for computers: let us assume that there is a huge, highly accurate atomic clock in the middle of the universe, transmitting time data across the Internet. One small problem: transmitting data takes time by itself. When a device receives time data over the Internet and applies it to its own systems, the universe global state (time) would have already changed. In other words, it is impossible for a networking device to be perfectly up-to-date with the actual global time value.
>
> (Hong, 2020)

Time in short defines agency and power. Clocks, blockchain ledgers, and other 'public' infrastructures represent the power of patrons and designers to define the future over new instruments. In order to resist the fate of the hungry parasites and slaves who lose their power to new clocks, we must restore agency and control over prototypes and Kairos in governance, as well as in technology.

Governance over Prototypes

Instruments as governance machines promise absolute and universal control over time and the future. They are the progeny of Thales' monopoly contraption that restore cosmology and rituals as means of governance. They also reintroduced cosmological cycles and other patterns in nature as means of limiting the agency of citizens.

Prototyping as an opportunity (Kairos) to governance transform the future is seized by patrons and inventors who impose Chronos on the parasites or citizens who do not participate in the design and creation of the new table, platform, machine, network, or ledger. To avoid the fate of hungry parasites and save the open future and time as a public good, we need to rethink practices and engagements with prototypes. These engagements should include Kairos and prototypes that make the future less predictable but more open and plural.

Inventors who design new infrastructures often parade their power as a public good, while serving the technocratic dream of a control through automation by means of machines, algorithms, and data. Their infrastructures reduce the experience of time as Kairos in governance to monopoly contraptions and instruments that rule the citizens and transform them into surpluses and parasites. To save agency over time and the future, we need to preserve the 'momentum' of Kairos and make technology more 'democratic' and open to interventions, rather than 'technologize' and automatize democracy.

In the next chapters, we will explore the forgotten examples of prototyping that support the ideal of open futures and time as Kairos in governance and technology. We will start by discussing the genealogy of Renaissance instruments (Chapter 6) and institutions (Chapter 7) that introduced future-making as a public effort and goal. The prototypes of instruments in the Renaissance period not only lead to the ideal of progress but also open future and exploratory prototyping practices in the hackerspaces (Chapter 9) that offer a model for sandboxes as environments where governance meets technology (Chapter 12).

We will use examples of artisanal Renaissance instruments (Chapters 6 and 7) and do-it-yourself and open science hardware (OSH) practices (Chapter 9) to illustrate how prototyping opens the future for engagement and deliberation. Artisanal instruments reenact the experience of Kairos in governance and technology that embody different practices of knowledge creation closer to the philosophical concepts of paradigms, exempla, and regula (Chapter 6) that connect 'living' with 'knowing' and Kairos with Chronos.

The Renaissance instruments and the OSH prototypes in hackerspaces (Chapters 6 and 9, respectively) revive the original mission of Thales. He used his time and agency as Kairos to define the power of time as Chronos (time measurement and prediction of cycles), while criticizing its absolute and universal control. His actions expressed the freedom to explore things that no one cares about and to resist the dangers of automation and monopoly. The ambiguous knowledge of Chronos created the monopoly but it also mocked the existing power structures.

Renaissance artisans and today's geeks, hackers, and makers revive the ambiguity of Thales' project, which offers a model for public engagement with science, technology, and governance. It is a model that challenges the idea of absolute and universal control over the future and time or Chronos by being free to design new prototypes and generate new knowledge. The ideal of automation defines history as a matter of progress or restoration (Instauratio, discussed in Chapters 6 and 7) that reduces governance to a ritual and a monopoly. To avoid the reduction of governance to a matter of automation, we should follow Thales and insist on the value of Kairos as the ability to discover new phenomena in nature that question the political status quo.

Thales' anecdotes capture the ambiguous origins of Western science, technology, and philosophy as a time control (via Kairos and Chronos). To answer the question of why and when Kairos was reduced to technology, we used the genealogy of clocks (Chapter 5) and showed how it imposed Chronos as matter of governance. In the next chapters, we will describe artisan instruments (Chapter 6) and today's open science hardware prototypes OSH (Chapter 9) that highlight the importance of Kairos in governance and not only technology. These examples of instruments that support Kairos in governance will inspire the proposal for exploratory and public sandboxes in Chapter 12. They show the importance of personal and social engagements with the future and time over prototypes that test and explore different views of technology and society or time as Kairos and Chronos.

Governance that uses algorithms, models, and decentralized ledgers reenacts the myth of automation. It is a myth that reduces politics to cosmology and ontology and imposes the rules of rituals, (timekeeping) instruments (Chapters 4 and 5), and infrastructures serving the patrons. Against the concept of governance as control and automation over patterns and cycles of Chronos, we emphasize the experience of time as Kairos. It defines governance as a problem of personal and social agency that involves radical uncertainty, improvisation, and the negotiation of the future. In the next chapters, we will discuss how Renaissance (artisan) prototypes of instruments both supported and problematized the ideal of governance as automation, monopoly, and control over the future.

6 Prototypes as Paradigms, Cosmoscopes, and Living Instruments

The two notions of governance as an engagement with the future that emerged in the anecdotes about Thales define the practices of prototyping discussed in the next chapter. On the one hand, prototypes of Renaissance instruments affirmed the ideal of Thales' monopoly. They became means of the Francis Bacon project of science serving the restoration of a promised order in nature and society (Instauratio or later (Latin) progress). On the other hand, Renaissance prototypes also echo Thales' gesture of using knowledge of cosmology and Chronos to challenge society. Such instruments reject the teleological ideal of progress or restoration (Instauratio) and emphasize overlooked practices of meaning-making supportive of personal and social agency, discussed here as paradigms, analogies, and models (Agamben, 2009b).

Prototypes define good governance as either the pursuit of automation and Chronos or the opportunity for change, transformation, and agency described as the experience of Kairos. We use the dichotomy of Chronos and Kairos to discuss the reduction of governance to patterns, cycles, algorithms, data, or ledgers that define promissory infrastructures for governance (Chapters 3–5). Against the rule of such infrastructures as 'governance machines' that reduce politics to cosmology, we will now investigate prototypes that open the future and technology to personal and social engagements.

Starting with Thales' prediction of the olive harvest, instruments began to reduce the experience of time as Kairos to disruptive innovation that monopolizes the future. This reduction of politics to cosmology supports the status quo of patrons and hungry parasites (Chapters 4 and 5), and closes citizens' futures to the rule of quantification, false scarcity, loss of agency, and slavery. Under Francis Bacon's 16th-century project of the Instauratio Magna (Great Restoration), the rule of Chronos and governance machines even extends to institutions entirely dedicated to controlling the future as progress.

Bacon's proposal for the Academy of Sciences defined modern governance as a project that supports science and technology serving the ideals of Chronos as control over the future and time. Knowledge of cycles (Chronos) enables a monopoly that became a model of disruptive innovation supporting the new patrons and further enslaving the parasites. According to Bacon, only powerful patrons guarantee the project of Instauratio,

DOI: 10.4324/9781003189411-8

the restoration that fulfills God's promise to humanity to rule over nature (Iliffe, 2000; Whitney, 1989). The ideal future is based on teleological promises of restoration that later morph into the enlightenment project of progress. It is a future that repeatedly reenacts the anecdotes about patrons and their parasites with new means and infrastructures.

Restoration and progress define the prototypes of instruments and infrastructures as new patron's tables. They pretend to be neutral and public infrastructures that promise free dinners to parasites while enslaving them. The ideal future as Instauratio and progress then reduces all questions of governance to issues of control over the innovation, discovery, and disruption. By extending control over time and the future from instruments and infrastructures to the institutions (Academy of Sciences), Bacon further strengthens innovation and discovery as the only goals of governance.

In what follows, we will investigate prototyping that resists the teleological ideal of instruments serving new monopolies and closing the future to one goal. Mechanical artists and natural philosophers in the Renaissance period explored various personal and social projects that preserved the value of time as matter of Kairos against the enchantment with Chronos.

From ancient clocks to blockchain technologies and models, prototypes define social expectations about science and technology in terms of the future and good governance. They promise scientific and technological progress, which reduces the question of governance to the control of the future and monopoly. However, the same instruments also enable new questions about values in society, new attempts to define the boundaries of the community, and common goals. Instead of reducing governance to issues of control, technology, and automation, such practices question the purpose of knowledge, prototyping, and innovation. Discovery and instrument-making become means of critical inquiry that open the future to new ideals and values.

Renaissance instruments reveal an alternative history of prototyping that is close to today's practices in hackerspaces and other liminal sites (Chapter 9–11). As a form of public engagement, prototyping of instruments serves the formation of new communities with various (often conflicting or playful) agendas. Prototyping in the service of Kairos opens up the future to citizens rather than disrupting anything to support investors, inventors, early adopters, and men of God. The prototypes in the liminal spaces discussed in Chapter 9–11 preserve the future as open to negotiation and experiments. They offer engagements that support Kairos in governance and technology and serve as an example for the sandbox model of innovation and policy discussed in Chapter 12 that opens up the future to public engagement.

Artisan Instruments versus Tools of Instauratio

In his descriptions of the future as a project of Instauratio (restoration), Francis Bacon uses examples of instruments without mentioning their designers (Colie, 1955; Keller, 2013), such as the 17th-century artisan and natural philosopher, Cornelius Drebbel. Bacon uses Drebbel's instruments to illustrate the work on the restoration of human powers over the creation defined as a governance project. He calls the actual designers of such instruments charlatans and magicians who do not understand the true purpose of their inventions, namely God's plan with humanity. Bacon then proposes an institution, the Academy of Sciences, that will define 'correct' prototyping in service of the teleological and theological goal of creation (Faulkner, 1993; Keller, 2012; McCarthy, 1995).

Bacon's whole project is defined as an opposition to artisans like Drebbel. He even accuses the artisans of being mere tricksters who manipulate wealthy patrons and the public without advancing the one true goal of governance and technology that will lead humanity to fulfill its purpose in the creation. The project of Instauratio reenacts the original conflict in Thales between the two uses of expert knowledge and time (Chronos and Kairos). Bacon insists that prototyping should serve only the goal of restoration, rather than exploring any new values that express the care for the 'whole' (holon) or 'open' future as that which might exist. Since Thales and then Bacon, the vision of an open and unpredictable future clashes with the agenda of automation or later algorithmic rule that limit the future to similar teleological projects, such as Instauratio.

The prototypes of instruments express the agency and freedom to invent, discover, and experience time as Kairos that transforms nature, technology, and society. Reduced to means of a 'technological' Kairos, disruptive prototypes of instruments support control and monopoly over the future – the projects of Instauratio or later Enlightenment ideas of progress. Such instruments reenact the original mission of the monopoly contraption in Thales (Chapter 4): to foreclose the future while supporting the rule of the patrons over parasites who lose all their political agency. Designers and investors in innovation become modern patrons who enslave precarious subjects as victims of the new infrastructures. They control the teleological project as 'progress', while the rest will only wait to be saved or served on the tables as parasites.

Renaissance artisans problematize this vision of the future in Bacon. They show examples of prototypes that preserve Kairos equally in technology and governance. Instead of the ideal of automation and the teleological promises of progress, these practices advance the critical use of Thales' inventions and the expert knowledge of Chronos to reform society and its values. The 16th-century artisans, alchemists, and mechanical philosophers, such as Cornelius Drebbel, Jakob Bornitz, and others, explore future(s) beyond the teleological promises of Instauratio. Their playful engagements with prototypes of new instruments are open-ended and equally concerned with transformation in science, technology, and society (governance). Rather than supporting Instauratio or further consolidating anyone's power over the future, these instruments encourage fellow artisans to experiment, discover, tinker, and imagine a future society.

Renaissance instruments thus set the stage for disruptive innovations that promise progress but also prototyping that performs Kairos, agency in governance and technology. Drebbel's handcrafted artisanal instruments, described here as cosmoscopes (Keller, 2010), merged expressive and creative ideas about how the universe works with reflections about society. Instead of preserving or restoring any plan, power, or promise, Drebbel's instruments define the future as a practice open to all citizens. The instruments become invitations to join the research and exploration of possible futures rather than to impose ontological, theological, or cosmological agendas on society.

Drebbel's prototypes had an explicit goal to engage fellow citizens in the understanding of nature and imagining what is possible in society. Instrument-making became a way to rethink and transform the human experience of the creation and define new roles for humanity, visions for the future, and engagements with the public. While Drebbel amused patrons and emperors with instruments generating 'miracles', he never promised any eternal rule, progress, or Instauratio that enslave the fellow citizens by new patrons, tables, automation, or some teleology of Instauratio.

Instead of asserting knowledge of God's plan with humanity (Chapter 7), Drebbel's creative instruments investigate and simulate the universe as a work of an artisan who include the fellow citizens as partners. Today's 'science artisans' (Chapter 9), with open hardware prototypes, extend this original mission of Drebbel. Prototypes as Drebbel's 'living instruments' embody the original Thales' ideal of free time to do research that nobody cares about. The artisans of the past and present combine the personal insight and knowledge with idiosyncratic future-making that preserves the future as open and public matter. Their instruments support personal and social action as an experience of Kairos against the teleology, automation, and the rule of Chronos closing the future to Instauratio.

Future-making as Instauratio and Desiderata

Renaissance artisan instruments, as well as present open science hardware, show prototyping that serves as personal and community probes into the future. To explain how prototyping supports the ideal of time and future as an open and public good (an experience of time as Kairos), we will start with Agamben's alternative views of (expert) knowledge and insights captured in his discussions of the obscure notions of paradigm, model, and analogy. Agamben used these concepts to describe a type of knowledge and practice that remain an open process of meaning-making resisting any final ontology, cosmology, or goals (Agamben, 2009a, 2009b).

Paradigms in language are like prototypes of new instruments. They embody the process of creation without claiming any finality or universality. By supporting practices of meaning-making and interpretation through paradigms and prototypes, time as Kairos remains an opportunity for transformation, without claiming any final truths, goals, or promise of progress or restoration. Prototypes as embodiments of Agamben's paradigms enable individuals and communities to reclaim the future beyond automation and define governance as an experience of Kairos against the power of Chronos, teleology, cosmology, and ontology.

Whereas Bacon's instruments supported restoration (Instauratio) and teleology of progress, Drebbel's artisan instruments explored ambiguous and open-ended objectives closer to Agamben's paradigms. Like Thales' discoveries (Chapter 9), artisan instruments entertain, surprise, and provoke fellow citizens with new ideas and insights that preserve the future and time as radically open. Instead of facilitating monopoly, they have no stakes in God's or patron's control over the future and time as Chronos. They are neither tables that host hungry parasites nor teleological means to impose a political order as a cosmological and ontological necessity. Like Agamben's paradigms or later prototypes of open science hardware (Chapter 9), Renaissance prototypes express idiosyncratic and creative experiments, personal explorations, and social actions.

Artisan instruments offer an alternative to Bacon's technocratic vision of science and technology as tools of Instauratio that intensify and institutionalize the control over the future. Bacon's new institution (the Academy of Science) secures the power of patrons as representatives of God's plan over the future and over time. Prototyping that serves R&D agenda only reinforces the power structures in society while undermining any personal and collective agency as Kairos. Instauratio or later progress reduce science and technology to means of a divine plan that includes the rule of patrons over the parasites. The new instruments serve as rituals of controlling the future.

Bacon transformed the teleological and theological promise of Instauratio into an actionable menu of desirable and lost inventions (desiderata) that patrons support to further God's plan (Keller, 2012, 2018). With desiderata, the future becomes a matter of investment in innovation that preserves the rule of patrons and further enslaves the parasites. Both Instauratio and desiderata make prototyping an act of shaping the future to serve the political status quo. They transform knowledge, technologies, and institutions into infrastructures and tables on which patrons 'host' new parasites.

To describe this mythical control over time and the future by means of science and technology, Bacon literally speaks of the 'time's masculine birth' (temporis partus masculus) (Iliffe, 2000). Prototyping in the service of innovation is an act of the 'time's masculine birth' (later defined as experimenta lucifera) that contrasts the natural flow of time that brings innovation by chance (experimenta fructifera). It is an act that is reminiscent of ancient rites of domination over time by mythical kings. The ritual control over time and the future then repeats with each new instrument and infrastructure, including today's algorithms.

Time's Masculine Birth

The 'masculine' birth of time is a synonym of automation. Through disruptive prototypes and knowledge representing this birth, humanity is promised efficiency, plan, and control over the future. The new knowledge and insights into Chronos control time as something with generative properties (Kairos) available to investors and patrons. Control over the generative properties of time as Kairos makes patrons 'godlike world transformers' (Iliffe, 2000) who bring forth new worlds and literally perform a power over life (as creation and birth).

Whereas Plautus cursed the inventor of the sundial for limiting citizens' agency and control over their time, Bacon celebrates the new inventors for restoring the imperial power over time and the future. The new patrons are world transformers 'giving birth' to time through new instruments that reduce all political, social, and individual decisions to one. They restore the ancient rites of the emperors over the calendar and time and connect cosmology, ontology, and politics to serve the teleological goal of restoration:

> Janus-like sense of instauro (establish/restore) accommodates this powerful complimentary paradox, emphatically suggesting masculine imperial power over time itself. Instauro here comes to be associated with the cyclical conception of history as a recurring pattern of fluorescence and decline, a conception that governed the historical consciousness of the Romans. Where before a priest or public official had the authority to extend public religious festivals by decreeing 'Instauration' or repetitions of them (as reported in Livy and Cicero), here it is the whole society and world that the highest official, the deified emperor, can revivify through festive rituals.
>
> (Ibid.)

Bacon's 'masculine' birth and Instauratio are only two of many competing visions in the 16th and 17th centuries that describe the political uses of science and technology. For Bacon, prototypes are tools of the 'masculine birth of time' whose purpose is to empower patrons who invest in science and technology. Instead of exploring various uses for cosmological, political, and social knowledge and values, such prototypes have only one goal: to hijack God's program and serve the patrons. The prototypes set the stage for the algorithmic rule and reduce all politics to control over the R&D process and innovation.

Against this reduction of politics to cosmology and a myth of automation, the forgotten artisans' projects bring alternative visions of science, technology, and society relations. They resist Bacon's metaphor of 'masculine birth' and governance as a matter of monopoly over the future through restoration (Instauratio). Instead of a teleological progress, prototyping of instruments supports experimental values and new classes of citizens called artisans, mechanics, natural philosophers, or alchemists with various ad hoc and open-ended goals.

Drebbel's instruments and related projects described in Chapter 7 show the future as an open project that emphasizes public engagement and experimentation that break the divisions between scientific, philosophical, and political metaphors. Teleology and the universal rule of Instauratio or automation are still dominant, but not only visions of the role of instruments and infrastructures in society. The fringe prototypes explicitly reject these visions of automation and governance based on rituals, machines, and algorithms. Instead of technologies becoming the new devil's bridges, these prototypes act as probes and experiments into diverse political, aesthetic, and social values and visions.

Prototyping as a material and conceptual engagement with science, technology, and governance has served various pragmatic, didactic, and even emancipatory purposes throughout history. It connects visions, concepts, and words with human actions and things outside of human agency. To explain how artisan prototypes of instruments transform society without falling into the trap of teleology, we based our definition of prototypes on Giorgio Agamben's discussion of paradigm, model, and exempla (Agamben, 2009b).

Agamben captured knowledge but also practice (prototyping) that combines ontology, cosmology, and politics without supporting any teleological notion of final ends. The paradigm or exempla emphasize knowledge as much as participation (political and social agency) and define meaning as something that has to remain open to iteration (discussed here as the need to view time and the future as a public or commons resource). Agamben uses the forgotten notion of paradigm to question the canonical concepts and interpretations of history and philosophy, which have lost their emancipatory power (in relation to the future and action).

Prototypes as Paradigms

In 'The Signature of All Things' (Agamben, 2009b), Agamben reminds us that the original meaning of the paradigms is 'singular objects that, standing equally for all others of the same class, define the intelligibility of the group of which it is part and which, at the same time, it constitutes.' The paradigm reveals as much as it creates, thus emphasizing the agency of the reader or interpreter who engages with the future:

> The paradigm... by exhibiting its own singularity, it makes intelligible a new ensemble, whose homogeneity it itself constitutes. That is to say, giving an example is a complex act which supposes that the term functioning as a paradigm is deactivated from its normal use, not in order to be moved into another context but, on the contrary, to present the canon–the rule–of that use, which cannot be shown in any other way.
> (Ibid.)

Paradigms as practices of meaning-making reject any finality of something predetermined or expected at the end of time (such as restoration or progress that guide most modern projects of prototyping in science and technology). As practices of meaning-making, paradigms create not only new concepts but also institutions and values without insisting on their universality. Agamben traces the origins of this concept in Aristotle's discussions of analogy and models, which led to later medieval concepts of exempla and regula (Agamben, 2009b). All these concepts (paradigm, analogy, and exempla) express practices that produce new knowledge, visions, or institutions as precedents without insisting on their finality. In the case of regulae, there are guiding principles of the monastic orders and describe practices of following the 'exemplary' life of Christ or the saints without claiming that there is only one possible and perfect form.

Paradigms as practice of prototyping preserve human agency over the future and the experience of time as Kairos. They become an opportunity to transform the meaning, institutions, and society, without seeking any certainty or finality of any insight or Chronos. Instead of turning citizens into obedient subjects of an ontology or cosmology identifying cycles and patterns of Chronos, paradigms as 'form(s) of life' (Ibid.) enable citizens to preserve their agency. When citizens prototype or engage with a new paradigm, they are free to connect knowing with living without being forced to adapt to any universal truth, value, or future goal.

The notions of exempla, analogy, or paradigm circumvent the traditional philosophical oppositions between what is universal and particular, or intelligible and sensible. As performative knowledge, paradigms and prototypes express the agency and Kairos, the possibility for new insights and action that emphasize transformation without universality, finality, or teleology. They are precedents that make new orders, objects, classes, or sets visible and intelligible as a 'singularity that, showing itself as such, produces a new ontological context' (Ibid.).

Agamben's discussion of paradigms even includes examples of prototypes, such as the art of weaving in Plato's 'Statesmen' or Michel Foucault's panopticon (Ibid.). Through these examples, Agamben shows how concrete artifacts become models of thinking about society, even changing the way we imagine governance. These metaphors define new relationships between power and everyday life or governance and technology. Prototypes as such paradigms thus explore the relationship between science, technology, and society without insisting on any teleology of desiderata or Instauratio consolidating the existing powers. As material, technological, and conceptual explorations, paradigms or prototypes define new values and visions for society and the future.

Prototypes as experiences of Kairos or paradigms are neither mere material objects nor intangible insights, ideas, or norms. They are precedents and examples of how things might be, including what communities we may create around them. Their purpose is to encourage individuals and communities to experiment and define their values and visions for the common future while remaining open to further exploration. As a means of Kairos, prototypes use knowledge and practice, science and technology, in an 'exemplary' way trans-forming present and future expectations. In the next sections, we will describe this as 'future anterior' and optatives that define how prototypes preserve the future(s) as open and public.

Prototyping for an open and public future connects politics to ontology or governance to technology without reducing one to the other. It emphasizes Kairos as an exploration of possible futures and forgotten genealogies that transform our notions of agency and time. Rather than fulfilling any teleolog-ical promise, such a 'paradigmatic' use of prototypes preserves the singularity and uniqueness of each action, and defines new perspective and rule.

The paradigms of Giorgio Agamben perform a hermeneutic understand-ing of the world and society based on human agency and action. Meaning, knowledge, and technology are open-ended practices and engagements that transform our institutions and values without closing them to one ideal form. In Chapter 9, we will discuss the present examples of such practices in the liminal environments of hackerspaces and makerspaces, which define the model of prototyping for governance via sandboxes in Chapter 12.

Prototypes as Regulae and Formae Vitae

The prototypes define the relationship between science, technology, and soci-ety as an opportunity for transformation and change beyond monopoly. They express Kairos rather than Chronos, interventions that lead to 'a new ensemble' (Agamben, 2009b) and 'heterogenous phenomena':

> Paradigms obey not only the logic of the metaphorical transfer but the analogical logic of the example. Here, we are not dealing with a signi-fier that is extended to designate heterogeneous phenomena by virtue of the same semantic structure; more akin to allegory than to metaphor, the paradigm is a singular case that is isolated from its context only insofar as, by exhibiting its own singularity, it makes intelligible a new ensemble, whose homogeneity it itself constitutes.
>
> (Ibid.)

The heterogeneous interventions and precedents define the future as a matter of personal and social agency rather than a matter of cycles and patterns that automate society. Prototypes as 'material' paradigms and exampla open up new ways to experience the world and society while preserving the future as open and public. The new meaning, reality, or experience become models of thought and action supporting further iterations. In this sense, prototypes articulate and perform rather than represent something pregiven, ideal, and perfect. They create new instruments, infrastructures, and ideas of govern-ance and technology as singularities and actions that take place in time as Kairos, an opportunity for change. They are invitation for everyone to join and transform their language, technologies, and institutions.

Prototypes that open the future to engagements connect what exists with what 'might exist' (future anterior) without insisting on Chronos or the teleology of Instauratio. What might exist is a process driven by actions rather than insights and the ideal of the future as open to new engagements and opportunities (Kairos) for personal and social agency. By letting others decide whether to replicate, iterate, or completely change the practices, technologies, and rules, this practice makes the future public and a common matter. The forgotten, repressed, neglected, or imagined future(s) become as important as the one that leads to automation and Chronos, ontology, or cosmology. Serving Kairos in technology, governance, and language over paradigms and prototypes is therefore about preserving time as an open and public resource.

Agamben's paradigms capture the importance of prototyping for restoring the time as Kairos in governance and technology. Prototypes link reflection to action in what Agamben calls the 'form(s) of life' (forma vitae), which transform institutions, culture, and language. Examples of monastic orders show how paradigms organize communities beyond the representation of an ideal meaning or regulation. The regulae of monastic orders presents the founder's way of life (forma vitae) as an interpretation of saint's' life, adapted to the context of the community. Only later in the Middle Ages did the regula become written rules of the monasteries, which lost this flexibility:

> at least until Saint Benedict, the rule does not indicate a general norm but the living community (koinos bios, cenobio) that results from an example and in which the life of each monk tends at the limit to become paradigmatic, that is, to constitute itself as forma vitae.
>
> (Ibid.)

The regula defined the monastic order as a living community in which members reinvent and adapt the rules rather than simply reproducing them. The rules express not only metaphysical commitments to cosmology, ontology, and Chronos (or saints in the case of the orders) but also Kairos, context, and opportunity for change. Instead of immutable structures that demand obedience, they become invitations to change lives and practices according to the new visions and insights of the community:

> The paradigm entails a movement that goes from singularity to singularity and, without ever leaving singularity, transforms every singular case into an exemplar of a general rule that can never be stated a priori
>
> (Ibid.)

Current prototypes in hackerspaces and makerspaces follow the logic of Agamben's regula and monastic orders, demanding performance rather than repetition of knowledge, insights, and know-how. Prototyping in the hackerspaces that we will discuss in Chapter 9–11 explores the future beyond the project of Instauration and desiderata. Instead of adhering to predefined key performance indicators (KPIs), ideals of progress or restoration, modern desiderata of further automation and algorithmic rules, prototypes remain open-ended explorations. The communities involved in prototyping resemble the monastic orders of the past. We discuss them in Chapter 9 by using the example of hackerspaces and similar fringe communities that define time as personal and collaborative work on open futures.

The regula in the hackerspaces could be their wiki pages describing the community projects and instruments as models for starting, funding, and maintaining a hackerspace. Rather than franchising an institution or infrastructure through a kit, monopoly or patent on some knowledge, the prototyping as regulae supports improvisation. The regulae or prototypes and kits become invitations to join, experience, change, rethink, or even misuse the technology. Under the logic of regulae, examples, and paradigms, every institution becomes a prototype without the need for a teleology or an Instauratio.

The prototypes in the hackerspaces explore the freedom and opportunity as Kairos and agency to transform both the technology and community. They define governance as an open-ended process, a performance instead of a repetition serving some ideal knowledge, insight (Chronos), Instauratio, or progress. Instead of materializing preexisting, teleological concepts, or modern KPIs, members of the hackerspaces create instances of the prototypes and explore new norms, aspirations, or futures as individuals and community.

Care and Curiosity for the Future

Renaissance instrument-making, represented by Cornelius Drebbel and similar artisans, performs the paradoxical temporality of Agamben's paradigm, exempla, and regulae as that which 'might exist' (future anterior). They are examples of future-making that embraces the possibility of change without insisting on its necessity or some teleology of progress. Prototypes as paradigms support personal and social agency, action, and meaning-making without repeating or claiming final goals. They preserve time as a public good and a medium for invention, discovery, and self-determination.

Agamben's paradigm and regulae thus show how individuals and collectives reinterpret the future from the past (the lives of the saints) and reuse it to define new visions and practices. They preserve continuity and meaning while engaging and recreating new ideas and insights (Chronos) in a particular context. Instead of repetition and obedience to an external structure that dictates the ideal future, prototypes become an opportunity for change and Kairos. The only goal is to increase participation, which will help individuals and communities define new goals and values through practice.

Whether as monastic orders in the past or today's hackerspaces, the sharing of knowledge and know-how is an invitation to try something without imposing teleological ideal of community or technology. Adapting the founder's way of life (forma vitae) or existing prototypes and technologies to different needs and ideas makes the legacy come alive without compromising the agency of the living.

Prototypes in the hackerspaces and liminal environments resemble in this sense Agamben's paradigms. They are props and probes into possible futures without imposing perfection and finality. They interpret time as a particular 'care' for what 'may exist' and an expression of agency. Through this care, citizens modify the future as something plural, imagined, and possible, but never final. Agamben described this as 'the future anterior', a concept borrowed from Foucault to describe a type of curiosity about a future without a definitive goal and agenda, such as progress (Agamben, 2009b).

The future anterior explains the paradoxical temporality of the paradigm – it is a care for what might exist, including the future forgotten in the past. It is a future that does not recreate or break with the past to fulfill some teleology of final or original goals. It only expresses the curiosity as agency or Kairos evoking Foucault's use of the term 'future anterior' as

> the care one takes of what exists and what might exist; a sharpened sense of reality, but one that is never immobilized before it; a readiness to find what surrounds us strange and odd; a certain determination to throw off familiar ways of thought and to look at the same things in a different way; a passion for seizing what is happening now and what is disappearing; a lack of respect for the traditional hierarchies of what is important and fundamental. I dream of a new age of curiosity.
>
> (Foucault, 2000)

Curiosity as an experience of an open future goes against cosmological or ontological certainty and truths (Chronos). It expresses human agency as the capacity to transform and change conditions, society, and the environment. Rather than disrupting or revealing the true meaning and purpose of technology, society, or history, prototyping guided by curiosity fulfills the paradoxical and aleatory function of the future anterior. As a care for what might exist, it is part of the experience of time as Kairos or the 'passion for seizing what is happening now and what is disappearing' (Ibid.). Foucault's insistence on curiosity and dreams as examples of such paradoxical temporality defines the possibility of knowledge outside power and teleology. Along with Agamben's paradigms and examples, Foucault's curiosity explains prototyping as a practice that liberates the future and time. Future anterior enables personal and social action as alternative to monopolies and other forms of patrons' control of the parasites.

The prototyping that expresses Kairos introduces metaphors, paradoxes, and unexpected uses of technology driven by curiosity. It supports future-making that rejects the rhetoric of innovation or the teleological views of the community. Prototyping that insists on time as an open and public resource is never controlled or closed by one goal, no matter how important and desirable it may sound. To think, envision, and prototype means to experience the paradoxes of the 'past in the future' as 'moments of arising' that can transform 'the unrealized into realized and the realized into unrealized' (Agamben, 2009b) or make the familiar look unfamiliar (Foucault's quote readiness to find what surrounds us strange and odd; a certain determination to throw off familiar ways of thought and to look at the same things in a different way').

Future anterior and Kairos contrast the use of time in prototyping with the goals of Instauratio, automation, and Chronos. They show us how we can 'gain access to the present for the first time, beyond memory and forgetting, or rather at the threshold of their indifference' (Ibid.) and to use prototypes as care for what might exist. Understanding time and the future as an open and public resource means insisting on preserving human agency, curiosity, creativity, and dreams. They are the only alternatives to the algorithmic rule and control over Chronos, Instauratio, and other teleological concepts of technology and governance.

Futures Worth of Trouble

Prototypes as paradigms, exempla, and regulae are technical, social, and political probes into the future driven by curiosity and dreams or uses of time as Kairos. They explore the relationships between science, technology, and society by connecting knowledge with living, structure with action, and Chronos with Kairos. Rather than representing predefined knowledge or normative systems, they materialize futures as dreamworks, opportunities and challenges that remain open to interventions:

> The essential point of the dream is not so much that it revives the past as that it announces the future. It foretells and announces the moment in which the patient will finally reveal to the analyst the secret (he or she) does not yet known, which is nevertheless the heaviest burden of (his or her) present... The dream anticipates the moment of freedom. It constitutes a harbinger of history, before being the compelled repetition of the traumatic past.
>
> (Foucault in Agamben, 2009b)

Dreamworks and prototypes liberate personal and social action from the constraints of Chronos such as history, forgotten trauma, or teleology of restoration and progress (Chapter 7). They reject the rule of Chronos that reduces both governance and technology to a project of Instauratio and other enactments of the myth of automation. Renaissance instruments (Chapter 7), including today's open science hardware (Chapter 3), work with the prototypes as dreamworks that oppose the eschatology, teleology, and utopia of Chronos. They support the ideals of an open and public future and experiences of time as Kairos.

To resist the teleological and metaphysical control over the future as Chronos, we must redefine the role of designers and lawmakers, as well as the connection between technology and governance. Foucault's curiosity and dreams offer a model how to do it by explicitly rejecting the roles of the wise man, the prophet, and the legislator that haunt our imagination of the future. To liberate time, as well as prototyping, from eschatology and teleology, we must go beyond these three roles and explore paradoxes and ruptures in time (another synonym of time as Kairos rather than Chronos): 'The Greek wise man, the Jewish prophet and the Roman legislator are still models that haunt those who today practice the profession of speaking and writing' (Ibid.).

Foucault's public intellectual resists the three roles and models of future-making and embraces the paradoxes and experiences of Kairos in governance and technology:

> I dream of the intellectual who destroys evidence and generalities, the one who, in the inertias and constraints of the present time, locates and marks the weak points, the openings, the lines of force, who is incessantly on the move, doesn't know exactly where he is heading nor what he will think tomorrow for he is too attentive to the present; who, wherever he moves, contributes to posing the question of knowing whether the revolution is worth the trouble and what kind (I mean, what revolution and what trouble), it being understood that the question can be answered only by those who are willing to risk their lives to bring it about.
>
> (Foucault, 1977)

Moving without knowing where we are going and what we will think tomorrow describes the experience of time as Kairos. It emphasizes personal and social agency over time. Time becomes a matter of open future and active resistance to any power and control of Chronos, telos, or automation. Knowing and prototyping as 'moving without knowing' and resisting the teleology of Instauratio and Chronos (represented by wise men, prophets, and legislators) means transcending the 'inertias and constraints of the present time' (Ibid.) and recognizing the 'weak points, openings' for change. These moments are opportunities of Kairos in technology and governance, in personal and public life, that we need to embrace by prototyping.

Prototyping without teleology becomes a plea for agency and freedom. It preserves an open future and public time for citizens to decide what type of future is 'worth the trouble' (Ibid.). Rather than accepting the certainty of automation and the prophecies of restoration (Instauratio), prototypes in the service of Kairos engage in what Foucault describes as 'troubles'. The radical uncertainty about the future described by the 'troubles' remains open to personal and collective interventions ('wherever he moves, contributes to the question of knowing whether the revolution is worth the trouble and what kind (I mean what revolution and what trouble), it being understood that the question can be answered only by those who are willing to risk their lives to bring it about.') (Ibid.).

Prototyping for governance means exploring the uncertain futures 'worth of trouble' that express individual and collective aspirations that are neither final nor controlled by any patron or God. The prototypes as means of governance serving Kairos follow Foucault's genealogical and archeological project, Agamben's paradigms, and Zielinsk's 'deep media'. They define future-making beyond any teleology.

Since Thales, science and technology have supported the experience of time as Chronos and Kairos, on the one side as control and automation and on the other as resistance, agency, transformation, and exploration. Using examples of Renaissance instruments (Chapters 6 and 7) and current open science hardware (Chapter 9), we will illustrate this radical future-making that is open to participation and engagement. Since Thales, we see how the same instruments and prototypes often serve opposite goals in society: on the one hand, the teleology and the establishment, and on the other the so-called folly of empiricism criticized by Bacon in the case of artisans and mechanical philosophers (discussed in the next chapters).

Prototypes as Living Instruments and Cosmoscopes

Instruments in the 17th century illustrate the 'folly of empiricism' as prototypes that open the future to many goals rather than closing it to one: Instauratio. They are examples of Agamben's paradigms that explore the future as that which might exist, or which is worth the troubles, against the ideas of necessary, predetermined, and close telos. For example, the prototypes made by the natural philosopher and artisan Cornelius Drebbel and described as 'cosmoscopes' or 'living instruments' represent such open-ended explorations that combine artistic, political, and scientific goals without a definitive agenda.

Drebbel's incubator or his simulator of weather cycles with a clock are material and creative engagements with philosophy, science, and society without one final goal (Keller, 2010, 2013). They are metaphysical models and philosophical reflections of the universe that paradoxically support practical use. They are explorations 'worth the troubles' showing the mysteries of nature to fellow citizens referred to as 'brothers' (Keller, 2011). While Bacon uses these instruments to support his bureaucratic takeover of power, for Drebbel, these instruments remain curiosity-driven explorations of the universe and our place in it.

In Bacon, science instruments help the elites to usurp the religious project of Instauratio supporting investments in science and technology to restore the human power over the creation (Colie, 1955). With his Instauratio project, Bacon imposed a political status quo as a metaphysical and theological necessity. The instruments became monopoly contraptions representing God's plan with humanity that ultimately serve the patrons. In contrast, Drebbel creates prototypes that serve various aesthetic and philosophical goals without one political agenda. As Vera Keller, a science historian who studies mechanical artists such as Drebbel, describes them, they are 'living instruments' (Keller, 2010) that demonstrate the universe as an invitation for everyone to become a maker and philosopher with their hands.

Instead of supporting patrons, Drebbel's hands-on experiences with nature empower everyone to become an artisan with direct and authentic relationship with the universe and the future:

> He prided himself on his ability to transmit his own bodily knowledge to others using things more than words... indicating to his readers how they might arrive at bodily knowledge through the manipulation of matter. He crafted his texts as material carriers transmitting his bodily knowledge to the bodies of his readers. Drebbel hoped to transform his readers into artisanal philosophers themselves, so that all may participate equally in knowledge of nature and of God.
>
> (Keller, 2011)

For example, Drebbel's weather simulator with a clock ('Archimedean sphere') encouraged the citizens to engage with a philosophical discussion about vitalism and imagine different uses for the 'perpetually moving chemical microcosms' (Keller, 2010). The instrument bridges the divides between vitalist and mechanical notions of life and machine, or chance and design (close to our dichotomy between Kairos and Chronos). Drebbel's Archimedean sphere paradoxically simulates a 'microcosm' with chemistry (example of vitalism) to power a mechanical clock, creating a precedent bridging the opposing values and divides.

With instruments based on opposing philosophies and value systems, Drebbel reconciles the idea of time as Kairos, an act of creation as a vitalist and chemical process, with Chronos, a control based on a mechanical contraption. This 'machine based on nonmechanical natural philosophy' (Keller, 2010) overcomes the tension between Kairos and Chronos to define new knowledge, as well as values and ideas about the universe and society. As a living instrument, it uses chemical processes to power a mechanical clock that performs Chronos without insisting on its rule. The instrument repeats the lesson of Thales' contraption, which also used time as Chronos to perform Kairos as an agency. It created a monopoly over olive presses to challenge the status quo in the society and common views of what is useful knowledge.

Another of Drebbel's 'living instruments' explored the function of a self-regulating mechanism later called a protothermoscope or thermometer, which enacts similar paradoxes (and precedes our cybernetic ideas of self-regulation in various systems). The purpose of the instrument was not to control anything but to demonstrate a perpetual motion and represent how the universe generates life. This early cybernetic feedback mechanism embodies the algorithmic and technocratic promises of control but claims to perform the values of life and Kairos itself, a 'simulacrum of the universe... living machine that could encapsulate, prove, and effortlessly convey universal knowledge of nature' (Keller, 2010).

With similar prototypes, Drebbel performs his ingenuity and agency as freedom to design and understand nature and the world with his hands and direct experiences that openly oppose the divisions of his time. His personal and direct engagement serves the goal of democratizing knowledge as such radical future-making:

> The cosmoscope suggested a single pansophic artisanal philosopher who based his knowledge in his own manual construction of a working microcosm that validated all of his theories. This model entailed a close association between the body of the artisan and the content of his own natural philosophy encapsulated within his single personal device. By contrast, the thermoscope/thermometer, as a specialized metric instrument rather than a universal demonstration, suggested a diverse range of individuals and an equally wide array of experiments. The instrument was not itself an experiment, but a tool to be used in many experiments. Different individuals might make the instrument from those who used it, noted down observations and collated those observations.
>
> (Ibid.)

Folly of Empiricism against the Rule of Automation

Drebbel's prototypes did not establish any universal rule or ideal future, such as Bacon's Instauratio project. Their purpose was to explore and demonstrate philosophical, aesthetic, and even political explorations that involve fellow citizens in the democratization of science and technology. Instead of imposing universal and absolute control over the future with each new clock and instrument, Drebbel's prototypes explore alternatives to automation and algorithmic rule.

They are dreams and performance that express Foucault's 'care' for what could exist and 'the future anterior' or Thales' things that no one 'cares about'. In this sense, the instruments define care as an experience of time, as Kairos, an opportunity for action that bridges the common divides, such as the ones between vitalism and mechanical philosophy, or between governance and technology.

Care for what might exist (or Thales interest in phenomena that 'no one cares about') defines the agency of the artisans like Drebbel. It is an agency of someone who creates, invents, and imagines a future without serving any patrons or gods. Instead of automatizing or controlling time and reducing governance to technology and one goal, Drebbels instruments serve various practical and impractical functions. The clock, for example, is even a musical instrument that performs what Plato's idea of a future as 'music that has never been played' (Plato, Theaetetus, Section 174a, n.d.). In short, prototypes are models of the universe that perform the processes of creation while supporting human agency.

Drebbel uses the instrument to connect various philosophical insights, knowledge, and creativity as forms of care for the future. The prototypes also become direct and authentic experiences of working with hands while sharing knowledge and know-how with others. They neither automate the political status quo nor embody any ideal future, but open it as a matter of Kairos, dreams, and curiosity that empower the artisans to experience the universe:

> Also associated with the machine at Eltham was a keyboard that played by itself when the sun shone. Thus, Drebbel's most famous installation of his motion was grafted onto mechanical objects (such as clocks or stringed instruments). It was not simply a glass orb that displayed the motions of the heavens, as in the classic Archimedean sphere, nor a purely alchemical 'element glass' showing the rota elementorum within a retort. However, within his texts, Drebbel stated that he could build a chemical microcosm in glass, and, as noted above, he compared his sphere himself to the Archimedean sphere.
>
> (Keller, 2010)

Vera Keller's research of mechanical artisans in the 16th and 17th centuries describes these instruments as open-ended tinkering that combines various ontological and political commitments (Keller, 2013). While Francis Bacon's instruments of Instauratio served only one purpose, institutionalizing knowledge and the rule of patrons, Drebbel's instruments repurpose various scientific, cosmological, political, aesthetic, and social commitments that he materializes into prototypes. Although Drebbel's instruments inspired Bacon's desiderata, wish lists and investment plans (Ibid.), they remain eclectic, holistic, and open-ended explorations – optatives serving 'future anterior' as the care for what might exist.

Living instruments define prototyping as experiments with possible futures without restoring or automating anything. Instead, they support personal and social agency as an experience of Kairos without the teleological goals of restoring human power over nature or closing the future to one project. Rather than promising innovation as a panacea for all social and political issues, living instruments balance transformation (as Kairos) in science, technology, and society.

Robert Fludd, a prominent physician and contemporary of Drebbel, describes such prototypes as 'demonstrative machine(s)' and 'experimentall Instrument or spirituall weapon' employed 'to demonstrate the verity of (his) Philosophicall Argument' (Ibid.).

The performative and demonstrative prototypes in the service of artisanal science helped alchemists and philosophers express their curiosity, imagination, and dreams. With their prototypes, the artisans preserved the experience of time as Kairos, an opportunity to iterate, experiment, and start anew, to create without any guarantees of success, finality, or universality.

Prototypes as living instruments were open-ended practices that capture a 'forgotten fantasy, a single living machine that encapsulates, proves, and effortlessly conveys universal knowledge of nature' (Keller, 2010). It is an old fantasy expressed in Thales' discovery and knowledge of Chronos (representing universal knowledge of nature) that supported monopoly and control, as well as his new and provocative visions of society questioning the values of merchants and aristocrats (Chapter 4).

The alternative to the teleological idea of the future under the rule of Chronos is the experience of time and the future as open-ended transformation (Kairos). While Bacon's prototypes (desiderata) serve the teleological ideals of science and technology as wish lists of discoveries and innovations that will fulfill the goals of Instauratio, artisan prototypes explore 'wonders no one could even imagine' (Keller, 2010). Artisan instruments are optatives, something 'yet to be discovered' that transforms society in ways we could not imagine, opposing the chiliastic ideals of Bacon's progress. Drebbel's or later Bornitz's projects embrace 'optatives' (sometimes also described as desiderata) as creative and provocative prototypes that combine vitalist and mechanical metaphors of 'living instruments' with pansophic 'living trees with living fruit' (Keller, 2015).

7 Future as Restoration or Transformation

Salomon's House, Academy of Games and Pleasures, and Hackerspaces

The prototyping of instruments in the 16th and 17th centuries inspired different projects and institutions dedicated to science and technology, such as Bacon's Academy of Science, Leibniz's Academy of Games and Pleasure, and less-known proposals by Drebbel or Bornitz (Keller, 2015). Bacon's academy defined science and technology as means of Instauratio. The purpose of the academy was to restore the knowledge and power over the creation that humanity lost after the original sin and fall. Bacon believed that science and technology will restore the control of humanity over the ontological and pre-given order in nature. This restoration of knowledge and power over the creation will then automatically bring moral and political advancement in society, which the later enlightenment project interpreted as progress.

The idea of the academy serving the teleological project of restoration contrasts sharply with Drebbel's 'folly of empiricism' (Keller, 2015) and his artisanal instruments (Chapter 6). Drebbel's instrument supported open-ended explorations of science, technology, and society. Unlike Bacon's academy, Drebbel's informal network of so-called book of friends (alba amicorum), something of Renaissance Facebook, had no fixed agendas nor ideals of a theological and teleological order in nature (or society). The informal networks of prototyping geeks showed science and technology as a matter of friendship and sharing of material, poetic, and social explorations similar to the hackerspace projects discussed in the next chapter.

Instead of imposing any teleological future, Drebbel's prototypes and informal networks support curiosity about what might exist. They combine mechanical arts, natural philosophy, and 'courts' (politics) to explore radical visions, for example Bornitz's transgender body politic (Keller, 2015). For Renaissance artisans, such as Drebbel, both nature and society are continuously transforming in ways we cannot predict nor fully control. Instead of restoring the pre-given order of Chronos, the goal is to embrace curiosity, openness, and opportunity of Kairos:

This idea was ingeniously encapsulated in a posthumous emblem book that illustrates Bornitz's key ideas through the figure of a transsexual. The Latin tag warned, 'Through a wonder of nature, a male appears in

DOI: 10.4324/9781003189411-9

place of the female/ and she who was your wife will now be your hus-
band (Mir a naturae vice faemina nasculus [*sic*] extat,/Et quae sponsa
fuit, jam tibi sponsus erit).' Chroniclers of wonders offered many
accounts of sudden sex changes that dramatically illustrated nature's
constant ability to surprise. Such transformations could not be predicted beforehand according to reason, as the German emblem indi-
cated, 'Nature often brings forth something new/Which Reason thinks
impossible (Offt die Natur was newes bringt/ So die Vernunfft unm o
glich findt)'.

(Keller, 2015)

The informal networks of artisans defined artistic and creative engagements
with science and technology as iterative and open-ended practice. Instead of
automation and algorithmic rule, these prototypes express curiosity for what
might exist. They are 'optatives' explored by informal and temporary networks of friends without predefined agenda.

While Instauratio reduces social progress to scientific and technological
innovations, the alchemist and artisan projects in Drebbel and Bornitz open
it to radical challenges. Under the 'folly of empiricism' and its 'book of
friends', science, technology, and society remain hybrid and paradoxical
experiments leading to radical transformation. Drebbel and Bornitz's playful
and creative projects combine social, political, and mythic images and metaphors to define their future as something no one can even imagine, let alone
control.

The emphasis on personal agency and tinkering practices, interpreted in this
book as the experience of time as Kairos, means an opportunity to transform
science, technology, and society. Instead of serving restoration, divine plan,
ontological and political certainty, or order of Chronos, prototypes open the
future to dreams and curiosity. Instead of Bacon's 'time masculine birth' that
brings Instauratio, the prototypes as optatives and desiderata (imagined and
desired projects) support the 'future anterior'. These forgotten engagements
with science, technology, and society, discussed here as artisanal prototypes,
explain the present functions of open hardware prototypes in the hackerspaces
in Chapter 9. We will use them as a model for defining public prototyping in
the sandboxes that support agency over the future in Chapter 12.

Republic of Artisans or Salomon's House

Bacon's metaphor of the Salomon's House (Colie, 1955; Whitney, 1989)
describes his proposal for an academy of science. Named after the mythical
king, the academy serves the project of Instauratio and fulfills God's promise
to humanity. Both science and technology as expert knowledge and experience of time as Chronos become means by which humanity restores its
power after the mythical fall. In contrast to Bacon's academy as Salomon's
House, Drebbel's folly of empiricism or Bornitz's transgender body politics

use instruments and prototypes to perform the future as open to engagement and radical visions. With their emphasis on public engagement and democratization, these projects dream of a society as a kind of republic of artisans (Keller, 2015).

Artisan projects by Drebbel or Bornitz are closer to Leibniz's vision of the Academy of Games and Pleasure (Wiener, 1940) than Bacon's academy. Leibniz's academy like Drebbel's folly of empiricism or Bornitz's transgender body politic demonstrates prototyping that does not reduce future to expert knowledge and Chronos. These projects represent forgotten alternatives to controllable and automated future (restoration and progress) and emphasize time as experience of Kairos, opportunity for new ideas and visions.

In contrast to Salomon's House that explicitly embraces political power as the only goal of science and technology, artisanal projects work with the alchemical ideals of transformation of nature and society (Newman, 2005; Smith, 2004). They refuse to follow teleological and theological dogma reducing science and technology to means (of Instauratio) rather than ends in themselves. Improvements in society and governance, according to Bacon, automatically follow the knowledge of nature and the universe that is closed and pre-given. Progress is then entirely dependent on the instruments, institutions, and infrastructures funded by the patrons who benefit from the teleological vision of the future and society. In this sense, Bacon's theological and teleological view of society only restored the rule of patrons over parasites by new means – instruments of science and technology.

Bacon's academy's role is to guarantee the correct and teleological uses of instruments and prototypes that support the Instauratio project. It combines the function of a laboratory with the court to define and control the main purpose of science and technology, which is to serve the political and social elites – kings chosen by God, such as Salomon. The instruments and prototypes that serve the goal of restoration of the human control over nature are even described as 'experimenta lucifera' (Bacon, Novum Organum, n.d.) contrasting the artisan's 'experimenta fructifera'. Instead of producing only effects (fruit), the main function of the experimenta lucifera is to produce light and knowledge about the real purpose of science and technology. It is a purpose that guarantees control over time and the future (as well as control over society by the patrons supporting this project).

Bacon's 'luciferous' instruments and methods of knowledge as control contrast the tinkering and open experiments of artisans and natural philosophers described as fructifera (experiments producing effects and fruit), serendipitous explorations that do not offer controllable knowledge and innovation that serve the elites. Prototypes producing effects and fruits (fructifera) do not bring any unity of the scientific, religious, and political goals under one project that claims to restore the human power over the creation (Perez-Ramos, 1988). They only offer random 'fruits' that many enjoy without bringing any light or unity and teleology of Instauratio and progress. (Ibid.).

Bacon detested the serendipitous experimenta fructifera that do not follow any commitment to Instauratio (Jardine, 1974), nor explicitly support the absolute rule of the patrons. Instead of controlling the public, the artisan prototypes only amuse and engage (democratize science and technology). To curb the influence of these powerful but vane experiments and instruments, Bacon proposes experimenta lucifera that control the purpose of knowledge and technology. They support the power of the patrons and political elites over the religious project of Instauratio that, according to Bacon, is the only legitimate goal of science, technology, and society.

The main purpose of Salomon's House is then to use science and technology to support the theological project of restoration. Bacon rejects the experimenta fructifera, the wild, poetic, and often creative experiments and visions of society that question the ideal of the predefined and closed future. Making prototypes without pre-given, political, and religious visions of an institution that serves the patrons who represent God's order on earth is irresponsible in Bacon's view. He wants to avoid any uncertainty about whose interest science, technology, and the new institution serve. He explicitly names the new institution after the mythical King Salomon to signal the conservative agenda of preserving the teleological (and monarchist) goals of science and technology as tools restoring religion, myth, and rituals.

Science and technology since Bacon follow this conservative, social, and political agenda of the religious and teleological project of Instauratio. In the Enlightenment period, the restoration is rebranded into the ideal of progress and later technocratic ideals of governance driven by experts. The teleology of God's plan with humanity informs all later concepts of governance as a problem of automation and algorithmic rule of some ideal pre-given order that science and technology both discover and reenact. The closing of the future to the idealized notion of society mirroring ontological or cosmological certainties reduces the issues of governance to Chronos and closes the future for 'parasites'.

We can trace similar teleological notions of governance as restoration and progress in the modern ideals of science, such as Polanyi's 'community of explorers' (Polanyi, 2009) or various technocratic proposals in cybernetics and present transhumanist ideas about singularity. Like Bacon's scientists in the Salomon House, Polanyi's explorers are allowed to experiment with science and technology only if they remain socially and politically conservative, obedient to the political status quo. The nature in Polyani is 'disobedient' and challenges the 'community of explorers' to search, discover, and experiment. However, as citizens, scientists have to follow the predefined goals that remain absolute (although democratic). Polyani rejects any 'moral' disobedience and experiments with governance, society, or politics (our example of the use of time as Kairos) that lead to existentialist and nihilistic philosophies that 'try to apply scientific rigor to matters of human nature and society' (Ibid.).

Disobedience becomes synonymous with freedom in science and technology that reduced governance to the rules of Chronos (knowledge, automation, algorithms serving the patrons).

Experimenta Fructifera and Living Trees with Living Fruit

The prototyping and instrument-making since the Renaissance period combines metaphysical, religious, and social aspirations that serve different ideas about the future. Philosophers and artisans, such as Cornelius Drebbel, Jakob Bornitz, or Robert Fludd, used prototypes to mimic the generative and unpredictable properties of nature (Kairos) and explore new values in society. They believed that they could transform the world, society, and even the body of the artisan with their work on instruments serving various political and social ideals.

The prototyping made cosmology and ontology (as expressions of Chronos) a part of personal and political projects, a matter of Kairos and open future. The biblical 'fall' like Thales' 'fall' before became an opportunity to question the existing status quo (Chapter 4) and transform rather than restore anything. In contrast, the fall in Bacon is a metaphor for degradation that the teleological and theological Instauratio claims to repair.

Artisan cosmoscopes and living instruments (Chapter 6) do not restore anything in society but transform society and even nature beyond anyone's ability to predict or even imagine. As 'living' or 'pansophical' prototypes, instruments define true knowledge as part of a 'living' universe that Comenius described as a tree with living fruit, independent of any institutional or political power and sources of authority (Keller, 2015). The purpose of the instruments and prototypes is to transform society beyond anyone's imagination and control:

> This living universe would not only supply knowledge of all nature with certainty, but it would also show how to produce that which did not yet exist, as a fountain of infinite ideas and inventions. Oh how much was this to be desired! This living universe would serve as an instrument of wisdom greater than the individuals who manipulated it, and thus it could not be led astray by the hand of the individual artisan ('artifi cis manum').
>
> (Ibid.)

Drebbel's living instruments or Comenius living trees of knowledge oppose the myth of automation and the predefined goals of restoration (Instauratio). As metaphors, prototypes, and paradigms, living instruments perform the power of Kairos in governance as well as technology. They support the agency of the artisans who resist the fate of the hungry parasites and perform their agency over the future. Their instruments and prototypes make the future unpredictable and open, inviting everyone to learn and engage with knowledge as part of a creative life and 'pansophism', insight into the whole (similar to Plato's holon discussed in Chapter 4).

This open and transformative role of knowledge and prototypes as an experience of Kairos rather than Chronos is well summarized by the 17th-century academic refugee Comenius,

> He was well aware of the many well-organized Encyclopedias, fashioned as chains of elegantly intertwined mechanisms, which look like automata. Such piles of wood, carefully disposed in order, appear like a tree, with roots that spring from itself and unfold through the power of its innate spirit into branches, leaves, and edible fruit. Yet, they are not truly alive. We desire the living roots of arts and sciences, a living tree, and living fruits. Pansophism, I say, is a living image of the world, cohering by itself, imparting energy to itself and filling itself with fruit. True movement in knowledge required fewer mechanisms and more vitality and spontaneity.
>
> (Ibid.)

Drebbel's mechanical clock or the Comenius living tree and fruit show how vitalist metaphors mix with mechanical contraptions and ideas. They summarize the hybrid and paradoxical role of prototypes and informal networks or scientists and artisans formed over the travelogues and personal inscriptions in the books of friends (album amicorum) that remind us of the present hackerspaces.

Alchemists, artisans, and philosophers in the 17th century captured an unsystematic but open and experimental knowledge that contrasts with Bacon's institutionalized science and teleological goals of Instauratio. Instead of supporting any political status quo that mirrors the ideal state before the Fall of Man, or reducing the social progress to technological and scientific advancements, their artisan prototypes emphasize time as Kairos that enables tinkering and networking.

The artisans' institutions of science, including Leibniz's proposal for the Academy of Games and Pleasure, then summarize the open and fluid experience of prototypes and time as Kairos. We will discuss several descriptions of such hybrid practices and institutions in the work of alchemists and scientists, such as Jakob Bornitz and Johan Joachim Becher. They provide a context for the discussion of hackerspaces in Chapter 9 and the role of prototypes in the sandboxes (Chapter 12) proposed as a model for governance over prototypes.

Future between Restoration and Transformation

Bacon's academy of sciences as Salomon's House define our expectations from institution serving science, technology, and society. The academy became an institution that reduces politics to ontology and cosmology and defines governance as a pursuit for knowledge that will automatically solve all social and political issues (Perez-Ramos, 1988). Under Bacon's vision, science and technology automatically bring a moral restoration that performs God's promise to humanity to rule nature. The enlightenment ideal of scientific progress appropriates this belief in moral advancements that follow the knowledge of nature. It leads to present ideals of algorithmic governance that imposes machines and algorithms reducing governance to a matter of new (trustless and automated) infrastructure.

The governance machines that embody the cybernetic and technocratic ideas of governance, including algorithmic governance, are all successors of Instauratio. They follow the theological reduction of governance to matters of ontological (and religious) justification. Bacon's Instauratio of knowledge that automatically brings moral certainty and provides social and political stability and progress remains the dominant reason for prototyping in science and technology.

The teleological vision of Instauratio contrasts with the artisan projects of Bornitz, Drebbel, or Comenius that use metaphors of alchemist transformation of nature and society to emphasize agency, opportunity, and Kairos in governance, science, and technology. Johann Becher (Smith, 2004) and Cornelius Drebbel (Keller, 2010, 2013) explicitly claim that this transformation includes 'inner' and personal work, or what we call personal and social agency.

Scientific experiments and prototypes increase the knowledge of nature and understanding of patterns and cycles of Chronos, but they also express human agency as an opportunity for transformation (summarized here as the experience of time as Kairos). Prototypes in the Renaissance context connected the work in the laboratory with society and the private life of the artisan. Instead of a restoration, artisans insisted on an alchemical transformation emphasizing personal and social agency. Instead of predefined certainty and stability of the Chronos, ontology, or cosmology, the alchemists embraced time as Kairos. Their experiments have social, political, and personal impacts (P. H. Smith, 2004) that define time and the future as open to personal interventions.

The folly of empiricism as an alternative to the project of Instauratio includes a complex web of aesthetic, theological, and political metaphors and iconography. They describe the alchemical work and transformation as something driven by curiosity and dreams bordering at time with insanity and transgressions. Instead of restoring any predefined ideals of a paradise, these transformations of nature and society embrace the paradoxes and transgressions, such as Bornitz's transgender body politic. The artisanal, speculative, and creative prototypes then define both knowledge and social action as paradigms that probe new social and ontological arrangements (Chapter 6).

Recent studies of alchemy (Newman, 2005; Nummedal, 2011) explicitly describe the tinkering and entrepreneurship as part of the artisanal and commercial culture of the Renaissance period. The complex system of symbolic, ethical, theological, and even personal images and metaphors was open to interpretation rather than serving any teleology. The prototypes incited paradoxes and provocations that transformed their readers, followers, and practitioners without sacrificing their agency:

> As the issue of practice increasingly has come to the fore, alchemy now appears to be a fitting emblem for studies that aim to incorporate a broad array of practitioners and forms of natural knowledge into narratives about the emergence of the 'new science' in the early modern period. Simultaneously bookish, experiential, and experimental, alchemy stubbornly resists any attempt to separate out the histories of reading, writing, making, and doing. In fact, it demands that these various engagements with nature, the relationships among them, and the people of all social strata who created them all be kept in play in any account of its history. In this sense, alchemy offers a model for thinking about early modern science more generally, particularly in light of recent work that has explored the intersection of scholarly, artisanal, and entrepreneurial forms of knowledge.
>
> (Nummedal, 2011)

The hybrid transformation (instead of restoration) is the primary goal of the political artisan (Artifex politicus) as imagined by Bornitz (Keller, 2015). Bornitz viewed governance as a material practice that opens opportunities and includes chance, all synonyms of Kairos (and close to our views of prototyping). Bornitz's political artisan designs 'body politics' to perfect and improve nature, society, and even his own body:

> Bornitz claimed to base his method for transforming the body politic upon nature. As was the case for Botero and as would later be the case for economic thinkers such as William Petty and Johann Joachim Becher, Bornitz drew his more innovative ideas from his thinking about society in terms of matter. It was an alchemical idea of the perfectibility of nature that spurred Bornitz to the so-called mercantilist idea that states should not export raw material, but rather improve upon nature through art to produce a more valuable commodity.
>
> (Ibid.)

The political artisan or similar ideas about governance as a work of art in Giovanni Botero (Ibid.) show close parallels between prototyping and alchemist practice. Governance is a work of transformation guided by vitalist metaphors close to our concept of Kairos rather than restoration defined by Chronos. It is an open-ended process of learning, failing, and experimenting outside the pre-given order. The tinkering with science, politics, and even business in these unique and utopian projects offers an open definition of the future as matter of optatives and opportunities that are always concrete and personal. While Instauratio brings a future as a matter of progress and control over time, for the artisans the future is a matter of transformation on many scales. While the project of restoration imposed the logic of time and knowledge as Chronos, the alchemist transformation embraces the time as Kairos, an open-ended and hybrid process.

To summarize these dichotomies, we will use the example of Leibniz's academy of sciences that emphasized tinkering and experiments that lead to the present hackerspaces and makerspaces. Present tinkering in the hackerspaces and makerspaces revives the complex relationship between personal agency and knowledge, or between science, community, business, even arts, and entertainment. The prototypes support creative and imaginative convergences that open science and society to plural uses, values, and futures against automation and algorithmic rule.

Academy of Games and Pleasures

G.W. Leibniz wrote his 'Odd Thought Concerning a New Sort of Exhibition (or rather an Academy of Sciences)' in 1675 (Wiener, 1940), a century after Bacon's vision of Salomon's House. In his essay, Leibniz described the interaction between science, technology, and the public as matter of transformation without mentioning any restoration of a pre-given order (Instauratio) or progress. Leibniz provocatively ceases to discuss the advancement of sciences and technology in terms of metaphysical and philosophical issues of truth, limits of human mind, nature of reality, or God's plan. He defines science and technology by their capacity to generate new 'ecologies' of interests and influences, new institutions, networks, and relations between different actors and stakeholders.

Renaissance prototypes and instruments in Leibniz, Bornitz, or Drebbel express neither cosmological truths of Chronos nor God's plans. They are opportunities to experiment with tools and institutions as forms of creative collectives rethinking the common future. Leibniz's 'Academy of Sciences', also described as 'Academy of Games and Pleasures', performs the inventions to engage everyone in raising money from the aristocrats, court, and even the general public (Ibid.). Instead of insisting on the teleology of some final ends, Leibniz compares the technological progress in different countries and shows alternative futures and values.

To describe the 'Academy of Games and pleasures', Leibniz uses the metaphor of a casino as a model of engagement with the public. The academy is an institution that tricks the naïve public into gambling and indulging in a complex mechanical toys designed by the scientist to fundraise and support their projects. Instead of serving the aristocrats like Salomon's House, Leibnz's academy engages the public and creates a space for scientific and technological wonders that perform various functions from entertainment to state surveillance. Leibniz describes this as a 'Theater of Nature and Art', mixing performances and operas with scientific experiments, exhibitions of mechanical toys, various new media, exotic plants, and animal species.

The goal of the scientific casino is to support the public interest in the future and bring together different 'stakeholders' to initiate various projects instead of only one, Instauratio. Leibniz describes this institution as a 'general clearing house for inventions' that matches potential investors with inventors and scientists. Coupled with a 'museum of everything that could be imagined', 'museums of rarities', a menagerie, observatory, anatomical theater, it entertains, educates, and shocks. The examples Leibniz uses to describe this hybrid and complex R&D institution form a unique 17th-century political and social experiment rather than a theological project.

The academy is something between a business incubator, a technological park, a science museum, a performance space, and even a tourist attraction. Leibniz's 'odd thought' (drôle de pensée) about this 'new sort of exhibition' (nouvelle sorte de representations) is a prophetic vision of the type of organizations we are starting to witness in the present. Start-up incubators, various science museums, and festivals promote innovation, but also hackerspaces and makerspaces, which more explicitly revive the goals of Leibniz's academy. The new formats of public participation connect not only science, technology, business, and even art to support research in science and technology but also business opportunities and entertainment. They demonstrate the uncanny ability of science and technology to bring together new actors and create new economies, institutions, and politics.

Progress in Leibniz's casino does not follow God's plan but the flow of money, intensity of attention, and levels of public support. It brings together different actors and stakeholders to imagine new futures instead of restoring one idealized future from the past. Inspired by 16th- and 17th-century cabinets of curiosities (Kunstkammer, Wunderkammer) with natural and artificial rarities (rerum naturalium, curiosa), Leibniz's academy mobilizes the political and economic elites via wonders of science and technology and engages the general public. It's main function is to democratize future-making over prototypes without insisting on any pre-given ideal.

In this sense, Leibniz's academy explores alternative visions to the myth of automation and Instauratio, or the present algorithmic governance. The Academy of sciences is a liminal environment closer to the hackerspaces discussed in Chapters 9–11, where prototypes generate new ecologies of interests and influences. Such hybrid environments support the emergence of new institutions, networks, and relations on various macro, meso, and microscales.

From the Academy to the Hackerspace

Leibniz's academy was a precedent that offered a model for open and democratized future-making. It used bottom-up engagements and prototypes common in today's incubators, community labs, and hackerspaces. The kinds of engagements Leibniz envisioned over prototypes are still critical to saving the future and time as a public good. As discussed in the next chapter, we still use prototypes to experiment with the social organization of research as much as with science and technology. In Leibniz and later, prototyping combines personal and social values and interests with knowledge of nature. It acts as a probe into shared futures negotiated through experimentation.

Leibniz explicitly summarized the importance of personal and social engagements with science and technology in the following passage:

> The use of this enterprise for the public and the individual, would be greater than could be imagined. As to the public, it would open people's eyes, stimulate inventions, present beautiful sights, and instruct people with an endless number of useful or ingenious novelties. All those who produce a new invention or ingenious design might come and find a medium for making their inventions known and obtain some profit from that. It would be a general clearing house for all inventions and would become a museum of everything that could be imagined.
>
> (Leibniz in Wiener, 1940)

He predicted not only the membership fee model common in hackerspaces but also the coworking model of hosting different innovative projects in one space: 'preferably different rooms like palace shops in the same house where private parties having rented the rooms, would show the rarities' (Ibid.).

In another note, Leibniz emphasizes the importance of financial autonomy of the new institution, which will be dedicated to the future as an open and public project: 'Having a fund, there would be a perpetual income from interest and from other sources, such as the formation of companies for new manufactures' (Ibid.). In short, Leibniz's academy does not support science and technology as God's plan for humanity, but mobilizes citizens to participate in a creative project that opens the future to diverse goals and ideas. It is a vision of a future-making environment that brings people from different backgrounds together to work on common goals, so that those who are good at 'defraying expenses' will help those who 'constantly invent new things' (Ibid.).

What is intriguing about this vision of the academy as an environment for prototyping and future-making is the emphasis on hybrid and experimental relationships between science, technology, business, and even art. All engagements depend on events and performances that emphasize Kairos, opportunity, agency, and even the transience of encounters. Rather than linear or cyclical restoration or promises of progress leading to an end, the institution depends on ephemeral, temporal, mundane, and pragmatic engagements that are open-ended.

Leibniz's academy embraces time as Kairos and opens the future to what Thales described as a free time to research phenomena no one cares about. The vivid descriptions of entertaining events such as the 'Ballets of horses. Races round a ring and Turkish head. Artificial machines, such as I have seen in Germany. Power of a mirror to kindle a fire' (Leibniz in Wiener, 1940) capture the temporal and ephemeral aspects. Leibniz's academy combines entertainment with more structured formats that remind us of TEDx conferences describing

> Comedies of the styles, debates of each country, a Hindu comedy, a Turkish, a Persian, etc. Comedies of the trades, one for each trade, which would show their skills, peculiarities, jokes, master-pieces, special and ridiculous styles. In other comedies, Italian and French clowns who would perform their buffooneries (Ibid.) and 'Amusing and colloquial disputes'.
>
> (Ibid.)

Events and performances stimulate public interest in science and technology and attract investment to support the experiments. They create a complex ecology of interests and interconnections between local and global actors. As a hybrid and liminal space for new networks, the academy becomes a monad of the universe and society, where new relationships are constantly being fostered. It reiterates Plato's vision of the whole, which we discussed in Chapter 4 as one of the first descriptions of future-making as a form of lawmaking and governance.

The monad as a model of a holistic (political and ontological) engagement becomes an institution in this essay by Leibniz describing his 'Odd Thought Concerning a New Sort of Exhibition (or rather, an Academy of Sciences') in September 1675. It is an institution that explores variety of interactions between nature and society without teleology and hierarchy 'smallest particle of matte is a world of creatures, living beings, animals, entelechies, souls' (Lebniz, 1898). This garden or pond of recursive gardens explores the relationships between different actors, without closing the future to one actor, project, instrument, or monopoly. In this 'strange thought' describing the future academy, Leibniz does not even attempt to reconcile his wild ontology and vitalism with teleology (as he does in the last passages of his monadology).

While Francis Bacon's Instauratio reduced politics to ontology and cosmology that supports the rule of patrons over the future, Lebniz's academy, like other artisan prototypes, democratizes the future and opens it to hybrid and open engagements. Artisans like Thales, Drebbel, and Leibniz revived the value of time as Kairos as essential for science, technology, and governance. Their open-ended, plural, and artisanal explorations offer an alternative to Instauratio and emphasize personal and social agency above the teleology in technology and governance.

From Giorgio Agamben's discussions of the paradigm and Middle Ages' exempla and regula (Agamben, 2009a) to Vera Keller's Renaissance cosmoscopes, living machines, and desiderata (Keller, 2010, 2013, 2015) or Leibniz's academy, prototypes perform hybrid, political, and ontological experiments. They combine Chronos with Kairos to support imaginative and open futures of science, technology, and governance. With this idiosyncratic genealogy of automation as one of many goals of prototyping, we hope to outline the possibility of experiments with governance over prototypes. Instead of closing the future to one project of Instauratio or progress, prototypes explore alternatives to automation or the absolute rule of Chronos and its governance machines. They explore a future as a monad that mirrors the various ontological and political commitments on macro, meso, and micro scales.

Renaissance artisans and present hackers and makers are the true heirs of Thales. They engage with prototypes that express their agency and visions for the future as open and public, questioning the rule of the patrons or gods. From the forgotten practices of instrument-making in the Renaissance period (Chapter 6) to present liminal practices in the hackerspaces (Chapter 9–11) and future sandboxes (Chapter 12), prototypes support the experience of agency and Kairos in governance and technology. In the next chapters, we will discuss examples of prototyping in the hackerspaces and liminal environments to explain how they support open future and time as a matter of personal and social agency against the myth of automation.

On the one hand, prototyping creates new instruments and infrastructures that close the future to one goal; on the other hand, it expresses agency, time, and future as open and 'autotelic' activity that contains its purpose within itself. The 'autotelic' role of prototypes in governance does not reduce governance to technological innovation, disruption, automation, or infrastructure. Against the rule governance machines, it supports Kairos in governance over various liminal environments that will serve as a model for the proposed exploratory sandboxes in Chapter 12.

Part III

Governance over Prototypes

8 From Governance over Rituals and Instruments to Governance over Prototypes

From sundials to blockchains to AI, promissory instruments and infrastructures define governance as a control over the future and time. It is a control over the stability and predictability of Chronos, external cycles and patterns in nature that become templates for society. The enchantment with Chronos replaces the experience of time as Kairos, which defines governance as an opportunity for personal and social action (Chapter 4). Under the ideal of Chronos as control and automation, politics becomes part of cosmology and ontology (Chapter 5). Chronos imposes the rule of rituals, instruments, and infrastructures on society. Instead of being the result of an action, negotiation, or deliberation, governance becomes a matter of designing and prototyping infrastructures that support further automation. We describe this in the part II (Chapters 3-7) as the rule of governance machines, which reinforce the myth of automation with promises of 'disruptive technology and innovation (DTI)' (Brennan et al., 2019), smart cities (Cugurullo, 2020; Gabrys, 2020), Industry 4.0 (Wofford et al., 2020), RegTech (Arner et al., 2017), and algorithmic rule (Atzori & Ulieru, 2017; Just & Latzer, 2017).

In the previous part II, we discussed the genealogy of the myth of automation in the early anecdotes about clocks as well as on the examples of science instruments in the Renaissance period. Promises of control over new instruments quickly evolved into teleological ideals of restoration (Instauratio) over science and technology and Enlightenment ideals of progress. These promises led to a resignation upon agency as Kairos in personal and public life. With every new instrument that promises automation or progress, citizens resign upon their agency over time and their future. Instead of an opportunity for action and transformation (Kairos), time becomes a linear and predictable Chronos, a means of a teleology of progress and restoration of predefined orders and goals.

Chronos imposes regularity, certainty, and stability from a nonhuman scale as an ideal for society. It reduces society to an epiphenomenon of models, data, and algorithms. To save politics and time as Kairos, the right time and moment for action and decision, we need to rethink the role

DOI: 10.4324/9781003189411-11

of prototyping in technology and governance which will be the goal of the next part III.

The prototyping of instruments since Thales (Chapters 3 and 4) served two functions in society. On the one hand, new instruments and ideas reduced politics to cosmology and ontology (Chapter 4) that imposed a monopoly over arbitrary patterns and cycles from nature as normative ideals. On the other hand, prototypes provoked visions for society that challenged existing values and power structures. Concepts, such as paradigm, analogy, model, and exempla in Agamben (Agamben, 2009b) or Renaissance visions of desiderata, living instruments, and cosmoscopes (Keller, 2015), as discussed in Chapters 6 and 7, clarified the emancipatory prototypes that oppose the monopoly contraptions and the ideals of restoration.

Cosmological time as Chronos enables predictions, clocks, and governance machines (Chapter 5), but time as Kairos leads us to challenge the monopolies and teleological ideals of restoration and progress (Chapter 6). The experience of Kairos and agency means that the future remains open to intervention rather than serving a single (predetermined) goal. The prototypes supporting the experience of Kairos in governance then emphasize the importance of curiosity, dreams, and ideas of the 'future anterior' (Chapter 6). Instead of predefined goals, prototypes that support Kairos combine cosmological, political, and social ideas. To reflect upon this alternative history of why we prototype and what is the purpose of science and technology, we will discuss the examples in the hackerspaces and makerspaces that are restoring the forgotten Renaissance practices of instrument-making.

Future-making and prototyping that embrace Kairos as part of governance and not just technology define the future as a public good that requires the democratization of science and technology. Rather than supporting governance based on algorithms, code, or promissory infrastructures, liminal practices and spaces support personal and social engagements with science and technology. We will use examples of open science hardware instruments in Chapter 9 and the open hardware innovation ecosystem in Shenzhen in Chapter 10 to demonstrate interventions that preserve the experience of time as Kairos. They represent the forgotten history of instrument-making and prototyping (Chapters 6 and 7), which informs our proposal for exploratory sandboxes in Chapter 12.

From Living Instruments to Open Science Hardware

The goal of modern scientific instruments is to reproduce and scale Thales' original success with olive presses while ignoring his original goals. Instead of a predictive control, his monopoly contraption served as a critique of the status quo and the values of society. Thales' knowledge of cycles and Chronos performed the importance of his personal time as Kairos. His goal was to demonstrate the value of personal time to conduct research and formulate insights that challenge values and power structures in society (Chapters 3 and 4). He used the knowledge of Chronos (measurable orbits, patterns, and cycles) to express his agency as Kairos in politics as well as what we nowadays call science and technology.

Thales' monopoly over olive presses is the founding act of Western philosophy, technology, and governance. It describes a control over the patterns and cycles in nature (Chronos) that define all later teleological promises of progress and Instauratio (Chapter 6). While Thales' insights enabled monopoly, their purpose was 'autotelic': to enhance Thales' agency over the future and time, rather than to embody an ideal future.

Thales' insights into Chronos were meant to empower fellow citizens to realize the importance of doing something that no one else cared about and having agency over their time as Kairos, an opportunity to discover and question. Instead, the clocks as a product of this insight into Chronos turned citizens into parasites of future infrastructures and monopolies. This is contrary to the original purpose, which was to question the social values and status quo of the merchants and aristocrats and to create an opportunity for an alternative vision of society and the future.

We traced the 'autotelic' idea of prototyping serving Kairos back to Thales (Chapter 5) and the concepts of living instruments and cosmoscopes in the Renaissance period (Chapters 6 and 7) that lead to the present experiments with open science hardware discussed in Part III. Through technological innovation and disruption, prototypes change society, but they also explore radical ideas about governance. Instead of reducing Kairos to innovation, prototypes also embrace the freedom to experiment and engage with open future as an equally important expression of agency. We will demonstrate this on the present grassroots movements of makerspaces, hackerspace, and citizen laboratories that experiment with governance and technology. In these spaces, prototypes support personal and communal engagements with science and technology that become opportunities to rethink the future of society and experience time without obeying the Chronos or teleology of predefined goas.

Community-driven and do-it-yourself (DIY) instruments revive the practices of artisans and natural philosophers that we discussed as the folly of empiricism and experimenta fructifera (Chapter 6). Artisans in the past and present redefine the relations between science, technology, and society as a matter of an open future that does not impose any final goals. Projects calling for algorithmic sovereignty (Roio, 2018) platform cooperativism (Sandoval, 2019; Schneider & Scholz, 2016), various data co-ops (Micheli et al., 2020; Staub, 2016), and other self-governance experiments show the importance of prototyping as not only a technological but also a political action. They represent an effort to save agency and Kairos in governance and emphasize participation and empowerment through prototyping.

Prototypes that democratize future-making support the ideal of an open future that makes science, technology, and time personal and political matter rather than a cosmological or ontological insight. Based on the examples of prototyping, such as Kairos supporting personal and social agency in Chapter 9, we will propose an environment for exploratory governance of emerging science and technology infrastructures in the sandboxes in Chapter 12.

Autotelic Prototypes

The tensions between the agency as action and transformation (Kairos) versus cycles and patterns to obey (Chronos) is crucial for our definition of prototyping. While Chronos is linear, regular, and measurable time predicting phenomena and events on the nonhuman scale, Kairos is synonymous with our lived experiences and agency. It is the ability to change, transform, and define personal and common purpose and future.

We used the dichotomy of Kairos and Chronos to define the problem of automation and the rule of governance machines. Against this resignation upon personal and social control over time and the future, we placed the experiments with prototyping that support Kairos in governance as much as in technology. The insistence on Kairos in governance means resisting any reduction of future to predictable and predefined goals serving the patrons while defining the rests as parasites.

Barbara Cassin's interpretation of the two concepts of time in ancient Greek philosophy (Cassin, 2014) inspired this view of prototyping as the expression of Kairos in technology and governance. Cassin describes Kairos as the rule of language and meaning (logos) in politics that contrasts with the static cosmos, ontology, and Chronos. The dichotomy between structure and opportunity, insight and action, summarizes the original clash between the sophists and philosophers as a conflict between politics and ontology. She describes Kairos as an 'autotelic' and immanent time containing its own purpose within itself. The purpose is a political 'plurality that is at once conflictual and temporalized' (Ibid.) rather transcendental or ontological.

Preserving the value of Kairos is crucial for prototyping not only because it characterizes time as an expression of agency but also the original prototype of governance, the democratic city is a structure that emerges from the "wilderness". Cassin defines Kairos as a 'continuous creation, contradiction after contradiction... perpetual construction of the artifact that is the city and bears witness to the fact that the city is first of all a performance' (2014). The city as the original prototype and medium of Kairos emphasizes the precedence of performance, agency, and risk-taking over the certainty and ontology.

The discussions of Chronos and Kairos in Cassin pertain to Hannah Arendt's insistence on vita activa (Arendt, 2013) opposing ontological and cosmological facts defined by instruments. The imperfect but necessary actions of citizens who must figure out how to live together in an open and democratic society involve but do not reduce to the various infrastructures and instruments. Kairos as vita activa expresses the ideal of a free society, city, and infrastructure that are always open to transformation and action. Instead of reducing the choices of citizens to ontology or cosmology, political agency and Kairos expresses their personal and social agency.

The original artifact and infrastructure defining citizens' agency is the free society, the city, that embodies the Kairos. In Cassin, this view of the city as a space for Kairos is in sharp opposition to the premodern ideals that define the city as a mirror of the cosmos or celestial hierarchies of gods, rulers, and later Plato's 'ideal souls'. As an autotelic prototype, the city performs the governance as social and individual practice without reducing it to cosmos, Chronos, or an ideal soul. The city as the original prototype is an effect of active life (vita activa) and expression of agency and opportunity, in which we define our values and goals while living and experimenting together.

The prototypes, as Cassin shows on the example of the city, do not mirror any external and cosmological ideals of chronology or teleological projects of Instauratio (6). They express the personal and social preferences and actions of its inhabitants and users. The ultimate autotelic prototype and "paradigm" of a democratic society is the city state in ancient Greece. It is an example of an experimental and liminal environment connecting agency with external structures governance with technology, and Kairos with Chronos. We need prototypes that support Kairos in technology and governance to oppose the regressive teleological ideals of progress that only preserve the status quo while claiming to embody some organic unity, organism, perfect souls, or God's promises.

Instead of God's plan or Plato's souls that represent natural unity and one goal (telos), the prototypes and infrastructures in this book embody Cassin's view of the city as an autotelic Kairos. They perform politics by artifacts and infrastructures that disrupt and innovate without imposing any goal or model (Chronos, cosmos) on society. Kairos in governance and technology means plurality of goals and projects by citizens that use their space and time to express various personal and social agendas.

If we reduce politics and Kairos to ontology, cosmology, Chronos, or other ideals of automation, we only close the future to one rule. We impose something that philosophers like Barbora Cassin and Hannah Arendt describe as the 'Syracuse syndrome' after the infamous enslavement of Plato by Diogenes. It means imposing cosmos or Chronos as the ideal goals of bios theoretikos' contemplative life rather than action. Against this, we have to insist that philosophical and scientific insights into the micro and macro scales should not define the political life, 'bios politikos', 'the political way of life' (Arendt in Cassin, 2014). The insights and knowledge of bios theoretikos, (and Chronos) including the instruments and governance machines, lead to a loss of personal and social agency and opportunities for change, action, and transformation.

Instead of opening the future to various interventions, the governance machines close the future to one rule of an idealized cosmos and Chronos. It is a rule that defines the citizens as surplus, parasites, precarious, and jobless masses in a system that can run without them. Like the hungry parasites under the clocks in Rome (Chapter 4), the citizens adapt to the new instruments and algorithms that pretend to be without a political agenda, interests, and relations with Kairos. Algorithms, automation, and predictive analytics control their personal and public lives, including mundane activities and public institutions that serve the goals of the new cursed inventors and their patrons.

Saving Agency and Kairos in Future-Making

All governance machines start as prototypes that extend the insights from the nonhuman scale to human society. They become instruments that use cosmological knowledge of planetary revolutions, weather cycles, or other arbitrary patterns and phenomena in nature to support monopolies. The transformation of science instruments from prototypes that support curiosity to governance machines that impose control summarizes the problem of automation. It is a rule of an infrastructure as a ritual or a devil's bridge (Chapter 5) that reduces the experience of Kairos to a technological change that promises patterns, models, and other forms of Chronos. The patterns and structures of Chronos replace social action and politics with algorithms that claim power and control over the future as a matter of automation.

To save agency and Kairos, we need prototypes that support transitory and open interventions and deliberations by citizens. Instead of limiting citizens' choices to decisions made by innovators and their patrons, they need to increase engagements with science, technology, and society. To prevent the arbitrary power over the future by every new governance machine commodifying and quantifying the personal and social agency and time, autotelic prototypes democratize the future-making. They support the ideal of an open future as experiments with new infrastructures and policies, thinking and doing (acting, making), theoretical and practical reason.

Kairos as participation in future-making and prototyping presents an alternative to the rule of Chronos expressed as automation and algorithmic rule. Prototypes as practices, concepts, and products let citizens form new identities, institutions, and visions for the future. To discuss how instruments and tools support Kairos in governance and not only technology, we will introduce examples of open science instruments that save personal and social agency over the future (of science). Together with examples of innovation in the liminal zones, such as Shenzhen (Section 11), they will help us define a sandbox model for participatory future-making. Sandboxes will then define engagements with technology and governance beyond the calls for automation, prediction, and algorithmic rule (Chapter 12).

The Age of Prototypes and Demos

The age of prototypes and demos is challenging our understanding of the public good and common interest that include time and the future. Prototypes not only translate scientific and technical knowledge into useful products that serve the industry and transform the future of society. Their slow and indirect influence upon the future replaces governance and bulldozes society with new infrastructures, such as social networks or blockchain trustless networks and smart contracts. Technologies that serve automation as the only ideal enact an arbitrary power over public life, imagination, personal, and social agency.

The ideal of automated or algorithmic governance performs the power of prototypes over public imagination and future. They extend the original 1936 thesis by Walter Benjamin about the early 20th century as a convergence of mass production with politics (Benjamin, 2018) into the 21st-century convergence of mass automation and the end of politics. Benjamin described the 'age of mechanical reproduction' as automation that enabled mass political movements and novel mass production practices in factories and media, such as film and photography. The mechanical reproduction represented by the media and factories of the 20th century changed the idea of a political subject. It defined the citizens as an amorphic mass of viewers in the cinema, workers on the assembly line, or consumers of mass products.

The cinema and factory as sites that formed the new social identities reduced the citizens to members of classes and nations serving totalitarian and collectivist fantasies. Present automation seems to extend this 20th-century subjects into more isolated and predictable patterns of demographic data that are not even human. The 21st-century citizen is not part of any masses with historical agenda, but a swarm of data and molecules under persistent 24/7 surveillance. The 'subject' was atomized under various IT infrastructures, and recently also subjected to extreme for of biocontrol over PCR machines during the COVID-19 pandemic. The convergence of various modes of control and automation supports a political theology of purity, sacredness, and sacrifice (Kahn, 2012) with a totalitarian and regressive edge.

Instead of mass movements and collective identities, we are witnessing a pervasive micromanagement of arbitrary molecules and data that serve the new patrons and their infrastructures. While mechanical reproduction in the 20th century supported collectivist fantasies claiming historical missions of various classes and nations, the 21st-century automation serves a political theology of data and algorithms. It reduces citizens to parasites and dangerous reservoirs of germs that threaten the status quo by their mere existence. Prototypes of new infrastructures become tools to support monopolies, algocracy (Danaher, 2016), and surveillance capitalism (Zuboff, 2018). To save history, politics, and agency as expressions of Kairos against the pervasive power of Chronos, we need prototypes that empower the citizens to engage with science and technology as matter of politics and not only ontology or cosmology.

Prototypes in Hackerspaces and Makerspaces

In order to save history and politics from the rule of automation and algorithmic rule, we have to insist on Kairos in governance and not only technology. We defined Kairos as social and personal agency engaged in prototyping, described in Chapters 6 and 7 via the examples of Renaissance instrument-making. The same instruments that define the teleological project of progress and Instauratio, also define the possibility of plural and transformative visions of society represented by alchemists and natural philosophers, such as Drebbel or Bornitz. Present-day geeks, tinkerers, amateur scientists, and activists in the hackerspaces and makerspaces revive this tradition. They explore the alternatives to the teleological mission of Instauratio representing the control over time and the future as Chronos. Practices and prototypes outside the official R&D labs, industry, and university centers support plural goals and values that present experiments with the community, governance, and institutions preserving the open future.

While professional designers use prototypes to gather feedback on future services and products, hackerspace geeks and makers use prototyping to explore alternative uses and futures of various tools. They are stakeholders in the future and peers that demand democratization of innovation and control over the infrastructure. The geeks and tinkerers around the hackerspaces and makerspaces create tools without a clear agenda that have often surprising functions. They often solve problems of missing and expensive infrastructure, but also express their joy of making, as noted in the key reflections of these communities by Gabriella Coleman (Coleman, 2013) and Sarah Davies (Davies, 2017).

Hackerspace and makerspace prototypes are often creative but failed explorations performing the skills of the hackers who form communities around tools described as kits or open-source projects that never become real products or services. They are often only expressions of resistance and exploration of different (mis)uses that open time and future to personal agency. We describe such prototypes as autotelic and participatory. They support artists, philosophers, and other unexpected 'users' as future stakeholders who experiment with the tools to explore personal and communal futures Hackers and makers shape a global culture of alternative networks of knowledge production and sharing that serve plural and sometimes conflicting needs and goals, further discussed in Chapters 9–11.

On the one hand, hacking, making, and DIY activities support resilience and self-sufficiency. We see this on the projects such as open source Geiger counters helping grassroots radiation monitoring in Japan (Tokyo Hackerspace and Safecast[1]), or DIY drones supporting citizen journalism in Slovakia (Progressbar OccuCopter[2]), or DIY biology (DIYbio) wine-brewing protocols saving lives while protesting high alcohol taxation in Indonesia (HONF and Intelligent Bacteria project,[3] later Lifepatch[4]). On the other hand, many of the projects remain ambiguous, even mocking the effects of intrusive and sinister technologies, or testing the comfort levels around them. It could be the pizza printer in London Hackerspace,[5] which is an amusing and ominous look into the future of junk food merging with 3D printers and robotics. Another example is the intrusive AI automation system, the 'MOTHER' of hackerspace automation, designed and used by Louisville's Hackerspace LVL1[6] to monitor the productivity levels of its members and analyze how they use their time and space, even nagging them to remove trash and do daily chores.

The prototypes in hackerspaces provoke instead of solving world problems. They are leisure activities and 'practices streaked through with joy' (Davies, 2017) that remind us of the original purpose of Thales' monopoly over olive presses (Chapter 4). Making and tinkering are forms of personal reflections that often border with art performance. They support obstruse interests and ambitions, such as self-governance and autonomy through collective and open tinkering or pure pleasure of breaking the taboos, such as the neuromodulators in the hackerspace Brmlab[7] or the Hackerfleet, by Berlin-based c-base.[8] While Brmlab's brain hacking explored the effects of brain cortex electric stimulation (EBS) on individual cognitive abilities and moods, Hackerfleet was an open-source naval solution exploring the individual and group legal status of paperless entities in international waters. Both show prototypes as unique opportunities to engage, question, and push the boundaries of technology, society, and governance.

Makers and Hackers' Governance

Hackerspaces as liminal environments for prototyping preserve the experience of time as Kairos in technology and governance. To explore the future(s) beyond the promises of Chronos, automation, and algorithmic rule, these environments rely upon critical practices and inquiry, including creative experiments with technology, science, and society. DIY kits, workshops, and various novel formats of participation support explorations and expressions of individual and collective interests in emerging technologies.

Prototypes that support public engagement use the tension between governance and technology to search for new ways of thinking and living together in the age of prototypes. They embrace time as Kairos, an opportunity for social and personal agency that resists any teleology or search for fundamental and common ground from which to engage in thinking, speaking, making, or governing. In this sense, prototypes are like paradigms and living instruments discussed in Chapter 6 that question the divisions between practical and theoretical reason (Taylor, 2016), episteme and techne (Parry, 2020), theoria and praxis (Bénatouïl & Bonazzi, 2012).

Hackerspaces as hybrid environments for prototyping have an ambiguous relation to governance as much as technology, which makes them an important site for rethinking control over time and the future as Chronos and Kairos. Philosophy and politics since Plato's Republic excluded makers and artisans from good governance (Rosen, 2005; Salkever, 1992). Good governance was defined as the domain of norms, ideals, insights, and institutions, recently also ethical AI guidelines. This denigration of making and makers (Parry, 2020) is a continuation of the critique of practice in Aristotle's Politics, Book VII (Aristotle, 1944b), know-how or techné in book I (Aristotle, 1944a), and

Metaphysics book I (Aristotle, 1933) or the action or ergon in Plato's Menexenus, 236d-e (Plato, 1925).

Good governance as a matter of the right insight and knowledge since then relays on infrastructures, cosmological cycles and order of Chronos. It is never something we prototype, iterated upon, or experiment with. To define prototyping for governance as insistence on time as Kairos means including experiments and iteration on politics as much as science and technology (Chapter 12). The general exclusion of material engagements in politics still guides our ideals of political deliberation that is defined as a matter of communication. We prioritize knowledge, insights, and contemplation as expressions of Chronos over the actions and practices of Kairos.

The prototyping in the hackerspaces and makerspaces problematizes this exclusion of experimention from governance and brings back the importance of improvisation and tinkering as expressions of Kairos. Prototypes become a form of material deliberation on the common future as a political, and not only technical matter, as an experiment and project. Hybrid practices and environments even reject the divisions of theoretical and practical reason and define governance as an experience of prototyping, designing, and experimenting together.

From Ethnography to Engagements with Prototypes

Autotelic, civic, and participatory prototyping in hackerspaces and makerspaces is a model for governance whose goal is to preserve the future as open. This prototyping revives the values of artisanal and 'maker knowledge'. Instead of serving predefined and teleological goals that reinforce the status quo, the prototypes in the hackerspaces define their own agenda, commitments, and visions of the future. They combine the theoretical, aesthetic, political, and pragmatic interests of the local and global groups of geeks, hackers, and makers to initiate temporary but resilient networks and institutions and combine governance with prototyping.

Between 2010 and 2016, we followed emerging hackerspaces, makerspaces, fablabs, and citizen laboratories in various regions to understand how they use prototypes and experiment with science and technology for (self) governance. Over the years, we documented over 20 projects around the world that capture the role of prototyping in mobilizing different social, political, and aesthetic agendas (Kera, 2012b, 2012c, 2014a; Kera et al., 2013). The main insight was that many of the prototypes mock and subvert the techno-utopian agendas to create opportunities for personal and communal agency over the future. They combine learning and research with deliberation, artistic, and philosophical reflections.

The ethnographic research mapped these networks and identified an informal geek diplomacy (Kera, 2015, 2017) that combines private and public, even political and geopolitical, agendas. We engaged directly with the movement after 2012 by joining the Hackteria biohacker network in Yogyakarta,

Indonesia. This global network of scientists, artists, and designers goal was to introduce open biology hardware instruments to various Global South universities lacking infrastructure. Hackteria supported citizen science and open science projects through webcams turned into microscopes, bioreactors in plastic bottles, sterilization chambers with UV lights in an old scanning machine, etc.

We used all these prototypes in an early 2012 project that transformed a common Indonesian mobile food truck, so-called angkringan, into a scientific laboratory. The mobile angkringan laboratory enabled molecular gastronomy experiments as science engagements on the streets of Yogyakarta. Equipped with a DIY sterilization chamber, microscope, and bioreactor, it supported science communication and engagement with the public on the streets of Yogyakarta. By performing molecular gastronomy spherification techniques, it questioned the divisions between posh cuisine and street food, but also the idea that scientific work is independent from culture, everyday life, and interests.

Breaking the divides between lab, kitchen, and street in Yogyakarta opened new forms of engagement between science and society. By democratizing science in the streets, we connected the local food practices and materials with science experiments and adapted protocols and instruments to interpret the Sago pearl desert into 'spherified' wine-based pearls from a local fruit wine. The projects intentionally connected science to everyday life practice, such as cooking or playing, and explored the limits of personal agency in imagining different futures of (community) science.

To document such fringe practices and engagements, we often used a combination of design fiction movies, scenarios, and mockups. The initial angkringan project later developed into a scenario for synthetic biology and fermentation. It was presented during the EMERGE Festival of making and prototyping at Arizona State University in 2012. The project also inspired several prototypes exploring food commensality in Singapore (Kera & Sulaiman, 2014), nutrigenomics dinners (Kera, 2012a; Kera & Storni, 2011), citizen science experiments with fermentation under the GuthHub project (Dolejšová & Kera, 2016, 2017; Kera & Sulaiman, 2014) (Figures III.1–III.2 and III.9–III.11). All projects included collaborations with various hackerspaces and local art and food collectives.

The playful, artistic, and exploratory prototypes supported the experiences of (self) governance by breaking down the divisions between theoretical and practical reason, science and everyday life, time as Chronos and Kairos, structure, and agency. This is also visible in another project on 'brain uploading' performance with fMRI data in 2013 as part of a workshop on data liberation for citizen science projects in Brmlab Hackerspace Prague. In this workshop, we explored future extreme forms of quantification and produced a design fiction movie (which inspired a workshop on DIY Mind Machines in Singapore in 2016, Figure III.3–III.6).

The playful appropriations of science protocols and instruments continued in Switzerland and Singapore with microfluidics DIY kits, night hunts for fluorescent organisms, hacked spiritual chants automata, and open hardware using traditional crafts (Ausareny et al., 2014) (Figure III.7 and III.8). After 2013, this collaborative tinkering also included geopolitical lessons in the special economic zone and the capital of open hardware, Shenzhen, in China (Chapter 11). The hybrid environment supported experiments with open hardware in workshops organized by Silvia Lindtner in 2014 (Lindtner, 2020) and Dangerous Prototypes studio in 2015.

All projects aided the development of science infrastructure for the Global South (Hirosue et al., 2015; Kera et al., 2019) and challenged the view that discovery and innovation are something separated from culture and art. The exploratory prototypes would connect design, art, and traditional crafts by placing Russian Geiger counters in traditional Himeji windchimes in Japan or microfluidics boards into the Indonesian wayang kulit theater (Ausareny et al., 2014). Custom-made printed circuit boards became an ideal medium for connecting science and technology with traditional artisan techniques, ideas about the future with interpretations of the past.

In 2014 and 2015 in collaboration with the Tel Aviv Makerspace TAMI, we also used custom-made circuits to explore the media archeology of etching. It became a technique that connects the present and past functions of discovery and innovation, the origins of print culture (iron etching) with present electronics and microelectromechanical systems or MEMS (Kera, 2014b). The printed circuit boards reflected the early Renaissance prints, but also alchemist iconography that explores the relations between humans and the nonhuman on micro- and macroscales. By superimposing the original etched image of Albrecht Dürer (Landscape with a Cannon) on an open science hardware board that uses the so-called lickometer circuit common in behavioral science research, we explored the different functions of instruments. The project was a tribute to Dürer and also a probe into the connection between war machines and the idea of circuits, loops, and triggers. From Dürer's early prints teaching aristocrats how to fortify cities to cybernetics and behavioral circuits, we see how innovation serves power and war, as well as art and open inquiry into what is possible.

Against prototypes that divide society into patrons and parasites, we explored prototypes that connect the universe, human body, and society in projects rethinking the interactions on multiple scales. For example, we used magic circles and amulets designed as circuits and combined electronics with microfluidics and 21st-century Tarot cards.[9] The prototypes became a medium to connect the present and past ideas of interaction across the molecular, human, and planetary scales. Instead of war and defense, the engagements demonstrated the use of time as Kairos, an opportunity for personal and communal experiences with time and different 'scales' for creative projects. We will mention some of the examples of open science hardware projects from the Hackteria network (Chapter 9) and Shenzhen (Chapter 11) to illustrate how prototypes enable Kairos in governance and technology that will help us explain the proposal for sandboxes in Chapter 12.

Singapore Hackerspace 2010–2016

Figure III.1 Fermentation GutHub in Singapore show and taste meetup 2015

Figure III.2 Singapore Hackerspace SG DIYbio meeting 2009

Figure III.3–III.6 DIY Mind Machines workshop in Singapore Makerspace 2016

Notes

1 http://blog.safecast.org/2012/03/safecast-geiger-counter/
2 http://hackerspaces.org/wiki/OccuCopter
3 http://www.natural-fiber.com/
4 http://www.lifepatch.org/
5 http://wiki.london.hackspace.org.uk/view/Project:PizzaPrinter
6 http://www.lvl1.org/2012/02/15/mother/
7 http://brmlab.cz/project/brain_hacking/tdcs
8 http://www.hackerfleet.org/hackership.en.html
9 Parlor of Futures, 2017 https://github.com/anonette/futures

9 Grassroots Governance over Open Science Hardware*

Prototypes of open science hardware (OSH) instruments challenge not only the epistemic (improving the knowledge about nature) but also normative (improving society) ideals of science and technology. They emphasize the open exploration and various (mis)uses of instruments in personal and public life. The OSH instruments revive the hybrid Renaissance practices discussed in Chapters 5 and 6 and offer alternatives to automation as an ideal of governance. They support the experience of Kairos in governance and technology in various emancipatory, aesthetic, and exploratory projects.

The 'public' science instruments often explore surprising functions, such as political activism[1] over Hackteria microscopes[2] or incubators supporting science in the Global South, artistic explorations, and creative (mis)uses, such as the Wild OpenQCM tool,[3] which connects a quartz crystal biosensor with an artistic theremin in performances. Instead of a civil and military 'dual use' (Atlas & Dando, 2006), they confront us with complex, plural, and hybrid uses that rewrite the famous motto and assert that 'in the future, everyone will be a scientist for 15 minutes'.

The DIY instruments explore not only the hidden forces in nature that define the certainty and predictability of Chronos but also Kairos, as an individual and collective agency of the citizen scientists, geeks, and hackers who tinker to explore unexpected uses. When we compare the Renaissance artisan instruments and present OSH to the more classic examples of the vacuum air pump (Baudot, 2012; van Helden, 1991), we will notice the difference. The purpose of the DIY instruments is not to woo the public into worship of science but to invite everyone to take part in the tinkering and demystify the aura of science and technology. In this respect, OSH explores the idea of the artisanal origins of modern science and society described by the historian and

* This section uses parts of published articles: Kera, Denisa. "Science Artisans and Open Science Hardware." *Bulletin of Science, Technology & Society* 37, no.2 (June 2018): 97–111. Link. DOI 10.1177/0270467618774978.

   Kera, Denisa. "The Museum as a 21st Century Bestiary: Biotechnology, Nanotechnology and Art Between Protocols and Manifests." In Filippoupoliti, Anastasia (ed.) *Science Exhibitions: Curation & Design*, Edinburgh: MuseumsEtc (2010): 210–237, Link ISBN: 978-1-907697-03-6.

DOI: 10.4324/9781003189411-12

philosopher of science, Edgar Zilsel. His somehow forgotten 1942 thesis (Zilsel, 2000) describes the work of superior artisans in the Renaissance period as a practice that bridged the social, epistemic, and political divides crucial for any social transformation.

Instrument-making transformed the middle-age society. It aligned the interests of the different types of scholars (philosophers, mechanical artists, theologians) who bridged the disciplinary and social barriers in the 16th century. Renaissance instruments, as much as present OSH, perform time as an opportunity (Kairos) that combines technology with governance and leads to surprising and unexpected transformations. Time is an opportunity to experiment with new knowledge and tools that transform society without creating a monopoly or closing the future to one goal. As an artisanal practice, prototyping saves the agency as ability to decide the future of society while generating new knowledge and creating new tools.

The present hackers, makers, and citizen scientists revive Zilsel's thesis that claims that social transformation in the Renaissance period was the result of convergence of artisanal and scholarly knowledge, practice, and theory (Ibid.). According to Zilsel, the work on the instruments combined the theoretical and experimental interests of the three classes of citizens and defined a new political order and agenda. Secular humanists, scholastic academics, and pragmatic artisans represented the social and epistemic divisions in the Renaissance period. Their work on the instruments transformed the status quo leading to modernity.

Instrument prototypes transformed science as much as society, as we discussed on the examples of Francis Bacon and Cornelius Drebbel in Chapters 6 and 7. In Bacon, science and technology imposed the rule of science as knowledge of Chronos upon society to serve the ideals of restoring God's promise to humanity guarded by patrons (Instauratio). In Drebbel, the instruments defined a new class of philosophers and artisans experimenting with political, cosmological, and ontological ideas as expression of time as Kairos. Drebbel's instruments ignored the common divisions between mechanical arts and vitalism, cosmology and politics, and even Chronos and Kairos. They democratized knowledge to serve various social and political projects expressed as wish lists (desiderata and optativa).

Drebbel's prototypes and present DIY instruments are unique and creative projects that bridge various divides and explore the future anterior as a care for what might exist. They do not serve any status quo or teleological goal but concrete citizens that combine their skills and concerns about nature and society, personal and public matters.

The idiosyncratic instruments bring a convergence of not only technical and social but also scientific and artistic processes and practices. Instead of embodying insights into the cycles and patterns of Chronos that serve automation as the ideal of governance, artisan prototypes combine epistemic and normative interests and express Kairos in governance as much as technology. Citizens engage in decision-making over the tools and define various ideas about not only science and technology but also society and the future. Instead of only communicating and representing scientific ideas to the public (the classic painting about the air pump experiment), the instruments become an integral part of the activities and lives of the citizens. We will discuss this on the examples of OpenDrop electrowetting[4] or the OSH manifesto in the next chapters.

Prototyping for governance responds to science and technology controversies by increasing participation rather than insisting on expert knowledge and visions. It opens the future to new visions, as we can see in another example, the 'Open Source Estrogen'[5] project. The direct engagement with prototypes articulates a full spectrum of ideas and values between emancipation and open exploration in science as in much as society, in knowledge as in much as governance. The Renaissance instruments or present DIY prototypes, therefore, serve the experience of time as Kairos, an opportunity for change and action that resist the reduction of governance to technology, algorithms, or other forms of Chronos. These instruments mobilize citizens to respond to the promissory, dystopian, and uncertain futures with more action and even provocations. They bridge the present divides in the pursuit of democratic governance and agency over time and the future.

Open Science Hardware

Prototyping for governance supports time as an experience of personal and social agency or Kairos. It serves the ideal of an open future connecting various actors and agendas that bridge the present divides. Governance becomes material and social engagement and practices that define the future as open to anyone willing to tinker and work on the instruments. We can see this in the example of Hackteria's OpenDrop electrowetting platform.

OpenDrop is a DIY tool that moves molecules and cells in an electric field through a gamelike console that supports experiments with science and art. The community around the tool uses it for game design, artistic performances with molecules, and also serious pursuit providing tools for cheaper experiments that support drug discovery. Similarly, the reverse osmosis filtration system and DIY spectrometry in the 'Open Source Estrogen' project connect science, politics, and art. DIY sensors monitoring xenoestrogen pollution in the environment become a medium to implement 'estrogen' politics and allow the public to rethink the (trans) gender.

Most DIY prototypes from the hackerspaces and citizen futures labs support such creative engagements with science, politics, and art that bring together different actors and agendas and define the future as an experience of Kairos rather than automation and Chronos. The work on incubators, microscopes, and 3D printed instruments by a Spanish collective 'GYNEpunk: Autonomous gynecologyLAB'[6] also enacts gender and science politics, including patient rights and the future of clinical trials. Hackteria prototypes of DIY instruments support citizen science as much as science infrastructure in the Global South and ambiguous concepts of governance and geopolitics.

The HONF's work[7] with bioreactors and satellites uses the gallery space as a laboratory for rethinking the common future of communities dependent on agriculture. The prototypes connected art with future scenarios and functional solutions. In Thailand, DIY spectrometers supported the pursuit of 'big data' in organic and urban agriculture[8] and the search for new economic models. The project connected emerging technologies and scientific research with business opportunities in the Global South. In Nepal, the microsatellites for space exploration[9] aimed at reforming education to include more hands-on practice, but they also challenge the stereotypes of developing countries' ambitions when it comes to space.

The document that summarizes the purpose and values of these open and ambiguous uses of science instruments is the OSH manifesto - Global Open Science Hardware (GOSH) Manifesto formulated in 2016 during the first meeting of OSH geeks, makers, and citizen scientists in CERN. In this meeting, we defined the challenges of OSH prototyping that serves research as much as the 'technological transparency and public oversight' (Global Open Science Hardware (GOSH) Manifesto, 2016) of research. OSH became an explicit example of prototyping that connects science, technology, and governance. It not only improves the oversight and public perception of science but also engages citizens and enables them to 'create, obtain, study, modify, distribute, use and share (science instruments) designs' (Ibid.) in a variety of contexts. Instead of mobilizing citizens to accept new entities, such as vacuum in the case of the air pump, or new sources of authority, such as the expert scientists, OSH prototypes support sharing, working together, and reflecting science and technology with friends in various formal and informal settings.

Science Artisans as Modern Thaleses

The prototyping of open science and DIY instruments revives the artisanal approach to science and technology that emphasizes Kairos. It bridges the divides between various domains of knowledge (engineering, humanities, art, science) and civic virtues (libertarian DIY-making and self-reliance vs peer culture of collaboration and communitarian values). With direct access to instruments and policy discussions, citizens gain agency and disperse the asymmetries of power. They actively define their future by connecting prototyping with governance.

Instead of closing the future to predefined projects of innovation or further automation of society, citizens engage with time and the future as open and commons resources. To contextualize this open future, we will use Zilsel's thesis to describe how prototyping bridges various disciplinary divides and transforms society. Prototyping becomes a means of personal and social agency and example of Hannah Arendt's active life. To capture this ambiguity of prototyping creating monopolies, on one side, or exploring the open future, on the other, we will use Arendt's division between action (leisure), labor, and work (2013). The prototypes express Kairos as a personal and social agency that influences the future. They bring not only new discoveries but also misuses and creative projects. This emphasis on science artisans then responds to Arendt's critique of instruments as a resignation from politics and society and revives Zilsel's thesis.

DIY makers, hackers, and present artisans use prototypes to interact, define, and perform what living together means in the changing sociotechnical milieu. They use tools to define their future while facing various risks and challenges, such as estrogen pollution, antibiotic crisis, emerging, and disruptive technologies. Instead of reducing society to the rule of Chronos as automation, innovation, or disruption, reducing human agency to what Arendt describes as labor and work (2013), scientists embrace the 'action' and vita activa (Arendt, 2013). They dare to take personal risks, provoke, and engage the general public with emerging science. Their work on the instruments performs the experience of time as Kairos in governance and not only technology. Instead of communicating science or conducting philosophical discussions about the nature of scientific knowledge and deep structure of reality (Chronos), science artisans perform what is called 'little science' (Price, 1986). They engage in science as a 'way of life' (Ibid.) that depends on agency and Kairos. In practice, this means tinkering with friends while building instruments that remind us of Agamben's regulae and the orders of the early monks (Chapter 7).

The hybrid and small-scale projects of DIY science share the values of invisible colleges of the 17th century, in which papers (and instruments) were still 'social devices' (Ibid.) serving alternative alchemist networks and projects of transformation of society and the world. The instruments were means of building communities rather than citational fortresses that preserve the power of the institutions of 'big science' (Ibid.). They presented pragmatic and emancipatory reasons for breaking the cost barriers of doing science over DIY instruments. OSH thus enables research not only in informal spaces (hackerspaces, art galleries, etc.) but also in the Global South while supporting nonutilitarian, creative explorations and reflections. We will describe some of the prototypes to discuss how they engage citizens in defining their common and personal futures through building tools and infrastructures.

Idiosyncratic Prototypes

The prototypes of instruments that support private and public interests and aspirations simply express the experience of time as Kairos. They enable citizens as science artisans to regain sovereignty, dignity, and freedom in an age immersed in science and technology controversies. By combining the pursuit of knowledge with the diverse needs and ideals of individuals and communities (their vita activa), or even private interests (otium), they become tools of autonomy and freedom. The idiosyncratic connections between science, art, design, and politics transform the nature of scientific work and public action. They support activities outside of (scientific) work and labor in laboratories to define experiments as civic and public 'actions' and interventions in culture, art, and society (Arendt, 2013) happening in time as Kairos.

The prototypes supporting Kairos thus enable a form of 'citizenship' or scientific and hybrid public sphere that includes science protocols and instruments as a social action, for example, in monitoring pollution. The science artisans build instruments not only because of a necessity (searching for low-cost, customizable solutions) but also to express their freedom, curiosity, and creativity. The ambiguity and possible conflict in the decisions upon the common future become part of governance of technology over OSH. We can see this on the collaboratively designed instruments made in the citizen science network Hackteria[10] or its affiliates (Pechblenda[11] lab, Lifepatch[12] etc.), which we followed and worked with since 2012. They show many examples of ambiguous engagements in which prototypes become tools of governance that define new identities and communities.

To follow the hybrid uses of instruments in community building, we also initiated the OCSDNET project 'Understanding Open Hardware and Citizen Science'[13] that supported open and citizen science initiatives in the Global South. Between 2015 and 2017, we organized workshops in Indonesia, Thailand, and Nepal on how to build DIY instruments and engage with science. Although the engagements supported science communication, education, and 'serious' scientific work, the workshops showed many unexpected uses beyond research. The various idiosyncratic, creative, and niche concepts, scenarios, and aspirations made clear that we need to rethink the science beyond the deficit model (Lewenstein, 2003; Sturgis & Allum, 2004). They inspired us to reflect on the exploratory, artistic, and speculative (mis)uses of instruments as equally important as their use in 'official' science.

The present DIYbio (Delgado, 2013; Landrain et al., 2013; Meyer, 2015) and open hardware for science scholarships (Delgado, 2013; Landrain et al., 2013; Meyer, 2015; Pearce, 2012, 2014) often reflect upon the scientific, activist, artistic, and sometimes idiosyncratic uses of prototypes instruments. Researchers focus on how such practices change the roles of the (science) museums and science communication (Davies et al., 2015; Selin, 2015; Selin et al., 2016), how they enable the new infrastructure of independent science (DIYbio) institutions (Delfanti, 2013; Kera, 2011), or how they support a global movement of hackerspaces and makerspaces (Kera, 2012b; Moilanen, 2012; Seyfried et al., 2014).

The convergences between social, political, scientific, and technical processes are an important topic for laboratory studies (Galison, 1997; Knorr-Cetina, 1995; Latour & Woolgar, 1986) and history of science accounts of instruments (Keller, 2013a; Ratcliff, 2007; Schaffer, 1987). While they reflect upon the convergences only ex post, we followed the actual design and making of the instruments as an important moment for understanding the convergence of governance with prototyping. The prototypes in this sense become a medium of Kairos in technology and governance. During construction, makers and artisans also rethink the function of instruments in the society. The prototypes become tools of (self)governance and future-making that offer an alternative to the teleological projects, such as progress or present algorithmic governance.

Emancipatory and Exploratory Prototypes

Hackteria microfluidics prototypes, such as OpenDrop electrowetting, capture hybrid and artisanal engagements with Kairos in governance and technology. The prototypes are results of Kairos, an opportunity and chance, because as we see on the example of the OpenDrop tool it was literally envisioned on a napkin during one of the open science and DIYbio meetings in Vienna. It was then developed through a series of workshops in Italy, Finland, and Switzerland, described by one of the early participants, Eugenio Battaglia, who later designed a blockchain governance and funding model on top of it:

> I was following the whole thing since Biofiction Vienna 2014 when we all met Mirela. That night in a cafe Rudi and Mirela were already sketching first prototypes on a napkin… Then we went to Helsinki for a group teaching to Pia's student. That is when we sort of sneaked into a lab where DropBot was in use… Then in spring I brought some Italians to GaudiLabs and we did the hack/coating/art sprint… So much fun. Then I organized the biocommons meeting in the south of Italy at RuralHub, where interest around this tech raised from many different parties. So I thought that starting thinking seriously about strategy and governance is something that would have provided value to this project.
> (E. Battaglia, personal communication, 26 July 2016)

The serendipitous account of the OpenDrop history shows the artisanal origins of the prototype. It also explains the importance of the workshops, where different groups of people meet to define a future application. As a prototype of instrument, but also a future community, the OpenDrop brought together various people, domains, disciplines, and interests. It created an informal network closer to the Renaissance networks of friends than an institutionalized science. It was a direct result of serendipitous and creative encounters with microfludics in the Hackteria network with a long history and various goals described by Urs Gaudenz, its main hardware developer, followingly:

> Rüdiger and I were talking about the idea of a compact integrated desktop biolab for many years. We wanted the device to be able to do oligo synthesis, different bio assays, PCR, spectrometry, just all the synbio and crazy stuff, more like a long-term vision… A first idea of technical implementation was to use the laser trap (or laser tweezer, as we call it),

a device that can move around tiny plastic beads or cells using the force of a laser beam. After many attempts, including hacksprint in Lausanne with Sachiko, hack session at HackteriaLab Bangalore and in GaudiLabs, we got the device working. … Then Rüdiger came up with this electro-wetting technology and we gave up on the laser tweezer and launched our self into this even more promising technology… we first met in Helsinki in Aalto University with Eugenio, Miri, and Pieter to look into possibilities and to have a look at the DropBot, a device by the Wheeler Labs in Toronto that is also OpenSource and a big inspiration for us… Other attempts and hack sessions by the Waag Society, Rüdiger, and Miri (with a visit to Korea) pushed the project forward. Then I built the OpenDrop V1 that first spawned interest also in the institutional research community.

(U. Gaudenz, personal communication, 24 July 2016)

The emancipatory goals of cheaper diagnostic tools and platforms for development of new drugs closely followed various nonutilitarian explorations. Since 2015, OpenDrop supported an artistic search for a new medium of expression (Alice Grassi's electrowetting cat performing an eponymous meme),[14] a political and activist project on open antibiotics and phage research ('Bicommons'[15] and 'Biostrike'[16] projects), basic design explorations of bioelectronics,[17] and also scenario on future model for decentralized and blockchain supported science (E. Battaglia, personal communication, 26 July 26, 2016). In that late phase, the project also tested a new model of bitcoin-driven investment in science over a 'pay-per-play' model of laboratory automation[18] and public participation in science.

The OpenDrop in this sense is not another 18th-century air pump used by experts to understand and manipulate nature or to enlighten and educate the public. It challenges the conventional ways in which we think about science, technology, and society, where instruments (technolog), experiments (science), and governance (politics, national objectives, policy, and oversight) are strictly separated. The microfluidic protocols in the case of OpenDrop merge directly with the diverse practices and interests beyond the research and communication of science. They include speculations on the governance model and economic conditions of doing science, reflections on the social and political goals involved in research, and aesthetic, cosmological, and metaphysical interests in biology and electronics. In this sense, it shows a model of hybrid engagement with technology and governance over the prototype that serves Kairos and Chronos, governance and technology.

The OpenDrop shows how participants connect various domains of knowledge and action, nature and culture, to define future scenarios and engage in open explorations. They use their time as Kairos to denies new relations between science, technology, and governance. Participants then document their ideas, hacks, and scenarios on social media (rather than official journals) and present them as part of exhibitions in museums and galleries (rather than conferences). The GaudiLabs YouTube channel documented strange uses ranging from speculations on space research in microgravity to 'pay-per-play' entertainment formats of engagement with laboratory automatization over the so-called smart contracts and other blockchain speculations.[19]

From the documentation available on the Hackteria website and social media, the most common motivation seems to be the pure joy of connecting biology with electronics. The interest in connecting wet, biological media with electronics goes back to the origins of the network in 2009, the Interactivos09 Garage Science workshop at Medialab Prado in Madrid. The interest in quirky games and performances with molecules, microorganisms, and cells on bioelectronics boards led to the first microfluidics prototypes that became an official tool for research. The OpenDrop is just the latest tool in this quest for bioelectronic experiments with friends and members of the network[20] that reimagine the community around science as much as science.

Governance over Institutional Hacks

The hybrid function of prototypes bridging divides is also visible in the way OSH connects the work in the laboratories with environments, such as the artistic studios, galleries, and hackerspaces. In these liminal spaces, we can follow practices which are personal, social, political, and artistic and involve not only emancipatory but also exploratory (design and art) goals (bioelectronics, blockchain governance, etc.). Exploratory interests (hacks, projects, uses) often challenge the common bioethical and biosafety standards that mainly serve industry interests and profits. They are free in a sense, in which Hannah Arendt describes vita activa, meaning 'being able to begin something new and not being able to control or even predict its consequences' (2013).

The freedom to make instruments and conduct experiments that transform and provoke defines the agency as the ability to influence the future rather than obey predefined goals. For hackers and makers, the practices with instruments are close to everyday actions, interests, and aspirations, where they are directly and personally responsible to other humans and institutions. The prototypes transform anonymous scientific labor in laboratories characterized by strict adherence to bioethical and biosafety protocols into 'artisan science' 'actions' with political, artistic, and other consequences. The OpenDrop enables citizens to directly experience and manipulate some aspect of nature (hydrophobic surfaces, electrocapillary forces, interactions between molecules or organisms) and discuss with their peers the ethical dilemmas, political goals, or some other aspects of such action. What defines prototypes and artisan science are exactly these uses that go beyond the common laboratory work and labor. They form not only genuine civic actions but also private explorations and creative misuses.

Urs Gaudens, the developer of OpenDrop, summarized the spectrum of these obvious and less obvious uses behind prototypes, including what he calls 'institutional hacks' and collaborations between formal and informal institutions, serious and exploratory projects:

> The applications people have in mind are very diverse, from single cell isolation to multi-organ on a chip to automation in a human micro-biome project, and so on. It was clear to me that there is a need for easily accessible hardware in this technology. Although it has been around for almost 20 years, the interest in this kind of lab automation seems to be big and open devices are not available. The patent situation is quite difficult as there seem to be many patents and the most impor-tant probably with Illumina, which also released its first commercial product about a year ago… So for me the project was also interesting in terms of 'institution hacking' – before we tried to convince tradi-tional research laboratories to work with us and use our network and skills in a fast prototype, and they never took us too seriously, as you know. Now all of a sudden, we were contacted by them, and they were eager to collaborate and even started sharing information on their research project more openly. I think we should do more of these hack-teria network projects, like now also the gyne-punk and open estrogen. We even got contacted by Head Technology Assessment and Chief Technology Office at Roche Diagnostics; he was surprised to see a new development coming out of nowhere and having connections to institu-tions like Wheeler Lab or MIT.
>
> (U. Gaudenz, personal communication, 5 July 2016)

Although the economic and educational benefits of affordable instruments support the values of inclusion and justice, they preserve the 'big science' status quo. They do not challenge the current status of laboratories, which interact with society over technology assessment, R&D transfer offices, or other intermediaries. What Urs Gaudenz describes as 'institutional hacks' and 'network projects' challenge this 'big science' (Price, 1986) power dynamics and status quo (Price, 1986). They show how the work on the instruments can directly support social and political agendas defined by the participants of the workshops and even lead to new organizations and initiatives. Prototyping in this sense becomes a means of Kairos in govern-ance as much as technology that opens the future and democratizes the control.

Governance over Informal Repositories

Hackteria instruments are prototypes that do not replicate the goals of pro-fessional ('big') science with cheaper tools. They bring science to new places outside professional laboratories to test new relations between science, technology, and society (described as 'little science' or 'artisan science'). It means improving the participation of actors and stakeholders in science and also connecting science to new domains of knowledge and action. The plural and complex uses of instruments happening not only in workshops and hacker-spaces but also in the Global South (Hirosue et al., 2015; Kera, 2015) support the values of curiosity and inspiration. They drive artistic and exploratory experiments with governance and technology. The democratization of instruments creates conditions for science to connect with everyday life and interests of citizens. It transforms the quest for knowledge into unique epistemic adventures with political, aesthetic, and even metaphysical challenges.

The current OSH prototype repositories emphasize mainly the pragmatic and emancipatory functions of lowering the costs of science. They bridge the various technological and scientific divides to support education, research, and entrepreneurship (Joshua Pearces' OSAT entries, also Bryan Bishop projects,[21] Open Source Ecology[22] and Open Manufacturing[23] initiative, TEKLA lab,[24] etc.). The idiosyncratic and exploratory uses of prototypes are difficult to document because they include personal narratives or documentation of one-time events, such as workshops, exhibitions, and performances. In the various Wikis and websites created by the collectives and laboratories, such as Hackteria, Gaudi lab,[25] Biodesign,[26] Pecheblenda, the documentation is inconsistent and sketchy. It is similar to the Renaissance book of friends with hybrid connections that opens the future to creative interpretations and engagements rather than closing it under the projects of Instauratio or Chronos.

Compared to typical examples of well-documented prototypes for science projects, such as Joshua M. Pearce's Open Sustainability Lab[27] at Michigan Technological University, which lists instruments in its 'Open Source Appropriate Technology' (OSAT)[28] wiki, these repositories lack structure and logic. The OSAT Wiki offers a blueprint for more efficient science infrastructure in the context of a larger project that aims to open-source the entire technological infrastructure (OSAT). When we compare this to Hackteria's 'Generic Lab Equipment'[29] project, we will find similar instruments, but the context is rather open and exploratory, often connected to art. Another[30] repository of tools developed by anarchofeminists and transhackfeminists from Pecheblenda biolab[31] in Calafou, Spain, also uses the instruments to address gender issues through art, science, politics, and philosophy. The differences in these repositories well summarize the differences between emancipatory versus exploratory, aesthetic, and idiosyncratic uses of prototypes. The more technical and structured OSH prototype repositories, such as OSAT, emphasize the scientific interests, which are partially emancipatory and try to improve science reproducibility and access to tools. The less structured, Hackteria, and GynePunk prototype repositories also include political actions and aesthetic pleasures, which are part of exploratory uses of prototypes.

Prototyping for Otium and Vita Activa

Plural uses and 'actions' beyond OSH prototyping are essential to preserve the open future and the experience of Kairos. They show that no one should have absolute control over the facts, values, and time. When a science artisan prototypes, she or he 'never remains the master of his acts as it is to maintain that human sovereignty is possible because of the incontestable fact of human freedom' (Arendt, 2013). Prototypes enable unique collaborations and inter-actions that support the ideal of an open future and freedom without guarantees.

Science artisans not only engage and inspire each other but also involve various other actors and stakeholders, such as researchers, artists, farmers, etc., in rethinking the future. They redefine what science and technology can mean in various contexts and communities. Instead of only supporting pro-fessional scientists to communicate or help 'big science' with cheaper tools, the prototypes enable science artisans to embrace the freedom and plurality of exploratory science 'actions'. They become a medium of political vita activa or leisurely otium outside of labor and work. They use time as Kairos, an opportunity for unique networks and communities, rather than Chronos, a call for control and algorithmic rule over new infrastructures.

To elaborate on the nonutilitarian, exploratory, and artistic uses of 'action' or otium over prototypes as a form of genuine science outside the labor and work, we will mention several examples of projects. On then, we can show how they democratize not only science but also decisions about science in the case of hormones and the politics related to insulin and estrogen issues.

Hormones play an essential role in the social, medical, and economic issues with male infertility, diabetes, (trans)gender identities, patient rights, etc. While the two insulin projects (Hypodiabetic blog[32] by Timothy Olmer and 'Open Insulin Project'[33] by Counter Culture Labs) delineate the possibil-ities and limits of pragmatic and emancipatory prototypes, the project on 'Open Source Estrogen' questions the whole idea of public good and emanci-pation by medical and technological means. They enact different engage-ments with the future and questions of agency.

The 'hacked' insulin pump by biohacker and geek, Timothy Omer, who documented his tinkering with air pumps on his Hypodiabetic blog, shows individual empowerment over a prototype. Omer reused several medical devices to create his own 'artificial pancreas', an insulin pump using an algo-rithm he designed to manage his diabetes. The personalized and disruptive device monitors in real time the insulin levels and microdoses of the patient. With this, he changed the usual model of uploading data and waiting for expert advice on insulin uptake. He enabled patients to live more self-reliant lives over the prototype.

The limits of the insulin 'agency' are also explored in another 'Open Insulin project' by a group of biohackers from Counter Culture Labs in Oakland. They tried to democratize not only the management of insulin but also its production. The crowdfunding campaign[34] introduced the idea of an independent and affordable insulin[35] production that would disrupt a $176 billion per year industry in the US. While Olmer managed to create a relatively functional tool for real-time insulin application, the 'Open Insulin project' shows the impossibility of insulin production due to standardization and safety. The 'open' insulin project showed that it is impossible to create the tool regulations without parallel changes in our policy, regulations, and, most importantly, the patent system.

This self-defeating project perfromed how science is deeply embedded in social, economic, and political processes. Rather than being a cheap, fast, and disruptive solution, the prototype became a critique of current models of production of medicine. In this, it reminds us of the original function of Thales' disruptive knowledge and prototype: to reveal the limits of governance and values in society. The insulin project defines a scenario that is emancipatory (anyone anywhere producing insulin) but impossible to achieve by technical means without policy changes. It is close to the third attempt to 'democratize' hormones (Open Estrogen Project), which directly addresses the sociotechnical conundrum as a scientific but also artistic and political problem.

Contradictions in the Open Hormones Public

The nonutilitarian, artistic, and exploratory uses of prototypes in the 'Open Estrogen Project' are openly ambiguous. The two biohackers and artists (Marry Magic and Byron Rich) behind the project address xenoestrogen pollution as an issue with gender politics, patient rights, and future transgender scenarios. The ontological status of the estrogen molecules is directly connected to political decisions; it is a matter of Kairos rather than only knowledge and insight. Furthermore, open-source tools for the synthesis and monitoring of estrogen serve personal explorations of estrogen issues but also as a tool to mobilize the public and rethink the possibility of collective action.

The prototypes in this project support performances and workshops that follow estrogen molecules in our environment and bodies and capture attitudes, fears, and hopes related to this molecular 'invasion'. The artists refuse to think of their project as a solution to a particular problem: 'We have no interest in techno-solutionism. For us, the project is more a vector for critiquing the systemic issues, environmental or biopolitical, around estrogen and estrogenic compounds as powerful, 'socially resonant' biomolecules (B. Rich, personal communication, 25 July 2016). Their goal is to let everyone experience the full complexity of estrogen issues and the relationships between industrial pollution, gender identity, DIY self-experimentation, and access to hormones.

Workshops and experiments explore the ambiguous status of estrogen not only in society but also in our bodies and nature. The prototype shows how the hormone can free women to decide when and if they want to get pregnant, but also transgender and transsexual individuals to achieve the sex characteristics they want. It is also an ambiguous tool that shows uncontrolled industrial pollution, where xenoestrogens cause long-term mutagenesis of animals and humans that ingest them through the waters. The pragmatic and emancipatory goals beyond the design of a cheap yeast biosensor to detect estrogen prevent the 'invasion' as much as support it.

The project 'Open Source Estrogen' thus explores the contradictions of estrogen in the public imagination, species evolution, and nature. It does not define the ideal future of estrogen but leaves it open to interventions and Kairos of political, social, and individual actions. The prototypes can serve not only as a form of 'molecular colonization' and 'feminization' of the male population but also as attempts to prevent this. They point out environmental toxicity or perform 'body and gender sovereignty' and act as 'biotechnical civil disobedience' to 'increase the range of bioqueer options'.[36] The whole project simply enables citizens to have direct experience with their responsibility and stakes in the scientific, as well as political, and social controversies surrounding estrogen over the prototypes.

Open Hormones Public Rituals

The public formed around the workshops uses prototypes to reflect, question, and enjoy the ambiguity of the 'invasion' of estrogens rather than to search for a solution. Although the insulin 'public' demanded a disruptive solution to empower patients and bring better and cheaper access to medicine, the estrogen 'public' remains plural and conflicted. The combination of laboratory work, public discussions, and science exhibitions leads to acts of disobedience and experiences of time as Kairos. The labor of executing the science protocols in the estrogen project serves artistic and exploratory goals that rethink the status of estrogen in our history, evolution, and future.

The workshops even mock the possibility of a special 'cult' or ritual of estrogen, which is our 'oldest molecule' showing the unity of all life on Earth and reminding us of this 'oldest' communication channel of interaction with our environment. In these workshops, the prototypes connected the idea of ritual, civic action, and citizen science projects to define plural futures and scenarios of estrogen politics. The unique combination of science and politics, experiment and ritual, theory and action, communication and direct engagement over instruments shows how prototypes can enact different politics.

DIY activities around estrogen supported everyone to have a say or stake in data collection, but also collective and private interventions related to the synthesis of the molecule. They enabled agency in terms of estrogen futures as a direct and material engagement that remained ambiguous. The estrogen sensor prototypes became a tool of emancipation, but also aesthetic, exploratory, and metaphysical questions of what it means to have a gender, how we connect with the environment and other species. They embraced the freedom, politics, and community around the molecules as a matter of agency to negotiate and decide rather than obeying an ideal future.

The prototypes in the three hormone hacking projects supported communities seeking to explore the new relations between nature, culture, technology, and politics. They combined open technology standards with emancipatory, political, and aesthetic agendas, even philosophical and metaphysical concerns (estrogen cult, unity of life, apocalyptic future, transgender dystopia) and led to provocations. On the one hand, the prototypes supported cheaper and better tools for managing insulin or estrogen in our bodies and the environment (biosensors to monitor water pollution or insulin levels). On the other hand, prototypes became critical and emancipatory tools that question the decisions and management of hormones in our bodies, society, and nature. They became means of rethinking access to insulin and estrogen, extraction and synthesis of hormones, individual and collective responsibilities, and risks. They opened the philosophical and ontological questions about molecules creating politics.

The prototypes in these projects help citizens to research natural phenomena and also probe social and political processes beyond science as means of negotiating decisions in controversies. They engage the public with Chronos as new knowledge and Kairos as action in both technology and governance. Practical work on the prototypes intricately connected future-making to defining alternative scenarios experienced in the workshops. Although prototypes enabled more people to do science, they also defined new forms of public participation and material engagements with science, where the pursuit of knowledge supports deliberation and creative explorations. This opened the future to public imagination and curiosity, which became material, conceptual, but also political practice with an open future.

The hybrid and idiosyncratic prototypes supported the experiences of time as Kairos, an opportunity for social and political change and agency that is initiated by individuals and communities. We used the dichotomy of emancipatory and exploratory projects to capture the ambiguity of prototyping public- and open-science hardware engagements similar to the one described in the case of Renaissance instrument making in Chapters 6 and 7. The examples confirm and extend the canonical reflections on instruments in laboratory studies (Galison, 1987, 1997; K. Knorr-Cetina, 1995; Knorr-Cetina, 1983; Latour & Woolgar, 1986), history of science (Heilbron, 1989; Ratcliff, 2007; Schaffer, 1987; Shapin & Schaffer, 2011; Werrett, 2001), and recent DIYbio scholarship (Delgado, 2013; Meyer, 2015). We view these hybrid engagements as part of long discussions on how we control time and the future over prototypes. They show alternatives to the ideal of automation and teleology of progress. The engagements with science and technology over prototypes support an open future and control over time as a matter of personal and social agency.

Hackerspace Prague 2012

Figure III.7 GaudiLabs 'Lab in suitcase' demo in Singapore Hackerspace 2015

Figure III.8 Wayang Kulit Microfludicics hacks in the Singapore Hackerspace 2014

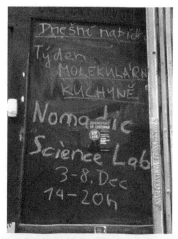

Figure III.9–III.11 Nomadic Science Lab in Prague 2012

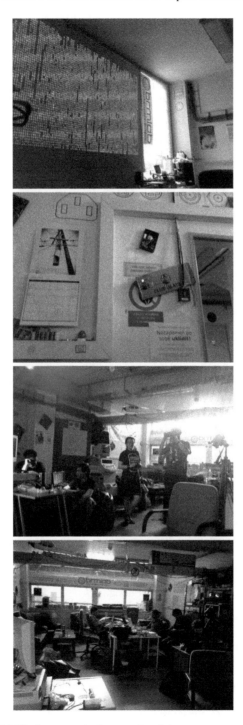

Figure III.12–III.15 Hackerspace in Prague, Brmlab.cz

Notes

1 Open Public lab tools https://publiclab.org/
2 Hackteria wiki documentation: https://hackteria.org/wiki/DIY_microscopy
3 Hackteria wiki documentation: http://hackteria.org/wiki/Wild_openQCM
4 OpenDrop platform website: http://www.gaudi.ch/OpenDrop/
5 Open Source Estrogen official documentation: http://maggic.ooo/Open-Source-Estrogen-2015
6 Documentation of the GYNEpunk project on Hackteria wiki: http://hackteria.org/wiki/BIO-reSEARCH
7 Micronation/Macronation official project documentation: http://www.natural-fiber.com/index.php?option=com_content&view=category&layout=blog&id=63&Itemid=65
8 Bryan Huggil from Raitong Organics Farm. Interview. April 2016. Official website of the Raitong Organics Farm: https://www.facebook.com/RaitongOrganicsFarm.
9 Blog following the DIY satellite project of the Karkhana innovators club: http://www.karkhana.asia/stories/tag/satellite/
10 Hackteria official website: http://hackteria.org/
11 Pecheblenda official website: http://pechblenda.hotglue.me/
12 Lifepatch official website: http://lifepatch.org/
13 OCSDNET project 'Understanding Open Hardware and Citizen Science' website: http://ocsdnet.org/projects/hita-ordo-natural-fiber-honf-foundation/
14 YouTube documentation of Alice Grassi experiment: https://www.youtube.com/watch?v=9IyDf5BUmfw
15 Git documentation of the BioCommons project: https://github.com/Bio-Commons/Bio-Commons
16 Git documentation of the BioStrike project: https://github.com/DennisAng/BioStrike
17 YouTube documentation of OpenDrop uses on the GaudiLab channel: https://www.youtube.com/watch?v=1Xnj35fqz9w; also https://www.youtube.com/watch?v=r6IdbnS-ie
18 Bittie Dapnia bitcoin account: https://onename.com/bittie
19 In March 2016, we designed a scenario for a 'Bittie' bitcoin account for a daphnia zooplankton https://onename.com/bittie connected to the OpenDrop platform, where funding could trigger the science experiment on the microfluidics. This interest in the blockchain technology is independently explored by another Hackteria member, Eugenio Battaglia, who is trying make such crowdfunding platform directly embedded in the OpenDrop instrument.
20 Hackteria wiki documentation: http://hackteria.org/wiki/Bioelectronix
21 Bryan Bishop official website: http://heybryan.org/
22 Open Source Ecology wiki: http://opensourceecology.org/wiki/
23 Open Manufacturing official website: http://openmanufacturing.net/
24 Tekla Lab repository of designs: http://www.teklalabs.org/
25 GaudiLab official website: http://www.gaudi.ch/
26 Biodesign official website: http://biodesign.cc/
27 Open Sustainability Lab website: http://www.mse.mtu.edu/~pearce/People.html
28 OSAT project repository wiki: http://www.appropedia.org/Category:Open_source_scientific_hardware
29 Generic Lab Equipment documentation website: http://www.gaudi.ch/GaudiLabs/?page_id=328
30 GynePunk offcial documentation website: http://gynepunk.tumblr.com/
31 Pecheblenda official documentation: https://pechblenda.hotglue.me/diwo
32 Hypodiabetic blog: http://www.hypodiabetic.co.uk/
33 Open Insulin Project official website: http://openinsulin.org/

34 Experiment official crowdfunding website of the Open Insulin project: https://experiment.com/projects/open-insulin

35 Open Insulin Project official website: http://www.openinsulin.org/

36 YouTube documentation of Marry Magic and Byron Rich presentation of the project: https://www.youtube.com/watch?v=urbm8e3gunE

10 Public and Open Futures between Labor, Action, and Leisure

Philosophy, religion, politics, and business have influenced the development of science instruments since the 16th century. They transformed the instruments into infrastructures and governance machines that include science institutions defining the goal of governance as automation and control. The instruments control time as Chronos by reducing various phenomena to patterns and cycles (Part II). They define the future as a matter of Instauratio, a teleological project of restoration of the human power over nature as promised by God.

Not all instruments follow this logic of governance machines. Some of the early prototypes express vitalist metaphors of living instruments and alternative wishlists, desiderata, and optatives (Chapter 7) preserving the idea of time as a public and open resource. Together with more recent examples of open science hardware OSH (Chapter 9), they reject teleology and insist on hybrid functions of instruments that refuse to demarcate science from its other. Instead of demarcating science from its other or promising progress and restoration, prototyping democratizes science and technology to explore contradictions in future-making. The artisanal prototypes in present hackerspace projects support the use of time as Kairos, an opportunity for personal and social agency that leads to hybrid and experimental futures. They offer alternatives to automation and the teleology of Instauratio, including algorithmic governance.

While in the industry, prototypes still serve what we described as monopoly contraptions (Chapter 3) and the teleology of progress and restoration (Chapter 5), in the hackerspaces, makerspaces, and similar liminal environments they show the possibility of personal and social agency through prototyping (Chapter 7 and 9). The important aspect of Renaissance future-making, which prototypes in the hackerspaces and makerspaces revive, is what Zilsel (Zilsel, 2000) describes as bridging the disciplinary and social divides in the process of designing and making new tools.

Edgar Zilsel's thesis on how prototypes bridged the various divides and transformed society (Zilsel, 2000) was further elaborated by Pamela H. Smith (Smith, 2004) and Vera Keller (Keller, 2010). Keller explicitly shows how artisanal practices represent the agency and embodied experiences of the

DOI: 10.4324/9781003189411-13

maker and scientist who transforms nature and society by democratizing knowledge and opening discussions about the goals of governance. In a study by Smith (2004), it is the work of Flemish painters and their artisanal techniques of observation and perspective that defined the modern scientific 'method'. Scientific knowledge was modeled after the artistic experiences of capturing the world with 'instruments' of perspective. Paintings are not only art but performances of the knowledge of nature. They perform the ability of the artist to imitate nature by organizing the perceptions via instruments. This original 'artisanal epistemology' defined the later experimental knowledge and organization of science and society.

Smith and Keller's artisanal instruments validate Zilsel's thesis about the importance of bridging the divides between the empirical knowledge of the new artisans and the superior, deductive, and theoretical reasoning performed in universities (Zilsel, 2000). The idea of knowledge as tinkering with instruments and prototypes that break social and other barriers and divides is further extrapolated by Peter Galison and Pamela O. Long's concept of 'trading zones' (Galison, 1997; Long, 2015), which we will use as a metaphor for our proposal for public sandboxes in Chapter 12.

The prototyping of science instruments plays an essential role in the formation of the modern public sphere engaged in future-making. It defines the public expectations from science and technology as not only a matter of personal and social agency but also a transpersonal and metaphysical teleology. It bridges the social and disciplinary divides in various periods and environments, including present hackerspaces and makerspaces (Chapters 3 and 7 and 9) which show the importance of liminal and experimental spaces and formats that we will discuss as sandboxes in Chapter 12.

While sociology of science and laboratory studies emphasized the role of the historical, social, political and cultural circumstances beyond various instruments, it is the history of science and present DIYbio scholarship that focus on how engagements with instruments transform society. Science artisans in the past and present connect their instruments with various agendas in society. They bring not only science closer to public life but also private explorations discussed here via the dichotomy of vita activa and otium (Arendt, 2013), emancipatory and exploratory uses of instruments. As intermediaries between science, technology, and governance, direct and often serendipitous engagements in prototypes use scientific labor and work to perform free 'actions'.

The emancipatory and exploratory uses of instruments enable a type of active science 'citizenship' insisting on time as Kairos rather than knowledge of Chronos promising control. As we could see from the examples of open hormones (Chapter 10) and other OSH tools, science artisans create their own public sphere and techno-social organization that questions the existing status quo. The public sphere of science artisans remains ambiguous about its agenda and reminds us of the origin story of Western science and philosophy - Thales monopoly and fall.

Even when prototypes tackle public issues, such as the measurement of pollution or the search for green energy, they rarely have a well-measured impact on science or society at large. The limits of public prototyping as a form of action, leisure, and sociotechnical 'initiation' into future-making are discussed in the present scholarship on critical-making and convergences of design and politics (Dantec & DiSalvo, 2013; Ratto, 2011; Ratto & Boler, 2014), various calls for object-oriented politics (Marres, 2012; Weibel & Latour, 2005), or the DIYbio scholarship discussed in the next chapters (Delgado, 2013; Kaiying & Lindtner, 2016; Meyer, 2015; Seyfried et al., 2014).

The contradictions are what we claim saves politics and agency from the rule of Chronos and teleology of Instauratio. We need experimental and participatory practices to democratize the future and bridge various divides that will support curiosity and dreams against automation with its visions of total control over time and the future.

Demarcating Science and Technology from Society

Laboratory studies and the history of scientific show that all science instruments are deeply embedded in the social, political, and religious projects that are often controversial and ambiguous. In this sense, the emancipatory and exploratory uses of the OSH prototypes make this process visible and accessible to the public. This 'extension' of the function and use of prototypes in science includes religion, philosophy, business, politics, and art as a norm rather than an exception. Providing controllable and sharable data to peers was always complemented by activities such as demonstrating philosophical claims, supporting religious concepts, mobilizing patrons and maecenas to invest in research, or initiating new institutions and power relations (Chapter 7).

Prototypes of science instruments also define various (failed) attempts to demarcate and emancipate science from religion, scholastic philosophy, politics, as well as crafts. The complex history of political, artistic, economic, and other (mis) uses of prototypes is well documented in the famous studies of Robert Boyle's air pump (Schaffer, 1987; Shapin & Schaffer, 2011), Samuel Morland's calculating machines (Ratcliff, 2007), Rene Descartes's garden machinery and automata fountain (Werrett, 2001), Cornelius Debbel's incubators and thermostates (Keller, 2010, 2013), and various aesthetic, metaphysical, poetic, and other uses of instruments in alchemy and mechanical arts (Keller, 2013; Newman, 2005; Nummedal, 2011).

For example, Morland's calculators were never only research instruments, but a commercial enterprise crossing the geopolitical barriers between London, Paris, and Florence and the social divisions between the court and artisan and craftsman studio. Descartes's garden machinery and fountain automata producing artificial rainbows performed the insights and genius of his philosophy instead of only testing a hypothesis (Werrett, 2001). Descartes used the prototypes to show the superiority of his method of natural philosophy over the empirical skills and experiences of the artisans and early engineers. In contrast to Descartes and also Bacon, Drebbel's incubators served as models of the universe along very practical uses, such as hatching of eggs or gaining financial support by impressing emperors. The 'living instrument' or the 'single, living machine that could encapsulate, prove and effortlessly convey universal knowledge of nature' (Keller, 2010) performed superior artisanal knowledge along Drebbel's insight into the universe to democratize knowledge and future-making (Chapter 6).

All prototypes of instruments performed various artistic, philosophical, and religious inclinations and interests of their inventors and scientists, which includes the hackerspaces and makerspaces in the present. We see this in the accounts of the conflicting and paradoxical uses of the well-known case of the air pump that define the modern function of instruments in science communication. Originally, the air pump served a radical philosophical agenda of atomism and a rather conservative notion of spirits (Schaffer, 1987). It performed the new philosophical and scientific theory of change as a process involving atoms, void, and chance that challenged the standard teleological explanations of nature based on a tedious debate with Aristotle's 'horror vacui' – nature fearing empty places (van Helden, 1991). The radical instrument performed atomism, but it also supported conservative (and vitalist) beliefs in spirits, understood as immaterial forces expressing the power of God (Brundtland, 2011; Heilbron, 1989; Shapin & Schaffer, 2011).

Simon Schaffer (1987) air-pump shows how the new experimental and epistemic practices and methods challenged but also helped to preserve the theological themes of spirits and souls. The air pump even created a new discipline dedicated to the agenda of pneumatics and pneumatology as a study of these spirits. Francis Bacon, Robert Boyle, as well as Robert Hook, and later even Isaac Newton, perceived their roles more as 'priests of nature' than men of science, and believed that science must be pious by proving the authority of divine power and plan (Ibid.). In Chapters 6 and 7, we explain how this led to the teleological and theological agenda of Instauratio advocating science and technology that support the rule of patrons and God over the future.

The complex connections between the instruments and their various political, social, and religious agendas are central topic in many sociology of science and laboratory studies discussing how instruments are deeply embedded in the present economic, social, and political orders (Ackermann, 2014; Galison, 1987, 1988; Krohn et al., 1981; Latour, 1993). Professional science instruments are described as 'inscription devices' or 'epistemic machines' and 'epistemic things' or 'machines to make the future' (Jacob in (Rheinberger, 2010) that mobilize forces and actors outside research to decide upon the future and governance of science and society. The sociologists and philosophers of science show the ambiguous role of instruments in negotiating the interests of various actors and later industries and stakeholders.

The hybrid and complex processes initiated with every instrument prove that prototyping is always a medium of Kairos, an opportunity that gradually transforms into a grand plan of Chronos or Instauratio. Peter Galison's 'epistemic machines' (Galison, 1997) of high energy physics (cloud chambers, nuclear emulsions, etc.) were part of a competition between the various industries and warfare efforts whose economic and political interests influenced the final instruments. The prototypes that form 'inscription devices' in the seminal work by Bruno Latour and Steve Woolgar (Latour & Woolgar, 1986) establish their authority through documentation rather than by design. They transformed the observed phenomena into graphs and journal papers to mobilize other actors and stakeholders from science to policy. They express Kairos, the opportunity to generate new knowledge and networks that is equally important as the actual knowledge of Chronos, cycles, and patterns that we discover in our decisions about the future and governance.

Socio-Technical Initiations over Air Pumps

The revival of instrument-making in the hackerspaces and makerspaces challenges the idea of public perception of science defined by Joseph Wright's classic 18th-century painting 'An Experiment on a Bird in the Air Pump'. The painting shows laboratory equipment that not only provides data to the scientists but also forms the public opinion and response to science (Baudot, 2012; van Helden, 1991). On the painting, a scientist, supposedly Robert Boyle, performs the new instrument suffocating a bird in the vacuum in front of a lay audience that includes women and children. The terrifying and visceral experience not only reveals the hidden forces in nature but also forms the public opinion of science through fear and awe. The vacuum pump serves not only science but also certain politics forming an obedient public that will support the project of progress or Instauratio to restore human power over the life and death and the whole 'creation'.

The 18th-century image represents the docility of the public facing new science discoveries and technological innovation. Science and technology as the results of Kairos reduced politics in this painting to the power of new knowledge and instruments over life and death. They serve teleological agenda of progress and other variations of Instauratio supporting the political status quo of new instruments.

In a sharp contrast to the 18th-century air pumps representing the power over time and the future, the present air pumps are part of everyday, mundane activities depicted on various websites and social media supporting tinkering and do-it-yourself (DIY) and do-it-with-others (DIWO) practices.

Services, such as Instructables,[1] let anyone with a 3D printer design and print air pumps and use them in various contexts. The growing number of hobbyists, citizen scientists, hackers, makers, academics, and entrepreneurs then design and democratize various 'open' laboratory instruments. They engage not only with science outside of the official laboratories but also with the rhetoric of progress and innovation, and bridge various interests, disciplines, and divides in diversity of contexts.

Instead of wooing or scaring off the public with new instruments and challenging scientific hypotheses produced by experts, the low-tech, digitally fabricated, and repurposed air-pumps support personal and social uses of time as Kairos, personal explorations, family activities, and community-based projects. While the main result of the air pumps of the 18th century was a docile public waiting to be saved by science and technology, nowadays the air pumps are parts of soda bottles and fish tanks, even more serious, sustainable energy projects and experiments with algae biofuel reactors.[2] The DIY syringe pump even serves as a self-experiment with microdosing of legal (Hurley, 2016) and illegal substances[3] or playful uses of microfluidics[4] in Hackteria's projects.

The hackers, makers, and geeks in these sociotechnical rites of passage remind us of Thales and his use of instruments and time. In a similar manner in which he performed the power of the new knowledge as a result of his free time and open future, the present prototypes explore, rethink, and tinker with nature, politics, society, and technology. Through private experiments and creative explorations, open hardware instruments define the public aspirations of science as activity that restores active citizenship and the public sphere through prototyping.

From the civic and independent monitoring of water[5] and air quality[6] to sound[7] and VJing performances,[8] artistic and conceptual explorations,[9] and also entrepreneurial[10] and educational uses,[11] OSH shows alternatives to academic and professional research. The plural, hybrid, and often ambiguous (mis)uses of instruments show science as an everyday activity, directly connected to private but also public, cultural, economic, and political lives and interests of the citizens.

Future-making ceases to be reduced to professional science, policymaking, and science communication, and becomes an experiment open to anyone who tries to define their place in the world and future. The work on the 3D printed DIY pumps in the biofuel and algae bioreactors,[12] as captured on Google search results, shows citizens exploring sustainable scenarios of future food and energy production.[13] It also shows individuals protesting against the patent system, which leaches on the open-source designs as expressed in this disclaimer.[14] The miniaturized DIY syringe pump is also essential in the microfluidic experiments of Hackteria's research into electrowetting and its creative (mis)uses for art performances described in Chapter 9.

Whether as a hobby item, educational tool, new form of a protest, or a probe into the future, DIY air pumps and prototypes rethink the roles of instruments in public life. Designed and made by citizens themselves rather than industry professionals protected by ISO norms, the imprecise and uncalibrated tools support something between a science 'cargo cult' and a genuine attempt to democratize science and involve diverse publics. The transformation of the Robert Boyle air pump, a tool of privileged access to not only nature but also political power, into a myriad of hobby items, citizen science projects, and artistic and design experiments captures the role of prototyping in defining governance.

The prototypes explore Kairos in governance as much as technology and support diversity, paradoxes, hybridity, and even liminality, such as the one we see on the example of the DIY air pumps. Tools express various private and public interests and uses of time that keep the future open to interventions that save social and personal agency. Building DIY instruments, such as air pumps, is a form of sociotechnical initiation rather than a submission to any teleology and control over time as restoration or progress. Instead of replicating any industry, academia, or policy standards, the makers and geeks experience the ambiguities inherent in every technology and its relation to society to make decisions about their personal and collective future.

Hybrid, Convivial, and Promissory Prototypes

Prototypes make the pursuit of understanding nature as important as the ability to create new institutions and express different views on society, industry, academia, etc. described here as phenomena of Kairos and transformation. The Renaissance instruments (Chapters 6, 7, and 10) as well as present OSH (Chapters 9 and 10) show sociotechnical hybrids that bridge various divides. The instruments express personal and social agency as future-making and insist on time as experience of Kairos, an opportunity for action and transformation rather than teleology of Chronos, knowledge serving restoration and progress.

The present DIYbio scholarship discusses this ambiguous ability of prototypes and open hardware instruments to bridge divides and transform society. DIY instruments such as the air pump are 'boundary objects' that negotiate conflicting goals (robust/fragile, material/digital, amateur/professional) while performing 'social-political work' along scientific research (Meyer, 2015). The instruments are 'convivial and materialized tools' (Ibid.), supporting not only cross-platform, digital and analogue, material and immaterial production of knowledge but also decentralized, egalitarian, and open uses leading to 'deinstitutionalization' of science (Ibid.).

Although history of science and laboratory studies show that the hybrid uses and contexts of the instruments remain often unacknowledged, hidden, or even suppressed, the DIYbio scholarship embraces the ability to bridge such divides. The imperfect and work-in-progress qualities of instruments, such as OpenDrop and the self-defeating strategies of the 'Open Source Estrogen' project (Chapter 9), emphasize the processes and engagements above the results produced by the instruments. Open hardware instruments are what Delgrado describes as 'promisory and evocative objects' (2013) flexibly linking material experimentation with discourse, deliberation, and reflection or 'material practices' with 'moral visions' (Meyer, 2015). The 'punk, unruly, domestic and unfinished character (of the instruments)… hail heterogeneity and precariousness' (Delgado, 2013) to make 'mundane futures in every-day practices of composing and recomposing things' (Ibid.). Their imperfections and ephemerality allow citizens to define and test their future expectations and stakes in science, technology, and society. By bridging the divides between science, politics, and design, as Delgado shows, they support governance as 'transitory associations of people, technologies, and natural entities, provisional encounters of otherwise heterogeneous elements' (Ibid.).

The pioneering work of Delgrado and Meyer on DIYbio prototypes illustrates the values of liminal and hybrid environments and prototypes. We claim that such values and environments should become a model of governance over prototypes and exploratory sandboxes (Chapter 12) that support alternative research communities, agendas, and ideas about the future. Delgrado's work inspired by Heidegger's notion of the 'thinginess of the thing' is particularly important because it clarifies the temporal aspect of building instruments and connecting them with lived experiences that we describe here as 'Kairos'.

Instruments in Delgrado reveal their origins in everyday life through tinkering practices that explore personal and social agency of people who take part in their development. The experience of engaging with instruments is about understanding their connection to different everyday activities (Delgrado mentions food hacking projects) rather than the 'higher truth' of patterns and signals resulting in religious or cosmological communion with Chronos or Instauratio. Instead of serving the myth of automation that 'ritualizes' science and technology through infrastructures closing the opportunities for the individual and communal agency, DIY prototypes allow citizens to imagine and explore different futures for science and society.

Delgrado remains ambiguous about the empowerment over such DIY tools, which she sees as symptoms of a crises rather than hope: 'current publics echoes a situation of institutional crisis of Western societies, and it reveals a generalized disbelieve in public institutions and in their capacity to make futures' (Ibid.). To restore this agency over the future, the publics needs to have a say in the processes how we define values and create new infrastructures. Prototypes by a science artisan, described in Chapter 9, or the early example of Renaissance instrument-making (Chapters 6 and 7) support the governance of emerging infrastructure by connecting what Delgrado describes as 'a certain civic positioning' in DIY practices and tools (promisory and evocative objects) with Meyer's 'promissory equipment'.

Delgrado defines the civic aspirations of DIYbio instruments (OSH) as a personal 'vision of a 'self' that can make futures by doing things' (Ibid.), which we find essential for any attempt to save agency as control over time and the future. The aspirational, private, and often contradictory goals of the public expressed through instruments are elaborated further by Meyer. He uses Lévi-Strauss' notion of 'bricolage' along with Ivan Illich's 'tools of conviviality' to capture the processes of making and using DIY tools for future-making on the example of OpenPRC and the Open Gel Box (Meyer, 2015).

In Mayer's opinion, the democratization of science instruments creates strong tensions between the communal and commercial goals of prototypes that often lead to disappointments rather than success. In our opinion, all prototyping must remain similarly agonistic to preserve active vita (vita activa) and agency. The combination of entrepreneurial and community-oriented aspirations defines what Meyer describes as the aspiration for 'citizen biotech economies' (Ibid.), where on one side they foster 'material redistribution, democratization and an alternative to established science' and on the other they feed the neoliberal agenda of start-ups and techno-deterministic illusions. The 'promisory equipment' is caught up in this tension between the fetishization and community goals, which Meyer describes as a 'convergence between material practices and moral visions, between the redesign of scientific objects and the articulation of political objectives'. (Ibid.)

Prototypes Serving Labor, Work, Action, and Leisure

Although we agree with Delgrado and Meyer on the ambiguity of the democratization and empowerment efforts via prototypes described as a tension between the emancipatory (pragmatic and practical) and exploratory (promisory) uses (community- and industry-oriented applications), we find this uncertainty essential for preserving the value of open future and time as public resource. The uncertainty and ambiguity of these practices defines the 'citizenship' of science artisans as vita activa happening in time as Kairos, the opportunity to express agency, and conflicting ideas about the future of science and society.

The prototypes as sociotechnical actions must remain ambiguous and agonistic to preserve the political and personal freedom of connecting science with various goals. This means using time as Kairos to freely explore the new knowledge or Chronos and envision the future beyond the status quo or teleology of Instauratio. Hybrid, at times silly and trivial uses of microscopes, air pumps, etc. may have little scientific or political value, but they give citizens freedom and creativity to organize workshops and form new networks.

The hacking of estrogen or the use of electrowetting to break the barriers between biology and electronics probes the different fantasies, discourses, and scenarios about our common future in a complex milieu of not only social, political, and economic but also technical and scientific influences and interests. They bridge the present divides between amateur (DIY) and professional science, libertarian and communitarian values, in the way that Zilsel describes science in the 16th century. The interventions living instruments and paradigms define the future through Kairos, individual and communal practices exploring rather than reducing everything to the Chronos and to teleology of Instauratio.

The prototypes problematize and bridge the divides between the work and labor performed in the laboratories and the practices and actions which define the free citizens as Thales. Present science artisans who design and build prototypes perform their citizenship as deeply embedded in various scientific controversies and visions of a common good. They combine design, science, and politics to express their concern about health and environment, and explore normative ideals (better and more accessible science or hormones), reflect upon possible futures (the Open Estrogen project's view on transgender identities), or engage with metaphysical, aesthetic, and exploratory values of the blockchain technologies (OpenDrop).

In this sense, prototypes of instruments support activities outside the monotonous work and labor in the research laboratories that serve the economic, political, and social status quo. They define the possibility of civil action by citizen scientists who refuse to become homo faber or homo laborans (Arendt, 2013), parasites and slaves on someone else's table or laboratory bench meeting future targets without any opportunity to question them or define new ones. The prototyping embraces the value of freedom as vita activa and also pure enjoyment of free time, which Arendt describes as otium. We discuss such use of free time as Kairos that defines that original prototypes of Thales as hacks that challenged to rather than preserve the political status quo discussed in Chapter 3.

The OSH instruments (Chapter 9) explore the aesthetic and political values of the estrogen public that break taboos and divisions between pursuit of knowledge and new values. They connect the labor and work on the science protocols with narratives and personal videos, community actions, and workshops. Instead of transforming the instruments into governance machines promising automated future biopolitics, they emphasize personal and community actions resulting in plural futures.

The emerging and hybrid public of science artisans revives the importance of artisanal knowledge based on tinkering that embraces Kairos over Chronos in governance and technology and open future over the project of Instauratio. The resulting hybrid practices and instruments define active citizenship through personal and communal agency that uses time for not only leisure or otium but also politics and vita activa (Arendt, 2013).

Stoic and Epicurean Technologies

Present tinkering and prototyping in hackerspaces support the experience of time as Kairos, a public and open resource for defining personal and communal projects and futures while experimenting with science and technology. Time becomes an opportunity for civic, communal, as well as private and leisurely interventions that question and resist the infrastructures that close and automatize the future. Instead of control over the Chronos, technologies become a form of individual and collective action over so called 'kits' of DIY, open tools for learning, customizing tools, and engaging with others.

The insistence on Kairos in technology and governance means that time is a process of negotiating different aspirations, values, and visions for the future rather than a resource that someone monopolizes and controls. Instead of serving the project of restoration, progress, and predefined goal, prototyping becomes a tool of Kairos with unpredictable and ambiguous results. Examples of OSH manifesto (Global Open Science Hardware (GOSH) Manifesto, 2016) or discussions of promissory and aspirational instruments (Delgado, 2013; Meyer, 2015) resist the monopolization of the future and time, but their impact remains aspirational.

OSH, as part of the movement of hackerspace, citizen science laboratories, and makerspaces, creates conditions for public engagement beyond automation, algorithmic governance, or the 'big science' status quo. It resists the monopolization of the future by industries and institutions perpetuating various divides in access to science and technology over journals, university ranking systems, government grants, or corporate investment. Against the ancient and modern divides between patrons and parasites replicating problems with every infrastructure starting with the clocks, the direct engagement with prototypes supports personal and social agency as future-making and Kairos.

Science artisans use the instruments for collective action and acts of disobedience, such as self-experimentation with various substances or for mocking of sociotechnical issues (estrogen public). Fringe prototypes in the 'Open-Source Estrogen' or 'OpenDrop' projects support not only emancipatory but also imaginative and unexpected futures. Their ambiguous and even risky engagements define the possibility of vita activa and civic future-making as alternatives to monopolization.

From the tedious labor on science protocols with better and cheaper tools to the more artistic, parodic, and leisurely misuses of instruments, science artisans demonstrate the Kairos in technology and governance. Prototypes of new tools explore nature and also probe the institutions, ideologies, and our views of science. They support Hannah Arendt's call for vita activa and otium (Arendt, 2013) while challenging her critique of the scientific instruments, such as the telescope, for destroying the potential for public life and private imagination.

Arendt (Ibid.) condemned science and its instruments for their powerful mediation of certainty and agency outside the human action and deliberation. In her view, the science instruments, such as the telescope with its objective cosmic perspective, destroy the political vita activa and the freedom to act or make meaning in an uncertain world happening on Earth. According to Arendt, instruments mark the disappearance of the public sphere. Free citizens transform into homo faber destined to work under different clocks or, even worse, to conform to pure biological processes of the homo laborans (Ibid.).

Science artisans, including Thales (Chapters 3 and 4) and Renaissance alchemists (Chapters 6 and 7) show that thus was not always true. Kairos-serving prototypes in technology and governance support instruments with hybrid, ambitious, and complex functions in science and society. They combine contemplation with action, knowledge with politics, reflection, and control with contingency and risk. Science artisans use prototypes create a community dealing with risks and uncertainties on individual and personal and also communal levels in the hackerspaces and makerspaces. In this, they remind us of the early monastic orders and their regula discussed in Chapter 6 together with Agamben's concepts of the paradigm and exempla defining alternative uses of knowledge in future-making that we claim opposes automation and the ideal of progress.

DIY kits, workshops, and open-source development models assert not only freedom, autonomy, and self-organization close to Stoics values of autonomy but also idiosyncratic or 'Epicurean' artistic explorations. They resemble the Cornelius Drebbel and Robert Fludd instruments for transforming society and nature (Chapter 6) and the early visions of the academy of sciences described by Leibniz (Chapter 7). Their goal is to open the future to imaginative projects that combine science, technology, and society instead of reducing them to monopolies that serve the teleology of restoration and progress.

The emancipatory (Stoic) and exploratory (Epicurean) uses of prototypes show contempt for the productive labor supporting the existing scientific, social, or political status quo, 'innovation' goals, and other teleology of progress and restoration. They extend Arendt's insistence on the public sphere as free from both productive concerns and biological necessities of life to include technology and science open to risks and actions without any guarantees. Projects and instruments, such as 'Open Source Estrogen' or 'OpenDrop', are open, exploratory, as well as ambiguous in their impact and they test new relations between science, technology, and society.

Science Artisans Designing Open Futures

Open science hardware instruments support individual and communal experiments with nature and society. The geeks and makers use the instruments to define their social expectations from science and technology and balance the new knowledge and infrastructure with their agency, which we interpreted through Hannah Arendt's concepts of vita activa and otium. Instead of surrendering to the cosmological certainty and order of Chronos with its ontology of cycles and patterns in various phenomena, the citizens use the prototypes for action and leisure as expressions of Kairos.

Citizens, as science artisans, express their agency in various creative and activist projects. They search for alternatives to technocratic visions, under which all public issues will be solved with the right app, technology, or science discovery. Such visions are a relic of the insistence of Francis Bacon on Instauratio, which imagines that technological and scientific advancements automatically guarantee moral and political progress. We contrasted the Instauratio in Chapter 7 with the alchemist and mechanical arts experiments that remain open-ended and hybrid. Against the teleology of restoration of some pre-given ideal state, the alternative visions emphasize the transformation of the universe, society, and even the body of the artisans.

Science artisans mock Silicon Valley cliches and solutions as versions of the Renaissance desiderata that close the future to technocratic rule and Bacon's Instauratio. The interventions and experiments by science artisans emphasize Kairos as an open future in governance as much as technology, a form of political action, and expression of agency. To define prototyping as a democratic, public, and material engagement with the future(s), we have to reject the insistence on Chronos and automation in governance. We need to rethink the practices as well as the spaces and sites where we make decisions about the future and demand more fluid relations between parliament, public spaces, laboratories, and universities. As liminal engagements, the hackerspaces, makerspaces, or public sandboxes discussed in Chapter 12 support such personal agency and action.

The emphasis on Kairos in the fluid and liminal spaces and projects allows the interests in facts and values to challenge each other. Engagements with new technologies or infrastructures do not compromise personal and social agency, even if the impact of such interventions limited. We discussed the open and citizen science projects as a form of Stoic and Epicurean retreat to private interests and circles of friends. However, they restore a level of autonomy that challenges the technocratic and teleological project. The projects are precedents that question the reduction of technology and governance to automation and the rule of Chronos, imposing one ideal of a future. By supporting personal agency and communal efforts, hackerspace and makerspace projects connect the work on regulations and values directly with technology and innovation.

Prototyping of instruments described in Chapter 6, 7, 9, and 10 serves a similar purpose as the protestant Bible in the 16th-century reformation movement. It translates complex jargon and practices into tools and kits that allow everyone to interact with the important institutions and realities defining their present. Instead of privileged means of access to truth and power given to experts to serve the status quo, prototypes become personal and communal means of interacting with nature, facts, science institutions, and futures.

Individuals and groups use open science hardware to monitor their environment and bodies and bring to public attention various social, technological, and cultural challenges and implications of such practices. Designing, building, and using prototypes a way to interact with nature, as well as institutions and economic models, such as open-source development, promises of blockchain technologies, data cooperatives, etc. The prototypes bring science and technology closer to leisure, art, and everyday activities (otium), and also civic action and public life, or vita activa (Arendt, 2013). They support the experiment with the future and time as Kairos, an opportunity, risk, and action.

We followed OSH prototypes that break the divisions between lab, public space, art gallery, and policy institutions. They extend Zilsel's thesis (Zilsel, 2000) on instruments in the 16th century that define modern science and society through manual work on prototypes. The prototypes broke down the barriers between craftsmen (superior artisans), university scholars (scholastic), and emerging humanists in the 16th century that represented the different forms of power and organization of society. Today, prototypes in the hackerspaces probe the present relations between science, technology, and society that have a similar potential to engage, transform, and inspire.

While tinkering with instruments in the 16th century transformed rural and feudal fiefs into modern 'capitalist' societies, the present prototypes engage new political and social actors that connect design, policy, business, and technology. On examples of OSH, citizen laboratories, and hackerspaces, we discuss hybrid and ambiguous networks changing the understanding of science and society. To further reflect on the role of prototypes in governance, we will follow the global experiments in the special economic zones (SEZs), where prototypes foster transnational networks and projects described as 'geek diplomacy' (D. Kera, 2015).

Notes

1 Instructables official website: http://www.instructables.com/
2 Instructables documentation: http://www.instructables.com/id/Solar-powered-algae-bioreactor/
3 Reddit group on microdosing self-experiments documentation: https://www.reddit.com/r/microdosing/
4 wetPONG website documentation: http://wetpong.net/
5 Fixed sensor wiki documentation: http://wiki.biodesign.cc/wiki/Fixed_Sensor
6 Smart Citizen Science platform official website: https://smartcitizen.me/; List of Safecast radiation monitoring devices official webite: http://blog.safecast.org/devices/
7 Git of CocoMake7 (A jugaad and low-cost educational platform for digital inter-activity): https://cocomake7.github.io/ using Attiny microcontroller developed by Hackteria for scientific experiments. Nalareksa sound installation using O2 and CO2 monitoring on the official website of Andreas Siagian, a membet of Lifepacth citizen science network: https://andreassiagian.wordpress.com/category/installation/nalareksa/

8 YouTube video documentation by Lifepatch of a VJing experiment with DIY microscopes: https://www.youtube.com/watch?v=wE5oiwmpCA8. It is using a PureData tool developed by Hackteria for VJing and DJing with microscopic images, official wiki: http://hackteria.org/wiki/Pd_microscope

9 Gel electrophoresis apparatus used for artistic explorations of food colors in the agar medium, official Hakcteria wiki documentation: http://hackteria.org/wiki/Agar_is_the_Media; Artistic experiments with visualization and sonification of Daphnia zooplancton, official Hakcteria wiki documentation: http://hackteria.org/wiki/Daphniaology

10 Quartz Crystal Microbalance official website:http://openqcm.com/; Open-source PCR Thermocycler official website: http://openpcr.org/

11 The Amino One Desktop Biolab official website: http://www.amino.bio/; Open Source meteorological station wiki documentation: https://pt.wikiversity.org/wiki/Pesquisa:Ferramentas_livres:Work_group_for_development_of_the_hyper object_workbench for example the meterreological station http://cta.if.ufrgs.br/projects/estacao-meteorologica-modular/wiki/Wiki; Atomic Force Microscope official website: https://openafm.com/

12 Instructable documentatioon: http://www.instructables.com/id/How-To-Make-A-PVC-Water-Air-Vacuum-Pump/ and http://www.instructables.com/id/diy-small-water-pump/

13 Search of bioreactors and hackerspaccess oon Google.com gives roughly 3,000 results of projects in various degrees of completion, such as this Instructables documentation: http://www.instructables.com/id/Make-Biodiesel/. There was even a competition on such bioreactors for space: http://www.spacegambit.org/open-bioreactor/

14 Thingiverse documentation: http://www.thingiverse.com/thing:29623

> The design files for this thing (air-pump) have been removed as a protest against Stratasys after their decision to file a patent infringement lawsuit against Microboards Technology. Their decision is extremely destructive and also underlines that the patent system is obsolete as it no longer serves any purpose for the betterment of society. Its main role is as a blunt weapon used by incumbents to hamper innovation. I see absolutely no reason to continue indirectly supporting Stratasys by providing free content to Thingiverse.

11 Global Prototypes for Local Futures*

Open science hardware (OSH) prototypes connect the daily life and interests of citizens with tools and instruments exploring nature. They enable citizens to express personal and public visions for the future through material practices that challenge the conventional dichotomies of contemplative and practical reason and the related concepts of labor, work, action, and leisure (otium). As experiments with social and political institutions as well as nature, prototypes of instruments democratize and 'open' science as much as society to pragmatic, emancipatory, as well as ambiguous and idiosyncratic projects (described as exploratory and leisurely otium in the previous chapter).

Prototypes as tools of civic action (vita activa) or retreat into science otium, leisurely activities with friends, enact the Epicurean values of pleasure but also Stoic insistence on personal autonomy and resilience. We discussed them as examples of Kairos in governance and technology that support personal and collective engagements in the future, including what we will describe now as transnational and informal 'geek diplomacy'. Over the years, we have followed several collaborations that developed such global networks over prototypes in do-it-yourself (DIY) biology projects (Kera, 2014a, 2015), radiation monitoring kits in Japan (Kera et al., 2013), attempts to democratize thermocycling and microscopy in Indonesia or Nepal (Kera et al., 2019), and food hacking projects (Dolejšová & Kera, 2016).

The informal ad hoc networks of geeks, makers, and hackers often ignore the common disciplinary and geopolitical divides. To describe the paradoxes and tensions in this emerging public of hackers, tinkerers, and makers that connect their 'leisure' with activism on local and global levels,

* This section uses parts of published articles: Kera, Denisa. 'Maker Culture Liminality and Open Source (Science) Hardware: Instead of Making Anything Great Again, Keep Experimenting! | A Liminaridade Da Cultura Maker E O Hardware de Fonte (Na Ciência): Em Vez de Fazer Algo Ser Grande de Novo, Continue Experimentando.' Liinc em Revista (Laboratório Interdisciplinar em Inofrmação e Conhecimento) 13.1 (2017): n. pag. Web. 25 June 2017 DOI: 10.18617/liinc.v13i1.3875.

Kera, Denisa. (2015, December 14). Hackteria: open science prototypes. Magazine Des Cultures Digitales. https://www.digitalmcd.com/hackteria/

DOI: 10.4324/9781003189411-14

we will use the concept of 'geek diplomacy' (Kera, 2015, 2017). With this concept we will also show how hackers and makers use prototypes to reject the traditional degradation of makers (demiurgoi) as political actors since Plato's Republic.

The blueprint of the Western ideals of governance, Plato's Republic, reduced the making and tinkering to practices that serve only the biological necessities of life (work and work) with no political or social implications (action). Ever since the Republic, we think of governance as a contemplative, cognitive, and discursive achievement that is based on the right knowledge and insight (often culturally determined or defined as 'expertise') into the true nature of our soul, society, or universe. These cosmological and ontological views of governance (Chapter 5) insist on the rule of Chronos and infrastructures that enable automation and resignation upon Kairos and agency. Prototyping becomes a receptacle for predefined visions and teleological projects of innovation, growth, or restoration (Instauratio). Their purpose is to serve innovation policy that meets predefined targets and key performance indicators (KPIs) supporting the existing political and social structures as the only possible future.

The informal networks of friends and collaborators in the hackerspaces, makerspaces, and citizen labs challenge this insistence on innovation policy as the only goal of prototyping. They form a utopian 'republic of makers' that questions the reduction of politics to ontology and cosmology, contemplative insight, or knowledge. In the liminal and experimental settings of the hackerspaces and citizen science projects, governance and technology become open-ended and hands-on experiences. The prototypes become opportunities to decide on personal and collective futures rather than a medium for perpetuating the divides and status quo.

Prototypes supporting Kairos, time as an opportunity for action and transformation, oppose the political rule of insights into prearranged order, cycles, or patterns that we must restore and impose. Pragmatic deliberations on common and even global futures through the designing and testing testing tools provoke people and communities to define the futures worth of trouble (Chapter 6). The future-making public in the hackerspaces and other liminal environments actively explores the alternatives to the present educational research, government, and also corporate institutions, tools, and projects. Although the impact of participatory, low-cost, ad hoc, and grassroots engagements remains low, it still enacts an experimental governance open to various interventions and values.

Is There a Community of Virtuous Makers?

Experimental governance over prototypes in the liminal environments (Kera, 2012b, 2012c) illustrates how time as Kairos is the essence of decisions and agency as a means of future-making. Instead of insights into patterns and cycles that define an ideal future as an effect of Chronos, time as Kairos means an opportunity for action. Kairos opposes hierarchies and teleological (mis)uses of time and refuses to reduce politics to ontology, cosmology, transcendental world of ideas, or knowledge of cycles and patters (Chronos). The interactions and engagements remain transient and open-ended, prone to contradictions, paradoxes, and chance.

The discussions of geek and hacker governance, such as the pioneering work by Gabriella Coleman (Coleman, 2013) or the ethnographic accounts of Shenzhen geekdom by Silvia Lindtner (Lindtner, 2020), capture the ambiguities of these engagements with prototypes and governance. While Coleman shows that paradoxes are intrinsic to open and free software movements, Lindtner criticizes the emphasis on prototypes as 'displacements of technological promise' (2020) supporting the political and economic status quo.

Coleman's examples, such as 'Debian's governance', show how developers of the free Unix-like operating system mix 'divergent political and economic practices and imaginaries' (Coleman, 2013). Rules and decision-making in Linux communities do not represent any coherent system of values, but a unique mix of 'democratic majoritarian rule, guild-like meritocracy, and ad hoc deliberations' (Ibid.). We can describe them as improvisations that embody the importance of prototyping to restore Kairos in technology and governance. Prototypes express agency and opportunity rather than Chronos, predefined political, social, or cosmological structures.

Descriptions of free and open software movements in Coleman provoke us to ask whether prototypes 'express the liberal traditions of free speech, the communitarian longing for community based on shared forms of life, or some romantic delusion of self-creation and radical autonomy?' (Kera, 2013). Coleman's account emphasize the ambiguous and liminal governance over prototypes in these communities that is our opinion embody Kairos in governance and technology. Her account differs from Lindtner's description of present attempts to prototype and govern in the maker movements (Lindtner, 2020) that strengthen the neoliberal order and various exploitations.

The prototyping for Lindtner is an example of a promissory technology that serves the modernist colonial project and injustice. The prototypes promise to ameliorate the 'institutional structures of inequality, exploitation, and injustice' through technology, but they further the neoliberal agenda of 'individual self-upgrade and economic development' (Ibid.). Lindtner's ethnographic account of maker movements in the US and China shows various examples of how prototypes support colonization and modernization through 'technological dreams of future making' that strengthen only 'demand for a particular kind of future' (Ibid.).

The technological change generated by promissory prototypes then makes 'acts of violence and control in the name of innovation... less noticeable, occluded by the promise of modern technological progress and its associations with good life – the promise to be freed from colonial and racial "othering"' (Ibid.). While Coleman examines the tensions between communitarian and liberal (even libertarian) ideals in free and open-source software projects as a challenge to understand how governance and technology mix, Lindtner shows a cynical misuse of the rhetoric around prototyping to support further violence and exclusions.

In Lindtner's view, the insistence in the maker movement on prototypes as tools of governance is a case of 'ambivalent alliances and always (already) partially compromised ideals' that has the 'capacity to accommodate diverse, often contradictory, hopes and anxieties' (Ibid.). In our view (and partially supported by Coleman's analysis of the open source movements), this ambiguity and paradoxes are the reason for a more in-depth inquiry into the role of infrastructure and prototyping in society, not a reason to reject the whole idea of governance over prototypes. The debate about implicit, explicit, and failed attempts at maker and hackers' governance over prototypes repeats in this sense the classic 17th- and 18th-century political philosophy debate whether a state based on natural philosophy or atheism could exist (Devellennes, 2017; Schulman, 2009). With the disruption, promises, and threats, the prototypes and new infrastructures seem to challenge our idea of body politics, common good, or the stat as something predefined and clear in its meanings and purpose (the ideal community of Christians in the 17th and the 18th century).

Prototyping in liminal environments provokes us to 'imagine a state (community) based on something other than religion, body politics, or visions of perfect and natural unity' (Kera, 2013). Instead of an ideal community including utopias of classless society or social justice, prototypes support radically open, agonistic, and uncertain futures through practice and material engagements. They offer a critique of the hierarchical and closed world (and time) without stating a clear agenda for the future. The future becomes an effect of Kairos that brings back the atomist ideal of 'a completely new world, an ensemble of things about which we currently have absolutely no idea at all' (Warman, 2020).

The prototypes in this sense share this atomist and materialist agenda of a future beyond our imagination and control. We describe this insistence on Kairos as an opportunity and chance in technology and governance that should remain open-ended, agonistic, even unpredictable. This concept of governance over prototypes restates the radical materialism of Pierre Bayle, Denis Diderot, or Baron d'Holbach (Devellennes, 2017, 2021) and insists on pragmatic and open-ended engagements against the teleological agendas of restoration and progress, including the present insistence on social justice.

Time as Kairos in technology and governance brings insistence on pragmatic and open-ended engagements with time, history, and the future. It is the reason why we disagree with Lindtner's assessment of prototyping in governance. In our opinion, facilitating neoliberal order and displacement, violence, or misuse of the maker rhetoric is one of the many functions that prototyping serves. Lindtner's warnings against promissory prototypes and their unequally distributed 'futures', including the ambiguous agendas and loyalties, are valid, but we consider them as a proof of their political strength rather than weakness. The 'capacity to accommodate diverse, often contradictory, hopes and anxieties'

(Lindtner, 2020) is what defines Kairos in governance and technology. It is the reason why we embraced the political dimension of prototyping rather than abandoning such engagements because of an inherent risk of not serving the main agenda of social justice or other ideas of progress.

The agonistic ideal of future-making as a matter of Kairos serves open, even conflicting, political ends that are crucial for preserving the agency, plurality, and freedom of the political life. Closing time, the history, and the future to one teleological project, such as restoration, progress, or classless society even social justice, reduces matters of politics to cosmology, ontology, and the rule of Chronos. It makes governance a matter of automation and efficiency over the infrastructures that will meet the predefined and idealized goals and serve the group that defines them.

Political action with or without prototypes is not an epiphenomenon of some predefined future or version of the collective that is modeled after the higher truths or values dictated by some cycles, patterns, and insights. The prototypes are 'autotelic' expressions of the personal and social opportunities and engagements that occur between concrete individuals in time as Kairos, a medium that is open to human agency, experiments, and transformation. The autotelic quality of the prototypes and human agency means that we must preserve the Kairos in governance and technology as opportunity for personal and social agency without imposing any teleology. Kairos in governance means a future that is open to change and transformation without any final goals.

Prototyping in the Special Economic Zone

To illustrate our thesis how Kairos in governance and creates hybrid and experimental futures, we will use examples of international and informal collaborations on prototypes described as 'geek diplomacy' (Kera, 2015). Collaborations in hackerspaces and similar marginal environments complicate the linear ideal of innovation as an 'adoption cycle'. Under the 'adoption' cycle, prototypes are effects of discoveries in science laboratories that designers and engineers develop into products and then manufacturers scale, while sales departments simply 'diffuse' into the society.

The liminal engagements over prototyping in hackerspaces show a different, more decentralized, open, and global process of future-making with ambiguous and uncertain results. The prototypes rarely become products and often remain a documentation on Github or similar platforms that invite others to adapt, transform, and contribute to the efforts. Instead of an ideal technology or infrastructure for governance mirroring some cosmology, ontology, and value system, including the postcolonial utopias, the tinkering with hardware embraces various paradoxes, that we will describe as liminality (Turner, 1985). Kairos in technology and governance over prototypes a thrives in liminal environments, such as hackerspaces, makerspaces including cities like Shenzhen in the special economic zone (SEZ) in China, which we followed in the period between 2012 and 2015 (Figures III.12 – III.26).

In that period, Shenzhen was a mythical place of prototyping and hacker dreams, a capitol of a global network of hackerspaces and makerspaces revolving around open-source hardware (Ames et al., 2014; Mellis & Buechley, 2011; Weiss, 2008) and DIY practices (Lindtner et al., 2016; Ratto & Boler, 2014). While channeling the promises of automated and distributed fabrication (Gershenfeld et al., 2004; Ratto & Ree, 2012), it gave rise to an ambiguous political and design fantasy that became a victim of its own success. The open hardware hype provoked a surge of government and policy interests in the so-called maker movements in the US, China, Singapore, Taiwan, as well as, the EU leading directly to nationalist calls for 'Making (XYZ nation) great again'.

The niche, exploratory, and informal transnational prototypes and networks (Kaiying & Lindtner, 2016; Vertesi et al., 2011) described here as 'geek diplomacy' (Kera, 2015) became co-opted by different governments to serve nationalist innovation agendas. They became what Lindtner describes as 'displacement' and 'promissory' prototypes (Lindtner, 2020), in stark contract to the early stages when they were simply 'liminal'. By 'liminal', we define prototypes that preserve the ambiguities and dichotomies between individualism and collectivism, local and global interests, nationalism and cosmopolitanism. Before serving the nationalist agendas, prototypes were precedents that never became an actual infrastructure, but preserved the value of open future and opportunities as expressions of Kairos.

Many open hardware kits and maker projects fit this description of an opportunity and chance that embrace Kairos without becoming government innovation plans. They express the liminality of the (technological) 'communitas' balancing the emerging (infra)structure with agency (Turner, 1969) and negotiating conflicting goals and agendas behind politics, technology, and globalization. Hackerspaces and maker prototypes served isolationist as much as cosmopolitan agendas; they embraced open-source rhetoric while remaining partially patented, pirated, and hybrid. They mobilized the global south's hopes of low-cost technologies while performing the Silicon Valley clichés, and used migrant slave labor in China and African conflict minerals while claiming to have a liberatory agenda. Rather than empowering some idealized notion of a subject, community, or even nation, prototypes demarcated the limits and conditions of our engagements with governance and its relation to production, innovation, and design.

Casablanca of Prototyping: Shenzhen

Shenzhen in Southern China's Guangdong Province embodies the paradoxes and liminality of open hardware prototypes and innovation. The electronics manufacturing capital of the world is part of the SEZ (Gopinath, 2009; Liu et al., 2007) defined by tax incentives and relative autonomy in proximity to Hong Kong and Taiwan (Longyi & Lihua, 2009; Ng, 2003; Zacharias & Tang, 2010). Shenzhen's unique innovation ecosystem accommodates large multinational companies and patented technologies, but also small and medium enterprises (SMEs) with their pirated (so called shanzhai) products and open hardware start-ups claiming to be part of the Silicon Valley dream. The factories in the SEZ manufacture products for both developed and developing countries, small-scale open hardware start-ups and big corporations, patented as well as pirated, shanzhai and gonkai (B. Huang, 2013) products.

Back in 2010s, the shanzhai copycat products attracted a network of geeks visiting Shenzhen to question the geopolitical stereotypes of China and to explore a new model of how to 'create in (or with) China' (Lindtner & Lee, 2012). Before 2015, when China rebranded the maker movement into their official PR strategy, Shenzhen was something of a technological version of the 1940s Casablanca depicted in the famous Michael Curtiz film noire (Sennett, 2009). It was a relatively neutral zone, where everyone could come, prototype, and scale production by engaging with various local and global networks, actors, and visions beyond the geopolitical divides.

The network of geeks involved in this liminal prototyping communitas included the first hardware accelerator, HAXL8R, popular among hackerspace members and independent developers since 2011 that marketed Shenzhen as a place to start and scale hacker projects. Another important network was initiated by the open hardware hacker and developer Bunnie Huang, who would bring MIT students to work on their projects in Shenzhen while exploring the connections with local manufacturers as part of their residencies. While HAXL8R/HAX incubated numerous consumer products, Bunnie's network supported unique and innovative ideas, such as circuit stickers changing the ways in which we think and interact with, or the first open-source notebook, Novena (B. Huang, 2014), and similar ideas of a 'sovereign' infrastructure.

The lenient IP policies and relative autonomy created opportunities for rapid scaling of hardware projects that supported unexpected geopolitical networks and new markets. It became an open hardware Casablanca where makers, tinkerers, and developers, not only from the Bay Area and East Coast but also from Iran, EU, Israel, and South America, could flock and collaborate on products and offer them to a global market. The CEO of Seeed Studio, Eric Pan, once described Shenzhen as the 'Hollywood of hardware products' (Gomba, 2013), a place that breaks barriers. He also labeled his products with the proclamation 'Innovate with China'.

Seeed Studio emerged in 2008 as a global, open hardware facilitation company targeting EU and US markets. After 2013, it even hosted geeks from developing countries like Indonesia or Nepal and supported projects of open microscopy kit, DIY sound synthesizers, and robots. The prototypes in Seeed Studio became tools of an informal science diplomacy (Burns, 2013). They fostered unique South-to-South collaborations and projects that served educational and entertainment purposes, but indirectly connected politics with design and created conditions for a public of tinkerers to take new challenges from health to environmental monitoring, prospecting, or building independent infrastructures (Huang, 2015; Kera et al., 2019).

In a playful manner, the open hardware kits manufactured in Shenzhen allowed users and developers to think creatively about their agency and scale their informal projects. Most of the projects never became a solution to social, political, and economic problems, but the experience of building a technological infrastructure that people can modify supported unique collaborations across various divides. The emphasis on tinkering rather than solutions supported hackers and makers to define various futures of figure emerging technologies (wearable, drones, and robots).

Patents, Open Source, and Everything in Between

Shenzhen, as Casablanca or Hollywood, of open hardware kits and projects around 2013 showed prototypes that broke the common divisions between the developed and developing countries or other common (Platonic) dichotomies of designing and manufacturing. They embodied Zilsel's thesis on instrumentation-making and prototyping as a process that breaks social (and we can add geopolitical) divisions and transforms society. We discussed the value of hybrid practices on the examples of Renaissance instruments in Chapter 6 and 7 ignoring the common division between contemplative and theoretical reason.

The example that illustrates well Zilsel's thesis is the Safecast DIY radiation monitoring kit that bridged the divides between hackerspace and industry, patents and open-source technologies, but also Shenzhen and the global community of hackers.

Safecast was a radiation monitoring kit prototyped in 2011 by an international community around the Tokyo hackerspace with the help of hackerspace communities around the world (Kera et al., 2013). Shortly after the Fukushima disaster, many geeks living in Japan envisioned an independent tool for measuring radiation and initiated a global hackerspace response to the crisis. The result was a crowd-sourced DIY kit manufactured in Shenzhen, later developed into a nonprofit organization that improved industry standards in radiation monitoring and worked closely with an established company in this domain, International Medcom Inc.

Over a period of two years, the initial ad hoc network of radiation monitoring geeks and volunteers transformed into a global organization supporting open measurements and publication of various atmospheric data. While the original prototypes supported efforts for independent measurement and data through custom-built DIY tools, subsequent discussions about accuracy and calibration led to a collaboration with regulatory bodies and industry players. Safecast became a pioneering example of 'humanitarian' hardware

(Akiba, 2011) that demonstrates the hybrid and liminal possibilities of an emerging public engaged in technology and governance.

From a community-sourced project to a Medcom product, the kit explored a productive tension between open-source aspirations and patented technologies. It offers a counterexample to the misuses and scandals of the MakerBot 3-D printer saga discussed by Lindtner (Lindtner, 2020) as a cautionary story of a co-opted and patented open-source prototype that destroyed the community aspirations and ideals:

> The story of a coopted hacker movement (through making or investing) further naturalizes the idea that there exists first an innocent countercultural subject position (the hacktivist) that will eventually (and inevitably) be torqued to produce economic value. What if instead we began instead from the understanding that there are no innocent and ideal positions and that what is available to us is always already partially compromised? We might, then, be able to step sideways and out of the seemingly endless cycle of success and failure, resistance, and co-optation... Shenzhen, its economies of scale, its global supply chains and factories were included in this 'pitch' where the resistant capacities were being democratized through open source technologies and commitments. Radical resistance here serves the function of pitch: displaced into the innovator's toolkit for 'disruption', it becomes a market device to attract feeling and serve the anticipatory logics of investment.
>
> (Ibid.)

In contrast to Lindtner's views of 'partially compromised' prototypes prone to promises and disillusionments, we view their instability and uncertainty as condition for enabling Kairos as agency in governance and technology. Prototypes need to remain liminal and ambiguous experiences that challenge the way we navigate the conflicts and tensions between our agency and structure, community and technology, politics and ontology, or Chronos and Kairos. The MakerBot controversy shows how even a Marxist pitch can attract a VC investment, but this transgression did not close the future for the 3D printing open-source community nor for the industry. For Lindtner, the MakerBot misuse of the open source work is an example of the precarious logic of 'happiness labor' in the 'new' organizational models of tech production (incubators, coworking spaces, makerspaces, hackerspaces, design laboratories, open innovation laboratories) (Ibid.) that is exploitative but this reduces the reasons why some spend time and energy on such prototypes. For many it is not labor at all, but a form of action or leisure, genuine (even if failed) attempt to make a difference.

The example of Safecast shows how the ambiguity and even liminality of prototyping strengthen rather than weaken the personal and social agency invested in similar open-source projects. Safecast started as a prototype, which was developed into a kit that involves citizens through crowdfunding and workshops, in which citizens learn how to use the tool and calibrate it.

The kit gradually transformed into a product that improved quality while complying with industry standards and preserving its connection to the original maker community. This DIY Geiger counter throughout the prototyping, testing, and reiteration cycle enabled citizens to gather and share independent data on radiation and take an active part in discussing policies related to the future of nuclear energy (Kera et al., 2013).

The moment that shows the strength of this liminal and hybrid prototype is when Safecast decided to integrate a patented technology into its open-source kit. Instead of patenting the open-source design as MakerBot did or refusing to engage with the industry, Safecast created a better tool that serves both, the geek community and industry. In the process, both sides had to question their ideological biases and insistences on patents or open-source ideals and define a more hybrid and open future. The tool crossed ideological, economic, and other barriers and divides in a way that Zilsel described it in the case of Renaissance instruments. Collaboration with a 'friendly' patent owner benefited both sides without compromising on their original goals of democratizing technology and repurposing it. In Chapter 12, we will describe this hands-on liminal engagement with prototypes as activity supporting what we call experimental policy and 'regulation through disonancne'.

The final bGeigieNano Geiger counter was developed by the famous maker who organized tours in Shenzhen, Bunnie Huang, who is also an active open-source hardware hacker and activist. Bunnie worked closely with the community around Safecast to integrate patented part from Medcom into the final tool (the iRover high-voltage supply with 'front end', which processes signal from the Geiger tube) (Huang, 2012). Although it was produced and distributed by Medcom, the world leader in radiation monitoring, the tool remained a DIY open hardware kit.

The hybrid of open source and patented technology did what seizing an opportunity as Kairos means in terms of governance and technology. It means moving beyond the common divisions between open-source and patented ideologies, technologies, and even sites, such as hackerspaces and industry, West and Shenzhen. It means creating complex and resilient networks that use both technology and governance for new goals.

Although hardware innovation in Shenzhen will always include exploitative 'happiness labor' and cynical Marxist pitches, brilliantly described by Lindtner, it is also a complex and experimental geopolitical site for experiments that illustrate the importance of what we call in this book Kairos. Technological and political prototyping is not about fulfilling any socialist, communist, or neoliberal dreams, but performing the temporality of our engagement with prototypes and time. It is not about creating an idealized 'imagined community' beyond history and politics, nor about ideal technology and automation. The liminal prototype tactically explored a variety of networks, concepts, political and economic regimes, and agendas to empower very concrete communities, individuals, and projects, such as the final Geiger counter and its idea of decentralized environmental monitoring over similar tools.

Shenzhen as a liminal site for prototyping supports the complex connections between patented, open-source, and copycat production (shanzhai) and fuels the various expectations from innovation and politics. It embodies the potential of liminal environments to support Kairos in governance and technology that challenge the view of China's role in innovation and production:

> Based on shanzhai innovation, China's hackerspaces argue for an alternative version of 'created in China'. Rather than proposing to overcome manufacturing for the sake of knowledge production, they offer the view that China's existing manufacturing infrastructure could be used to accomplish in practice what so far has been a political vision.
>
> (Lindtner & Lee, 2012)

Shenzhen demonstrated an alternative geopolitical future of 'innovate with China' that remained open to various hackers, makers, and visionaries. Once China's policymakers co-opted this promise to serve the CCP nationalist agendas, it simply collapsed into a cynical PR campaign around 2015.

The pre-2015 liminal communitas was a complex milieu of patented, pirated, and open-sourced technologies that created an ecosystem between hackerspaces, open hardware accelerators, and manufacturers. It enabled makers, entrepreneurs, and hackers from all over the world to freely explore the new political and economic networks. Not all projects and networks lead to successes, but even the failures, as we will show in the next chapter, offered a valuable lesson on the importance of Kairos in governance and technology over prototypes.

Dream-Works in the Republic of Garages

Unique geopolitical experiments with open hardware communitas around Shenzhen prior to 2015 combined various ideologies and interests that generated ambiguous ideas of governance over prototypes. Kairos in governance and technology means accepting risk and uncertainty that guarantee an open future even when the projects fails as we could see in the example proposing a micro-solar factory, Solar Pocket Factory.[1] Solar Pocket Factory was a joint effort and network of MIT graduates from Haddock Invention,[2] a company based in Hong Kong that operated in Shenzhen with a complex network of affiliates such as Mantis Shrimp Invention[3] in Manila and other SMEs from Asia, EU, and South America.

The self-described 'network of workshops and garages' combined the hacker ethos with new models of crowdfunding and traditional business practices, such as patents and the multinational, networked affiliates almost mocking the corporate pan-global structures. The goal of the garage network was to produce disruptive, low-tech prototypes that provide solutions to developed and developing countries in terms of energy efficiency (such as small solar panels for mobile phones or other examples of leapfrogging).

MIT graduates Alex Hornstein and Shawn Frayne envisioned the network of garages as a cooperation with local teams of tinkerers in the developing countries interested in the design of future clean confluent technologies (Frayne, n.d.), such as the low-tech solar panels and wind turbines.

The green energy prototypes would power the wireless sensor nodes for environmental monitoring, but also mobile phones, and improve access to electricity in places with missing energy infrastructure. The iterative process and complex networks envisioned around the prototypes would connect technological and social change:

> We are developing this network because I believe that paradigm-shift-ing, disruptive, confluent (insert punditry here) technologies emerge from a different innovation machine than has traditionally been the engine of progress in the past. These new inventions are not churned out [by] the 'invention factories' that Edison created in 1876, where hundreds of engineers worked twenty-hour days on the same punch clock under one roof. Nowadays, the biggest problems are not near the wealthiest markets and creativity is too spread out across borders.
>
> (Hornstein, n.d.)

Cells (garage networks) around prototypes were supposed to create 'a global invention organism – the Ocean Invention Network' (LeCompte, 2013). Envisioned as small teams of four to five people from both sides of the wealth divide, their purpose was to test a new model of manufacturing, R&D and business. The cells bridging of the divides perform what we mean by the liminal qualities of prototyping and emphasize the opportunity as Kairos in both governance and technology. They tried to reproduce and exten the Shenzhen model to support South-to-South collaborations involving original networks between graduates from MIT prototyping with the developers from the Global South while exploring new business models.

The company was based in Hong Kong and Shenzhen, but mainly targeted Thailand and the Philippines and insisted on inclusive innovation and exper-iments with patented and open-source technologies. Shawn Frayne and Alex Hornstein described their confluent technologies as 'technological magic that happens when challenges faced in developing countries meet challenges faced in wealthy countries' (Frayne, n.d.; Hornstein, n.d.). The confluence of social and technical opportunities, or what we call here Kairos of prototyping, would tackle governance and technology challenges while supporting the personal and social agency in the different regions against the monopolies.

> The scarcity of resources, according to their original document, would push innovators to develop resilient and original solutions that create a leapfrog type effect in innovation and adoption: Whenever new prod-ucts are developed to serve new customers at radically different price points, something wonderful happens, a rupture breaches the status quo, where incremental innovation produced by incumbent industry

giants is wiped away by a leap forward... These confluent technologies were developed to solve some challenge in emerging markets, under the pressure of cost constraints very different from the constraints in Silicon Valley. Emerging markets are the breeding ground for new innovations that will topple industries, not despite their constraints but because of them. For the first time, the lack of electricity, scarcity of clean water and the great need for medical diagnostics in the small village of La Borgne, Haiti, can force into existence new solutions that have the power to overturn multi-billion dollar empires across the economic divide in rich cities like Tokyo and San Francisco. That is what the Ocean Invention Network is all about, teasing out great inventions from the confluence and making some trouble along the way.

(Frayne, n.d.)

The idea of innovation as a 'rupture that breaches the status quo' or a leap-frogging describes the type of transformation that prototypes initiate when supporting an open future. They can transform the relationship between developed and developing countries, innovation and society. Instead of automatizing and monopolizing the future, such projects support the idea of 'future worth the trouble' that we use to describe Kairos in governance and technology in Chapter 7. The quote by Frayne defines how liminal prototypes from Shenzhen broke down the geopolitical and other divides and challenged us to imagine new futures.

The Shenzhen designers and inventors, like modern Thaleses, made prototypes to question the status quo and the limits imposed by the present social and political divides. Their confluent prototypes like dreamworks enabled the conflicting desires and publics to unite around the design of the future instruments. The explicit use of the metaphors of unconscious and biological processes of crosspollination and symbiosis is driven by opportunity and Kairos rather than well-defined ideals of a system or model of launching a product, IPO, and licensing or patenting to diffuse innovation to the global South.

The project failed but brought visibility to the material conditions of design and production and its role in politics. The independent, ad hoc, and mobile R&D centers, the garages in Delhi, Shenzhen, and Manila, together with fablabs, hackerspaces, and similar institutions around the world, are still the sites where we can dream and experience the liminal prototypes, such as the nonturbine wind generators (Hong Kong/Hawaii),[4] underwater drones (Octo23 in Paris),[5] etc. They are sites and projects that opened our imagination about the future via engagement with prototypes.

Sociotechnical Rites of Passage

The Solar Pocket factory and other Shenzhen examples illustrate what we describe as experimental governance over prototypes that brings forth liminality and hybridity. Instead of progress and restoration of an ideal society, technology or future, the prototyping in these projects is a rite of passage.

It is a transition between different, often conflicting, desires and scales in technology and politics. While it sustains the 'precarious conditions of entrepreneurial life... the emotional and infrastructural conditions for flexible work and venture labor' (Lindtner, 2020), it also supports personal and social agency over the future, that includes failures reminding us of the anecdotes about Thales' fall into a ditch that performed his agency over time as Kairos (Chapter 4).

The radical engagements with time and future over prototypes mobilize actors and forces to reveal new technological and political challenges without imposing any teleological goals. Shenzhen prototypes with all their ambiguous attributes of conflict-based, but liberatory, semi-patented, and almost pirated but still open-source tools 'ritualize social (and we should add technological) and cultural transitions' (Turner, 1969) in the present. They represent the transitions and ambiguities of our technology and society in the age of prototypes. For some, the transition is transformative and challenges the technological status quo as much as governance, but for many, the prototypes preserve the old hierarchies and power relations with new means. Rather than looking for an ideal convergence of politics and design resolving these tensions and ambiguities, our goal in this book is to use prototypes to challenge politics and technology.

Open hardware 3D printing created the MakerBot[6] controversy and debacle (Dickel et al., 2014; Lindtner, 2020; Molitch-Hou, 2014), but also successful open hardware projects (Prusa Design). The 3D transforming and transitory communitas did not become a perfect society of digital fabrication, in which everyone prints objects and materials they need without costs. However, it is neither a victory of the patented business practices that misused open-source projects, which are results of expired patent.

The transition from expiring patent to open source technology and then back to new patents created many 'shades' of business models and communities around 3D printing that are still evolving. Some are open-source advocates, but others combine their design with patents and create parallel and plural futures of 3D printing (Pettis, 2014).

The MakerBot controversy exemplifies the liminal experiences and rite of passage connecting technology and governance over prototyping. 3D printing experienced something Turner describes as the 'limbo of statuslessness' (Turner, 1969) with all the 'high and low, homogeneity and differentiation, equality and inequality' (Ibid.) of the present politics and technology. The transition between the regulated, patented, and open forms of innovation and society did not bring the victory of one type of technology nor governance but radical plurality and future that various groups and individuals still explore in their businesses and projects.

Open hardware experiences of prototyping are liminal because they are 'neither here nor there; they are betwixt and between the positions assigned and arrayed by law, custom, convention, and ceremonial' (Ibid.). This 'oscillation', rather than a dialectic of the global open hardware communitas opens the future not only of 3D printing but also of various other technologies. More than other technologies, open hardware, with its insistence on prototyping and community-based, peer innovation, exposes the genealogical roots of our idea of politics and governance modeled after the activities of the 'free' citizens of Athens that 'have time' to engage with projects no one cares about (Chapter 3). The geeks, hackers, and makers will always insist on prototyping that preserves the possibility of an open future as personal and collective control over time as a public good.

The Paradoxes of the Open Hardware Communitas

Shenzhen, as a liminal environment for prototyping, supported the experience of Kairos in technology and governance. It facilitated playful but also serious engagements with technologies and governance in what we are trying to describe as a global 'rite of passage' or open hardware communitas. It was an environment where geeks, makers, and hackers explored open-source licenses as well as patents to create complex geopolitical relations and visions. The tinkering public in Shenzhen experienced Kairos in governance and technology over different global and local projects and networks. They formed what we describe here as a 'spontaneous communitas' (Turner, 1969), an experimental and liminal rather than reflective and recursive (Kelty, 2008) public. We claim that such liminal public preserves the value of time as Kairos in governance and technology rather than only embodying predefined goals in society, technology, or history.

Instead of defining an ideal international community engaged in innovation, Shenzhen's examples remain liminal, transitory, and often prone to excesses. The examples of prototypes support what Turner (Turner, 1969) defines as communitas, an alternative and temporary ambiguity, chaos, and antistructure that probe the limits of governance, agency, and technology. The prototyping communitas around Shenzhen explored the liminality and paradoxes of not only prototyping and designing but also scaling the production without insisting on any ideal state, community, or citizens and technology. It embodied the paradoxes of geek politics and diplomacy described by Gabriella Coleman as syncretic and productive in her study of the geeks and hackers engaged in open software (Coleman, 2013).

Shenzhen at least before 2015 represents a public of makers immersed in Kairos of governance and technology or open hardware communitas for experiencing rite of passage between open and closed technologies and models of governance. As the manufacturing capitol of the world, where many open hardware projects congregated, it became an important site of DIY-making and innovation (Lindtner, 2014; Lindtner & Lee, 2012). Although it did not fulfill the expectations of empowerment through such practices (Lindtner et al., 2016), it enabled everyone to experience the range of possibilities and futures of politics and technology.

Shenzhen hosted the transnational open hardware accelerators that tried to define the future of innovation, but also the copycat shanzhai production of mobile phones and factories supporting the official (patented) electronics industry. The equilibrium between the liberated open hardware, shanzhai and regulated Apple, Samsung, etc., consumer goods summarizes the paradoxes of this liminal SEZ catering the needs of both developed and developing worlds (Liu, 2010; Longyi & Lihua, 2009). For a brief time, migrants in the factories and miners working with conflict minerals could interact with the promissory futures explored by the start-up scene, including Silicon Valley, MIT research labs, and the idealistic networks of hackerspaces and makerspaces.

The prototyping communitas in Shenzhen embodied the liminal aspects of tinkering and making that include the paradoxes of pirated, patented, and open-source technologies and industries. More importantly, this 'republic of makers' questioned the views on governance based on the denigration of makers (demiurgoi) as political actors. Instead of a society embodying the right insight defined by enlightened guardians, philosophers, or technologies, prototyping remained an ambiguous effort to open the future to various (mis) uses and new actors. China, the Congo, and other places involved in the material production of electronics could never meet the ideals of responsible innovation or fair hardware in terms of minerals, sustainability, and workers' rights, but they explored and tested new relations. The dream of perfect hardware and just minerals, after all, served only the established actors like Intel.

The only serious attempt for conflict-free and transparent trade with minerals from Congo remains US[7] based and shows a cynical misuse of the concept of the good governance to serve the interest of a western corporation. Intel, in its attempt to regulate conflict minerals tried to preserve control not only over the market but also the rules define the only the 'ideal community' of (open) hardware users and consumers. Engagements with minerals or other materials in places like Shenzhen ignored this insistence on the right insight and intentions as a condition for good governance. They supported actors without the 'right insight' to probe different possibilities of how to develop and scale production or create communities around it. Instead of defining governance as a contemplative and discursive insight that serves the interest of the status quo, they created opportunities for ambiguity, liminality, and hybridity.

Makers as Demiurgoi

Shenzhen as well as hackerspaces, makerspaces, and similar communities express the agency and power through prototyping and material engagement in future-making that is liminal, agonistic, and ambiguous. The geeks, makers, and science artisans perform their agency and visions as Kairos rather than a search for monopoly and automation based on some idealized notion of Chronos. They act as Plato's 'demiurges' of the Timaeus dialogue (Plato, 1871) rather than as philosophers-kings from the Republic.

Demiurge was always a surprising metaphor to describe the creator and legislator of the universe due to the low social standing of the artisans and craftsmen (demiurgoi) in Athens. The artisanal creations of demiurge as a form of governance over the material universe are in direct opposition to Plato's earlier views of governance in the Republic.

While the philosopher-king rules by contemplating the ideal forms and governance that mimic his perfect soul, the demiurge rules as a craftsman through the messy practices experiencing the friction or chora, the material world. The demiurge paradox in Plato's views of governance (Esses, 2018) summarizes our reflections of the liminality and paradoxes involved in the technological experiments with governance, sovereignty, and autonomy. To rule over chora, the receptacle, material substrate, or even a womb means to engage with the wilderness and space beyond the walls of the well-governed city-state (Bigger, 2004), our original prototype connecting Kairos in governance and infrastructure (Chapter 8). To govern and prototype as a demiurge thus means urbanizing the wilderness or engaging with the uncertainties of the future to serve the values and needs of a specific community.

Governance over prototypes facing Kairos, such as uncertainty, chaos, and wilderness outside the safety of some 'walls', is a process with unclear and ambiguous ends. Instead of mirroring any ideal Chronos, the demiurge tames the wilderness and uncertainty into temporal and transitory equilibria over prototypes open to change. The demiurge metaphor for governance over prototypes makes politics a pragmatic and material engagement with the world and time as Kairos. Governance becomes the opposite of the idealized cosmology, chronology, or technology.

The two important dialogues on governance by Plato staged the paradoxes and challenges of prototyping for governance. The dialogues perform the value of liminal environments for engaging and experimenting with different concepts (but also tools) of governance, infrastructure, politics, and future. They explain why we need to preserve the quality of such environments that leave open the paradoxes and tensions of governance and technology, wilderness and domestication. To support this liminality and rite of passage quality of design and prototyping communitas, we are proposing the model of exploratory and public sandboxes for governance over prototypes in Chapter 12.

Like Plato's dialogues, the liminal sites of innovation discussed in in this chapter, or hybrid sandboxes discussed in the next Chapter 12 embrace time as Kairos, an opportunity to transform both governance and infrastructure through experiments. Hybrid and liminal environments keep the future open to change and opportunity that enable individuals and communities to define their purpose through their tools. Prototyping practices and environments in this sense oppose all predetermined and teleological goals and insights, such as the restoration of some paradise, classless society, and similar ideas of a closed and predefined future.

Interpreting and Changing the World with Prototypes

While the philosopher-king rules with insights mirroring his perfect soul and an ideal cosmology, the demiurge rules by prototyping the world and performing agency over time and the future. The insistence on Kairos in governance and technology means insisting on a future that is open and free from teleological ideals of progress and restoration. It is a future without an ideal subject, community, or goal in nature and history, open to explorations, negotiations, and temporary equilibria. Neither cosmology nor ontology defines the future of communities and individuals that preserve their time as a precious resource or Kairos.

With this proposal for governance over prototypes, we openly challenge the teleological interpretations of history, including the historical materialist ideals of social justice or other concepts inspired by Marx. The notions of division of labor and structure of production (Fuchs & Dyer-Witheford, 2012; Miller 1991) only reiterate the teleological ideals of progress. They close the future to one project based on the 'right' insight into history or nature that determines the goal of governance (and technology). Prototypes as liminal practice do not reduce any action to insight but combine both while emphasizing the importance of Kairos in governance and technology. Governance over prototypes then does not serve any ideal society, technology, or infrastructure. It embodies the experience of time and the future as open to personal and social agency.

While Marx and Engel's critique of consciousness and idealism (Marx & Engels, 1998) comes close to this emphasis on prototypes combining knowing (insight) and making (action), the focus here is on preserving rather than resolving their tensions. We reject the cosmology and ontology of cycles and pattern, or psychology (of needs) in defining governance. There are no bases or superstructures in this emphasis on prototyping for governance. We view these concepts as remnants of Plato's tripartite theory of the soul that inspired the ideals of governance driven by insights of the reason in the Republic. Against this tripartite view of the soul (reason, spirit, and appetites) and its different version (true needs and superficial desires, the base, and superstructures), that we claim are responsible for the hierarchical and static view of the society, we place our concept of agency over time and future as the main goal of politics.

It is tempting to read Marx's famous Eleventh Thesis on Feuerbach (Ibid.) as a makers' manifesto stating the convergence of politics and design. The philosophers have only interpreted the world in various ways and designers finally get the point that we have to change it. Equally tempting is to apply the famous passages from 'The German Ideology' to the sentiments voiced by critical making concept of DIY citizenship or other beliefs in creating a just society once we become more reflective while producing and making:

> In communist society, where nobody has one exclusive sphere of activity, but each can become accomplished in any branch he wishes, society regulates general production and thus makes it possible for me to do one thing today and another tomorrow, to hunt in the morning, fish in the afternoon, rear cattle in the evening, criticize after dinner, just as I have a mind, without ever becoming hunter, fisherman, herdsman or critic.
>
> (Ibid.)

The problem with these passages in Marx and similar reflections of maker culture and prototyping is the idealized (or demonized and alienated) notions of a community and its subjects. Prototyping for governance does not serve any emancipatory nor idealized notions of society and technology, but remains a liminal practice enabling transitions, transformations, and open-ended experiments between the existing and new configurations of power, resources, subjectivities, fears, or fantasies. Prototypes that express Kairos, as an opportunity for transformation, oppose the politics based on Chronos with its notions of an ideal ontological or cosmological state and history, including the psychology of collective and individual 'souls' and needs. Instead of searching for another ideal politics based on design, making or praxis, or obsessing over the right place and use of design and technology in politics, citizens as demiurges question why making and tinkering should be excluded from politics.

Prototyping for governance opposes the rhetoric of change as a path to any universality and collective in Marx and Engels (Marx & Engels, 1998) but also the present literature on the convergence of design and politics (Dantec & DiSalvo, 2013; Marres & Lezaun, 2011; Ratto, 2011; Ratto & Ree, 2012). The governance over prototypes is a defense of liminal, open-ended, plural, and, in the best case, experimental processes with complex relations to materiality and time (history and future), private, and public life. Prototyping as an expression of Kairos does not serve any idealized politics or community but defines the agency as an ability to step outside the status quo and, like Thales, perform the powers of knowledge and technology over the future.

Prototyping Communitas as a Model for Public Sandboxes

Makers and tinkerers organized around open-source hardware projects in hackerspaces, makerspaces, hardware accelerators, Maker Fairs, and Shenzhen form a heterogeneous and complex network with conflicting goals and agendas. Examples, such as DIY air pumps (Chapter 9), 3D printers, and Safecast Geiger counters, capture this liminality (Turner, 1969) of prototyping that connects patented and open products with personal and communal acts of resistance, acceptance, or even opportunism, as we saw in the infamous case of MakerBot scandal (Molitch-Hou, 2014).

Prototypes as rites of passage support liminality and the formation of a heterogeneous community with diverse political and design interests and agendas. We described these agendas as effects of Kairos as an opportunity to change governance and not only technology. They are opportunities to improve the existing tools, where open-source licenses become a form of governance supporting collaborative innovation,[8] as well as a more critical and activist attempt to build laboratory infrastructure in the Global South for open science[9] (Chapter 9) or respond to the environmental crisis with independent monitoring tools.[10] Instead of limiting the technical and normative expectations to issues of automation or autonomy and sovereignty, the prototypes remain liminal and liminoid (Turner, 1985) fostering Kairos as agency in technology and governance.

Prototypes are messy, complex, and ambiguous objects of our recent political and design fantasies that only demarcate the limits and conditions of technology and governance (Chapter 10). Instead of empowering the idealized notions of subject or community, they are in permanent transition and transformation, creating paradoxical and uncanny networks (communitas) difficult to describe or let alone judge. The prototypes for governance embrace open-source rhetoric while remaining partially patented, pirated, and hybrid. They mobilize Global South hopes while performing Silicon Valley clichés and exploiting migrant slave labor in China and African conflict minerals.

Even the most iconic open hardware projects, such as the 'TV-B-Gone Kit'[11] for switching off annoying LCD screens in public spaces or the 'Tweet-a-Watt'[12] for monitoring electricity consumption, which tests our willingness to regulate consumption, remain inherently playful and exploratory. They will never become solutions to social, political, and economic problems, such as Cisco or Intel's smart cities embedded in corporate sensors, while promising democratic IoT futures (Caragliu et al., 2011). They are not props and mock-ups enhancing public participation, debate, and deliberation through design, as in the case of critical design (Dunne, 2008; Dunne & Raby, 2013; Wilkie & Ward, 2009) or science communication (Kirby, 2009; Wilkie, 2010), but imperfect attempts at probing the future for concrete people and communities.

OSH instruments discussed in Chapters 9 and 10 or open hardware projects from Shenzhen in this chapter show prototyping that embraces time as Kairos, an opportunity for change and transformation against any final goals in governance or technology. Such prototyping does not share the exaggerated rhetoric of the 'exploits' from critical engineering (Oliver et al., n.d.) nor the interest in contested and 'adversarial' design (DiSalvo, 2012) with claims about emancipating and educating the masses about infrastructure through the work of enlightened designers, artists, engineers, or hackers.

We emphasize the liminal properties of prototyping because they accommodate even opposing goals and values. While they share some of the sentiments behind media archeology interest in forgotten and neglected futures, they remain mundane and close to some of the critical making experiments (DiSalvo, 2014; Ratto, 2011) that emphasize collaborative and participatory work. They support individual and communal projects that are open-ended without necessarily being 'critical' or mobilizing makers into empowered DIY citizens (Ratto & Boler, 2014). They support the agency of concrete individuals and communities to decide what 'small' and 'big' futures and projects to build around the prototypes without resigning on politics.

Although many criticize the recent vogue of connecting politics with design as 'solutionism' (Morozov, 2014b), a reimagined and softened version of the old technocratic rule (Feenberg, 1994; Habermas, 1989), or neoliberal mobilization over promissory futures (Lindtner, 2020), we disagree with these assessments. They reduce technology to an imperfect form of social action that needs to reflect the insights into the ideal community, the 'soul', or other characteristics of citizenship and society.

The complex and liminal nature of prototypes as technical, legal, geopolitical, and even geological experiments operates behind every electronic component, idea for a service, or emerging infrastructure. Hybrid, liminal, and open interventions embrace time as Kairos and give us a reason to rethink how 'making' and materials enact politics rather than insist on any pre-given values or ideals of a community or citizens. The prototypes express Kairos in governance and technology without serving any preconceived notions of liberal democracy, communitarism, or other political ideals. They remain practices through which we enact an individual and a common future.

We welcome prototypes that provoke clashes between ideas, values, and material possibilities or offer opportunities to rethink what we expect from governance and technology. They probe the degrees of control over the future and time through concrete interventions that serve concrete communities and individuals. They problematize our views of technology, patents, innovation, and, more importantly, even the concepts of social action, politics, or governance. To fully grasp the type of freedom and agency that we can experience over prototypes, we need liminal and hybrid environments, where we can explore how to bring together technology and governance. The proposal for public sandboxes discussed in Chapter 12 explains the hybrid and idiosyncratic engagements as a type of public work on the future.

Homo Faber and Homo Ludens

The prototyping in the liminal environments and special zones questions the ideal of governance as a separation of powers of thinking and making, politics and design, or governance and technology. In the previous chapters, we tried to show prototypes emphasize liminality, hybridity, and plurality of goals and values. Prototypes in these liminal environments define governance as an experimental iteration that mitigates the risks and benefits of technology without embracing any idealized notion of a subject or community.

Citizens as stakeholders in the future use prototypes to oppose the ideal of technocratic and algorithmic governance. Technology is not a means to resign upon normative expectations and values nor to outsource the decision-making to automation. By engaging with prototypes, citizens actively embed their values and ideals, such as the importance of open science in the global South (Chapters 9 and 10) or the new geopolitical networks for innovation (Chapter 11) while negotiating their common future. This does not guarantee any success, but preserves the agency even in a failure, such as the 'paradigmatic' Thales' fall into a ditch in Chapter 3 that explains best what innovation and discovery mean. The emphasis on open-ended experiments strengthens agency and imagination against the absolute truth or insight that only close the future of technology and governance. The future in the 'republic of makers' and technological communitas with its demiurgoi is liminal, plural, and transitory rather than final and perfect.

While governance machines insist on the idealized and teleological notions of a community and infrastructure, we advocate engagements with technology and governance that support Kairos. Kairos defines the future as a matter of agency over time that supports direct engagements, further explained in the proposed sandboxes in Chapter 12, extending the environments described in Chapter 9–11.

The proposal for public and exploratory sandboxes emphasizes open and public environments for experiments with open future as a matter of technology and governance. Instead of repeating the grand narratives of homo faber who will save and fix the world with every new technology promising to achieve the final ideal of a moral community or Instauratio, we define the makers as homo ludens. They are playful citizens who enjoy their free time as otium as much as an opportunity to engage with others in vita activa. The liminal environments offer a model how to design and govern without falling into the trap of teleological expectation about technology or society and preserve the future as open and public infrastructure.

Citizens as homo ludens build playful prototypes to explore their cosmologies and build niche communities. They resist the myth of automation and algorithmic governance as unimaginative and dangerous control over their time and common future. As playful and active makers, they transform their technologies into democratic and inclusive practices that preserve the ambiguities of human agency as Kairos, an ability to decide and negotiate personal and common futures. Instead of blind faith in progress or final ends including justice, homo ludens insist on experiments as the means preserving their agency as Kairos.

The playful image of home ludens as a maker opposes the ideal of the engineer that controls the future and destiny of the world described in the anecdote about the first homo faber. The anecdotes about the great Roman builder of roads and bridges, Appius Claudius Caecus (Macbain, 1980; McClintock, 2019), often emphasize that his name (Caesus) literally means 'blind' for reasons which remain obscure but seem to imply the brute force he used to impose a technological change without political consensus or process. Caecus as homo faber is the model engineer as a policymaker who uses investment in infrastructure (roads) and innovation to transform society. In the process, he misuses his power and imposes technology upon governance that corrupts the political values in order to save the grandiose infrastructure project.

Appius Caesus embodies the image of a man 'fighting' the capricious nature and chance in the universe (an example of Kairos) with a design that promises technological progress solving all human issues. In this, he preceded Francis Bacon and his project of Instauratio or the Middle Age ideal of a man as the privileged image of the God (Imago Dei) with its ability to create and exercise his will over the creation. This image of homo faber inspired Bacon's project of technological improvement of society and later 'enlightened' scientific and industrial revolutions. It leads directly to the excesses of the 20th-century communist, fascist, and capitalist technocrats and the more recent echoes in the singularity and transhumanist dreams of a (post)human/ AI controlling the world by creating new collectives and totalitarian politics of the singleton (Bostrom, 2006).

The homo faber as the maker and tinkerer controlling the future of the world clashes with the ideal of homo ludens embodied in the early Thales' provocations and the work of the Renaissance artisans. Makers, geeks, and hackers with their frivolous projects revive the forgotten and playful meta-phor of homo ludens and open-ended tinkering that preserves Kairos as free time without final goals. The fools and tricksters offer the alternative to the solipsistic 'creator of the world' (Artifex and homo faber). It is essential to remain free to generate various metaphysical and cosmological ideas of how humans relate to their cosmological origins and also 'offsprings' and 'proto-types'. Instead of singularity or apocalypse with world saviors, destroyers, and transformers that close the future to one rule, we need to welcome the tinkerers that use science, technology, and society as playgrounds for idio-syncratic goals.

There are many past and present examples of such tricksters and playful makers, including niche communities of tinkerers discussed in the previous chapters, but we will mention one at the end, the anarchofeminist and tran-shackfeminist 'GynePunk Mobile Labs and BioAutonomy' organized by Paula Pin and Klau Kinky of the PechBlenda (ES) collective. Their projects save the future as open and public with research that investigates the fron-tiers of biology, art, and queer science. By democratizing and 'liberating' instruments and protocols used in obstetrics and gynecology, the collective supports practical uses of low-cost diagnostics in places with missing instru-ments and also experiments with human sexuality and 'biological' freedom, for which they created an umbrella term 'BioAutonomy'.[13]

The transhackfeminist experiments and prototypes openly challenge insti-tutionalized women health policies with tools, such as GynePunkFuge for the analysis of various body fluids or the 3D-printable speculum designed in col-laboration with another open hardware geek mentioned in Chapters 9, Urs Gaudenz.[14] GynePunk prototypes challenge the patriarchal control hidden in the biopolitical health policies representing another homo faber project. Their playful prototypes support the geek ethos of breaking the black boxes and exploring new cosmologies and politics that invite marginal groups to demystify science and technologies and rethink how they serve their needs (e.g., by building affordable equipment and enabling amateur scientists everywhere to conduct research).

Collectives like PechBlenda and Hackteria, including the artists and arti-sans that we mentioned in Shenzhen, offer an alternative to the myth of Silicon Valley entrepreneurs fixing the planet with their 'exits' and 'singu-larities', that close the future and history. The geeks and tinkerers from present hackerspaces are like the 16th-century artisans combining science with art, literature, and even folklore to serve niche communities with obscure interests and politics. Like mechanical philosophers and alchemists in the past, they perform unique cosmologies and politics without claiming to save, redeem, or offer solutions for the end of the world. They question current goal and values in science, technology, and politics: Are the present technologies and institutions of science democratic enough? Do they create inflated expectations and new forms of slavery? Are they inclusive enough in terms of our agency over time and the future? Are they playful, engaging, and poetic? Do they empower and inspire individuals and different communities? Do they open the future to our personal and social agency or close it?

The geeks and tinkerers that embrace time as Kairos in technology and governance do not suffer from the mysterious 'blindness' attributed to homo faber or Appius Caecus imposing engineering and technological solutions on society. The anecdotes about homo faber blindness add something important to our discussion of Kairos as playful and reflective tinkering and freedom to design the future. Appius Caecus was accused of disrespecting traditional rites in the temples and conspiring with 'plebeians' (corruption) in the senate to seize power and build his legendary road and infrastructure. His infrastructure still defines the imperial power of Rome over the world, as well as the misused finances and lack of good governance that ultimately brought about the fall of Rome. His engineering project destroyed the institutions and communities that made it possible which is the warning that Plato and Aristotle captured in their anecdotes about Thales (Chapter 3). The anecdote about this blind 'prototype' summarizes the problem with all technologies and projects that promise progress but sacrifice culture, politics, and social institutions or, in one word, our agency.

The great engineering project of the past, Via Appia, named after Appius, was financed by misused public money that ruined the goals of good governance while achieving the imperial ends of the Roman Republic. This corruption case still haunts us because it shows how innovation (science and technology) often destroys good governance, which fully depends on personal and social agency. Public participation and inclusion in science and technology over prototypes is an alternative to this 'blind' prototyping that misuses power, institution, and time. We need prototyping that promises less in terms of an idealized future but does more for personal and social agency. This idea of prototyping supporting Kairos in technology and governance goes beyond calls for transparent and public funding, open patents, and strategies to overcome technological and digital divides. It is a call for practice that the power of the blind homo faber as a model of innovation and governance and remind us of the homo ludens achievements in the original work of Thales and Renaissance artisans. Homo faber and his 'fixes' will never compensate for the lack of good governance, virtue, and agency and teach us how to balance the pursuit of knowledge and Chronos with the pursuit of an open future and time as an opportunity, Kairos, for agency and change.

Shenzhen 2013–2014

Figure III.16 Shenzhen 1 – Poster celebrating Shenzhen as a city of migrant workers and factories

Figure III.17–III.21 Dangerous Prototypes DIY kit for reballing (a type of soldering used in repairing mobile phones) designed for Hacker Camp Shenzhen 2014

Figure III.22 and III.23 Soldering workshop Hacker Camp Shenzhen 2014

Figure III.24 and III.25 Shenzhen hardware marketplaces 2014

Figure III.26 Shenzhai phones manufactured in Shenzhen, associated with counter-
feiting or imitation of popular brand models that support DIY making
2013

Notes

1 'Solar Pocket Factory', accessed 12 December, http://solarpocketfactory.com/
2 'Haddock Invention', accessed 12 December, http://www.haddockinvention.com/
3 'Mantis Shrimp Invention', accessed 12 December, http://manilamantis.com/
4 'Windcell', accessed 12 December, http://www.haddockinvention.com/projects/clean-energy/windcell174
5 'Octo23,' accessed 12 December, http://www.octo23.com/about/
6 'MakerBot', accessed 12 December 2014, http://www.makerbot.com/
7 US Public Private Alliance for Responsible Minerals Trade (PPA), Electronics Industry Citizenship Coalition (EICC), Conflict-Free Sourcing Initiative (CFSI) in the 'GeSI search', accessed 12 December 2014, http://gesi.org/search/?recent=2417
8 'OLINUXINO - Single Board Linux Computer', accessed 12 December 2014, https://github.com/OLIMEX/OLINUXINO/
9 'Hackteria: Wiki collection of DIY Biology, Open Source Art Projects that use Biology, LifeSciences, Biotechnology', accessed 12 December 2014, http://hackteria.org/wiki/
10 'Smart Citizen kit: Open source technology for citizens' political participation in smarter cities', accessed 12 December 2014, https://www.smartcitizen.me/
11 'TV-B-Gone Kit', accessed 12 December 2014, http://www.ladyada.net/make/tvbgone/
12 'Tweet-a-Watt kit', accessed 12 December 2014, http://www.ladyada.net/make/tweetawatt/
13 BioAutonomy http://hackteria.org/wiki/BioAutonomy
14 3d-printable speculum http://www.thingiverse.com/thing:865593

Part IV

Governance over Exploratory Sandboxes

12 Experimental Governance over Metaphors, Prototypes, and Sandboxes*

In the previous chapters, we used the dichotomies of agency and structure, politics and cosmology, and time as Kairos and Chronos, to define the various uses of prototyping in governance. Since the ancient clocks, prototyping imposes an ideal of governance as control and automation over knowledge and instruments. It is a control based on cosmological cycles and patterns in various phenomena (Chronos) that conceals the arbitrary nature of their discovery and use (Kairos), especially in governance.

We have discussed this ideal of governance based on the insight into Chronos as a myth of automation (Chapters 2 and 5). It is a myth that imposes the teleology of progress and restoration as something necessary, natural, and eternal that defines the purpose of the society (Chapters 5–7). Governance reduced to automation closes the future to a project driven by insights, instruments, and Chronos, which divide society into patrons of future infrastructures and parasites.

Chronos as a quantifiable, controllable, and predictable time of cycles and patterns in nature or other nonhuman phenomena defines the insights into cosmology or ontology (Chapter 5) that reduce politics to control and automation. Measured by instruments, patterns and cycles become a model of how to govern, because they promise predictability, progress, and restoration of society to an ideal equilibrium or state. The infrastructures that measure and impose the rule of Chronos deprive the citizens of their agency to influence the future and time as Kairos, an opportunity to transform technology as well as governance.

Although all prototypes manifest human ingenuity, agency, and the use of time as Kairos (an opportunity for innovation, discovery, and transformation), they enforce the rule of Chronos in society. It is a rule of ontology and cosmology as the ideals of governance that diminishes the personal and social agency over the future and time. New infrastructures and machines automate

---

* This section uses parts of a published article: Kera, D. R. (2019). Dining Philosophers, Byzantine Generals, and the Various Nodes, Users, and Citizens under Blockchain Rule (SSRN Scholarly Paper No. 3543889). https://papers.ssrn.com/abstract=3543889

DOI: 10.4324/9781003189411-16

governance and outsource human decision-making about society to algorithms, patterns, and cycles, all manifestations of the rule of Chronos.

To restore the value of time as Kairos, including the open future, we revisited the early instrument-making in Chapters 6 and 7, as well as present prototyping in the hackerspaces, makerspaces, and citizen labs in Chapters 9–11. These forgotten and marginal practices of prototyping by artisans and their idiosyncratic instruments served various, often conflicting agendas that enact time as an experience of Kairos, an opportunity to transform society and technology (Chapter 5). They restore politics beyond the ideal of governance based on cosmology.

The personal and communal prototypes discussed in Chapters 9 and 11 support the experience of time as a medium of action, politics, and agency. The experience of personal and social control over the future and time as an open, public, and shared resource is essential to preserve the value of democratic governance. Rather than closing the future to a teleological project of progress and restoration that promises to reveal the meaning of history, nature, or humanity, 'artisan' prototyping works like metaphors in language. Prototypes as metaphors use the 'structure' of language, nature, or time (Chronos) to create new meanings and possibilities for individuals and communities to engage with the public resources, such as time, language, or emerging infrastructure.

To explain the generative function of prototypes that serve the personal and social experience of time as Kairos, we applied Agamben's definition of paradigm and exempla in Chapter 6 inspired by Aristotle. Paradigms like metaphors in the language offer a new model of thinking and speaking or (as we claim) also prototyping, all expressions of Kairos. Artisan prototypes use technology in a way that metaphors use the possibilities of our language. They destabilize the common meaning to express novel and experimental ideas, values, and goals. Today's hackers, makers, and geeks in Chapters 9–11 engage in prototyping that destabilizes the common uses of technology and our expectations of science and technology in order to support Kairos as a personal and social agency.

We described the hackers and makers as the heirs of Thales and Renaissance artisans who prototyped instruments to explore various social, political, and technological projects. The elusive and often unfinished prototypes open the future to further engagement while resisting the teleology of innovation as the 'technocratic' rule (Feenberg, 1991, 1994; Habermas, 1989) and 'solutionism' (Morozov, 2014a). In the liminal environments and cities discussed in Chapters 9–11, prototypes are means of transformation without monopolizing and closing the future. They enact time as a personal and social experience of Kairos, an agonistic and autotelic activity that explores the limits of our commitments toward different futures, technologies, and values.

In what follows, we will propose a way to scale the experience of prototyping in liminal environments, that combines design with policy process supporting Kairos and agency in technology and governance through the so-called exploratory sandboxes. The sandboxes extrapolate the uses of prototyping in governance that open rather than close the future. Rather than imposing an ontology or cosmology on politics, prototypes in the sandboxes become means of personal agency and social action. They enact Kairos as a condition of possibility for governance and technology that supports citizens in experiencing their agency while testing different visions for the future without the teleology of final and original goals.

Prototypes That Mediate the Dichotomies of Theoretical and Practical Reason

Many design theories, such as 'design fiction' and 'critical design' (Dunne, 2008; Dunne & Raby, 2013; Savransky et al., 2017; Wilkie & Ward, 2009), 'adversarial design' (DiSalvo, 2012), 'critical making' (DiSalvo, 2014; Ratto, 2011), and 'DIY citizenship' (Ratto & Boler, 2014), articulate the importance of public participation in prototyping. They capture how prototypes serve or betray different values and systems, such as neoliberalism, anticonsumerism, disobedience, resilience, and solidarity, but, nonetheless, they assume that the values are somehow predetermined. Instead of defining or negotiating the values and future goals, prototypes only enact and embed the predefined politics that represent different classes, historical struggles, or other conditions.

Since the dichotomy of episteme and techne, theoretical and practical reason (Parry, 2020), we define governance by subordinating the actions, practices, and prototypes to the insights and ideals of theoretical reason. Reason detached from our bodies, society, nature, or history has political priority over the practice and contingency of the material and social world. It affirms the ideals of time as Chronos, pattern and cycle, ontology, and cosmology, representing the eternal and predictable truths.

The insights of theoretical reason even transcend human and social life, practices, and history. They reduce personal or social action to the mere affirmation of the ontology or cosmology as the ultimate predetermined goals of the collective 'body', 'soul', 'planet', or other ideas of political unity. The insights of theoretical reason define all processes of making and prototyping as mere enactments of ontology, cosmology, or the reign of Chronos in society. Rather than enhancing human agency and capacity to act, imagine, and influence the future, governance becomes a matter of automation and technology to enact the rule of Chronos.

Embracing time as Kairos means prototyping that rejects the subordination of practical reason to theoretical insights in various 'manifestations' and dichotomies of knowledge and practice (action) or technology and governance. Instead of serving or betraying predefined insights, ideals, and values, we define governance over prototypes as a matter of agency and freedom to transform both society and technology. While prototyping that imposes Chronos upon governance leads to the myth of automation, as Kairos, it supports the ideal of an open future that remains unpredictable and uncontrollable. Such prototyping rejects the knowledge of ontology and cosmology as ideals for politics. It rejects the promises of progress and restoration that lead to monopolies in society and technology, as discussed in Chapters 3–5.

To prevent the undemocratic and arbitrary takeover of the future and time by every new instrument and infrastructure that restates the myth of automation, we need prototypes that support time as a public resource and matter of personal and social agency. Insisting on an open future means preserving the experience of time as Kairos, an act, a discovery, and an innovation in technology as much as in governance. We discussed the examples of such prototyping in support of Kairos in the Renaissance period (Chapters 6 and 7) and introduced hackerspaces and other liminal environments in Chapters 9–11. These examples inform our current proposal for governance over public and exploratory sandboxes, where prototypes become a means of governance for an open future.

Experimental Governance: From Living Instruments to Exploratory Sandboxes

Prototyping that supports experimental governance emphasizes the political and technological future as a matter of agency and participation in the experience of time as Kairos. The main purpose of the exploratory and public sandboxes is to prevent the future from closing in on a vision, value, or goal. By emphasizing time as Kairos, the future remains experimental in terms of the values and knowledge it generates. By enabling direct engagement with prototypes, the sandboxes make these personal and communal commitments and values visible in technology and society. The experimental and even creative engagement with technology and society offers a way to negotiate and define temporary and plural futures.

In the exploratory sandbox as a liminal space for design and policy interventions, participants do not follow any KPIs, innovation goals, or other predefined objectives. They immerse themselves in an agonistic, autotelic, and exploratory practice that supports collaborative and performative actions through prototypes. They explore alternatives to the rule of automation and resist the need for the governance machines described in Chapters 3–6. The playful practices of artisans and hackers described in Chapters 6 and 9 show that we can express our private and public interests and visions for society through prototyping. In the structured environment of the sandbox, the goal is to reflect on the governance and technology challenges beyond each new prototype that applies new knowledge, technology, or insight.

Thales' monopoly on olive presses (Chapter 3) and examples of Renaissance 'living instruments' (Chapters 6 and 7) demonstrate the inherent ambiguity of prototyping, which serves both the experience of time as Chronos and Kairos, of the future as monopoly, and as an opportunity to question and explore. Prototyping creates tools with which we can question and transform society, but it also allows individuals to monopolize and profit from insight, discovery, and innovation. To elaborate on the use of prototypes to support agency over the future beyond the lure of monopoly, we used Hannah Arendt's 1958 critique of homo laborans and homo faber in Chapters 8 and 10 (Arendt, 2013). The prototyping of citizen scientists and hackers as play-ful homo ludens discussed in Chapters 10 and 11 rejects the teleological pro-ject of restoration or progress. It presents the possibility of active citizenship and vita activa as a matter of agency over the future. It is citizenship that explores goals beyond the promises of a fully automated society and governance.

Prototyping in public and exploratory sandboxes follows the fringe exam-ples of the Renaissance artisans, contemporary hackerspaces or citizen sci-ence projects. They allow citizens to engage in civic vita activa and leisurely otium (Ibid.) outside of scientific labor and work. The prototypes in the sand-boxes explore the connections between scientific practice, public action, and private interests (including leisure) as a matter of sovereignty, dignity, and freedom in an age immersed in science and technology. Resisting the excesses of automation and any ideal predetermined future, sandboxes offer a strategy for saving agency, collective action, and politics as phenomena of Kairos. They engage citizens with an open future and time as a public resource.

Inspired by the genealogy of prototyping in Chapter 3 and the ethnogra-phy of hackerspaces in Chapters 9–11, we see sandboxes as environments where governance meets prototyping. As liminal environments, they support explorations of the material, social, and technological conditions of govern-ance over prototypes. To elaborate on sandboxes as a model for innovation and governance in society, we begin by discussing the overlooked function of metaphors in computing that guided the original algorithms defining current ideals of algorithmic governance.

We will show how prototypes and metaphors destabilize common mean-ings and uses (of words or technologies) to open up new possibilities (and futures). After discussing examples of computer metaphors, we will explore the misuse of algorithms as metaphors for governance. They capture the reduction of governance to technology and automation that occurs when algorithms are used as metaphors for society. Against this new myth of auto-mation that uses algorithms as metaphors for ideal governance, we place the work in regulatory and exploratory sandboxes. The sections on metaphors show how exploratory sandboxes extend the function of metaphors to sup-port experimental governance over prototypes.

Engaging with Kairos: Metaphors and Sandboxes

Prototypes engage citizens with technology and governance in a way similar to how metaphors engage us with language. Both metaphors and prototypes create transient, ephemeral, often imperfect, and fragile objects and mean-ings, similar to what we described in Chapter 6 as paradigms, exempla, and analogies. They capture personal and idiosyncratic fantasies in language or technology that, in the case of prototypes, explore various entrepreneurial, educational, and political aspirations. They also combine personal with public or shared meanings of words and technology to promote novel, unique, and 'paradigmatic' experiences.

Prototypes and metaphors express our agency as an experience of time as Kairos, an opportunity to transform meaning and practice, to break rules, to become disobedient or creative. While metaphors express imagination and agency via our language, prototypes use technologies and knowledge for the same purpose. To illustrate this function of prototypes supporting agency and Kairos, we propose public or exploratory sandboxes inspired by the function of metaphors in the history of computing.

We will show how metaphors defined the new possibilities for technology and governance, while losing this advantage once their relationship to algorithms was reversed. For example, the political metaphors of 'consensus' and 'protocol' led computer scientists to think of networks as a problem of sharing 'resources' or communicating in heterogeneous, even conflict-prone environments (diplomacy). Computing concepts and algorithms, such as 'consensus algorithm,' however, reduce rather than enhance our ideas of good governance.

The metaphors inspired powerful algorithms that define modern infrastructures (early computers with peripherals and also distributed computing). Before defining the new ways of sharing resources and synchronizing data in networks that use time as Chronos, 'consensus' and 'protocol' expressed our agency and time as Kairos, an opportunity to experiment and develop an idea. As metaphors, the early algorithms provoked us to imagine and rethink what sharing resources in a network could mean and how to program the agreements between nodes.

The transformation of metaphors into algorithms thus plays a crucial role in the development of computing paradigms and contemporary ideals of algorithmic governance. For example, 'concurrent programming' (sharing processor power and synchronizing processes) or 'distributed computing' (accessing and synchronizing data) are both results of famous metaphor-driven thought experiments. The metaphors precede the algorithms and express the experience of time as a Kairos, an opportunity to generate ideas, build prototypes and transform society. As prototypes became infrastructures, the relationship between algorithms and metaphors changed. The resulting computational concepts, such as 'consensus mechanism', 'smart contract', cryptocurrency, or blockchain protocols, paradoxically became the dominant metaphors for how we think about and describe actual governance. This misuse of algorithms as metaphors for governance captures the reduction of politics to ontology (cosmology) and the agency and experience of time as Kairos to Chronos.

The reversal of the relationship between metaphors and algorithms defines modern computing and our ideals of algorithmic governance: algorithms as products of metaphors have become a metaphor for governance. It defines the myth of automation (Chapter 3) and the ideal of governance as another monopoly over the future and time, reducing the experience of Kairos to the insights of time as Chronos. Instead of algorithms inspired by provocative social and political metaphors, the new algorithms claim to be metaphors for governance, reducing all decisions to automation. Examples include the 'consensus mechanism' in blockchain protocols, 'trustless networks', 'automated smart contracts', and calls for RegTech, LegalTech, and distributed autonomous organizations (DAOs). All these examples of algorithms replace political decision-making and economic, social, and political institutions (law, money, voting) with a particular code. While governance metaphors inspired modern algorithms, today's algorithms seem to regress and parade as original metaphors for governance.

The fantasies of algorithmic rule and automation reverse the relationship between metaphors and algorithms, governance and technology, and ultimately Kairos and Chronos. We call this misuse of algorithms as new metaphors for governance a myth. It makes something constructed and arbitrary (metaphor) seem natural and necessary (Chapter 5). Instead of challenging new metaphors that transform computing or introduce new ideas, values, and concepts of society, we let algorithms guide our expectations of governance. The resurgence of the myth of automation behind these fantasies of governance by blockchain and AI threatens personal and collective agency and the right to self-determination. Instead of original allegories, thought experiments, or metaphors, we are facing algorithms that reduce all questions of governance to technology.

The function of a public and exploratory sandbox is to preserve the differences between questions of governance and computing, metaphors and algorithms, software, and allegory. We need hybrid and liminal environments to experiment with metaphors and algorithms while preventing reduction to one side. While supporting the experience of agency (metaphors) and structure (code, rules) through iteration of policy and design, the sandboxes restore the importance of personal and social agency and time as a public and open resource. They show not only the limits of what it means to govern with algorithms but also the limits of what it means to design something 'ethically'. No infrastructure will ever embody ideal (trustless) governance, nor will any regulation or ethical framework ever 'democratize' technology.

Both algorithms and regulations are opportunities for different stakeholders to agree on a common purpose and a common future. The sandbox allows the stakeholders to balance their interests and agency over the infrastructure and define pragmatic goals for governance. In the sandbox, stakeholders combine prototyping with deliberation, algorithms with metaphors, code with regulation to find a pragmatic and temporary balance between their interests, needs, visions, and values. This proposal for an exploratory sandbox simply scales up what already exists as a model for (regulatory) sandboxes by involving the public and citizens in early decisions about emerging infrastructures (discussed in more detail in Chapter 13).

Saving Agency and Collective Action with Metaphors and Algorithms

Social and political metaphors have played an important role in the development of many algorithms and network infrastructures. Since the late 1960s, they have defined challenges such as resource sharing (concurrent computing), fault tolerance, coordination, and synchronization among nodes (distributed computing). Famous thought experiments such as the 'Dining Philosophers', 'Two Generals', and 'Byzantine Generals' attacks, and the 'flows, catch/throw' metaphors (Leppälä, 2007) have inspired generations of computer scientists to design new algorithms. They are sometimes described as 'unifying metaphors' (ibid.) that support 'collective' action and agency in the research community. We argue that this function of a good metaphor to provide a 'unifying' environment needs to be extended to sandboxes as environments that engage the public in not only the design but also the governance of emerging infrastructures.

Metaphors as unifying 'experiences' play an essential role in the 'orientation phase of technology transfer' (Ibid.). Using examples of parallel computing and transputers, Leppälä showed how metaphors mobilized the collective efforts of the research community. They created a common and coherent understanding of the possibilities and challenges of technology. By acting like mock-ups and 'proto'-types, they inspire members of the research community to define the future product:

> especially in the orientation phase of the technology transfer process, it is utmost important that a common and coherent understanding of characteristics and possibilities of the technology is created. A strong or commonly agreed concept enables researchers and engineers to perceive objects in a similar way and to concentrate efforts to solve problems or to create efficient technical artifacts. This requires powerful metaphoric structures.
>
> (Ibid.)

The 'powerful metaphorical structures' and allegories defined common problems in computing to allow a group of researchers to negotiate future products, namely, 'perceiving objects in a similar way' (ibid.). They helped the community agree on common goals while leaving open the means and tools needed to achieve them. The public and exploratory sandboxes extend this function of a good metaphor or allegory to issues of policy and governance. By making the technical, social, and political commitments of stakeholders visible, sandboxes enable decisions and experiments that define common goals. As metaphors or hybrid environments, they support 'paradigm shifts' (Colburn & Shute, 2008) and expand epistemological commitments 'to account for new knowledge of existing reality (new ways of looking at cats and fog)' (Ibid.).

Neither metaphors nor sandboxes describe technology or society that already exists. Instead, they mobilize participants to create something new in terms of technology, governance, and regulation. In this sense, sandboxes use prototypes as autotelic catalysts that induce new experiences.

Transistors, computers, and programming languages exist as results of prototyping and conceptualization by engineers and designers. This conceptualization does not consist of new knowledge of old reality, but of a new reality seeking a conceptual framework within which to situate itself (Ibid.) In this sense, the prototypes in the sandboxes are generative experiences of time as Kairos, rather than descriptions of a preexisting ontology leading to discovery, technology, or the rule of time as Chronos. We discussed these autotelic and generative functions of prototypes in the chapter on making futures through paradigms and living instruments (Chapter 6), extended to issues of governance.

To explain how we can operationalize prototypes as generative metaphors or hybrid practices in sandboxes, we will use Peter Galison's concept of 'trading zones' (Galison, 1997) in Chapter 13. This concept of liminal environments supporting ad hoc interactions and the construction of a common goal explains the purpose of an exploratory sandbox. It shows that not only discovery and innovation but also regulation could occur 'through dissonance' (Chapter 13).

Sandboxes, metaphors, and complex allegories never describe or reproduce something that already exists, but stimulate new connections between different actors and groups to create 'contact' rather than a common language, and to stimulate change through collaboration rather than unity. Such environments foster new ways of seeing and imagining both technology and governance, algorithms, and decision-making. The hybrid and agonistic processes in the sandbox as a 'trading zone' define prototyping as future-making, a liminal experience that preserves the tensions between what exists and what might exist, as discussed in Chapter 6.

Exploratory sandboxes scale what provocative metaphors and allegories do in computing: They increase the agency and imagination of developers and stakeholders, while obscuring the details and complexity of the phenomena. Instead of explaining or communicating something concrete and given, metaphors mobilized researchers to 'reason about relatively concrete and very complex domains (such as manipulating a runtime control stack) using the inferential structure of relatively simple and abstract domains (such as catching and throwing)' (Colburn & Shute, 2008). In this sense, the transformation initiated by a metaphor, allegory, or thought experiment (hopefully also a sandbox) emphasizes the agency of the interpreter rather than the discovery of some ontology and cosmology. The exploratory sandboxes extend this function of important metaphors that have become algorithms, emphasizing the importance of preserving the autonomy and sovereignty of citizens making decisions about the future of governance and infrastructure.

As products of good metaphors or exploratory sandboxes, algorithms and infrastructures will never become solutions to a puzzle or means of teleology and cosmology. They embody a new way of understanding the relationship between technology and society that preserves the value of open futures and agency over time, as both Kairos and Chronos. The exploratory and public sandboxes only amplify the effect of a good metaphor in computing, emphasizing agency as an experience of Kairos in both governance and technology. Like hybrid and liminal environments, sandboxes support experimentation with technology and governance while preventing any reduction or closure of the future. They make the encounters between agency and structure, algorithms and regulations, an effect of the history, deliberation, and social interaction that remain open to Kairos.

The metaphors, allegories, and, we argue, sandboxes generate new algorithms, technologies, and concepts of governance that go beyond the ideals of automation and cybernetic or technocratic control, including algorithmic governance. Although the metaphors and allegories of early computing played an essential role in the development of modern computers and networks, the problem with contemporary algorithms is that they have reversed this logic. They have become metaphors and even models for algorithmic governance. This reversal ignores the productive tension between a metaphor and an algorithm and reduces questions of governance to technology. In doing so, it only repeats the original 'sin' in the story of Thales' insight into Chronos, which created a monopoly over society instead of reforming it, which was its original purpose (Chapters 3 and 4).

Instead of metaphors that foster the development of new algorithms, we are witnessing algorithms that claim to be metaphors for governance. Blockchain protocols, consensus mechanisms, and predictive analytics are examples of algorithms that have become metaphors for good, trustless, evidence-based, and automated governance. Instead of being the effects of challenging and provocative metaphors for sharing resources or governing a community, they seek to reduce society to an insight and a technology. The paradoxical inversion of the relationship between algorithms and metaphors leads to a reduction of governance to technology and a lack of new challenges for both algorithms and governance.

Dining Philosophers and Byzantine Generals

Although metaphors in computing have cognitive and pedagogical functions, they also inspired new algorithms and visions of computing. For example, metaphors played an important role in communicating new types of interaction with the computers that supported their adoption, such as better GUIs, or Graphic User Interfaces (Izwaini, 2003; Jingfang & Rong, 2013; Lombard, 2005; Ratzan, n.d.; Wang & Huang, 2000). They defined radical challenges for developers to imagine the future of computing, such as the 'Dining Philosophers' allegory about philosophers thinking and eating from one plate that summarized modern computing: programs that use common resources in the processor and memory.

Most modern algorithms originated in the thought experiments or allegories from the 1960s and 1970s. The allegories defined the challenges of distributed computing, leading to the present blockchain protocols that reverse the relationship between a metaphor and its artifacts. Instead of metaphors that guide the future development of technology, we have technologies that close our notions of governance to automation and algorithmic rule. They limit expectations of governance but also of technology. They reduce governance and technology to a myth of automation, a status quo that closes off the possibilities of transformation. Instead of using prototypes to experiment with governance, these algorithms impose governance machines as a goal of good governance.

The two famous thought experiments in the last century – 'Dining Philosophers' (Dijkstra, 1971) and 'Byzantine Generals' (Lamport et al., 1982)– not only define modern computing but also demonstrate the importance of separating metaphors from algorithms. Their provocations of what it means to eat together or coordinate an attack inspired the development of powerful algorithms behind the personal computer and the early Internet. As original metaphors of collaboration and decision-making, they inspired the future design of all modern algorithms, leading to today's blockchain technologies. Today's technologies have forgotten their metaphorical origins and impose algorithms as metaphors of automated, untrusted, and 'smart' governance.

The reversal of the relationship between a metaphor and an algorithm also limits our ideals of governance and technology. Technology is standardized to one type of algorithm with small variations, while governance problems are reduced to automation. Instead of visions negotiating and deliberating upon a vision, governance becomes consensus mechanism that expresses the CPU or stakes in the tokens and management of nodes. To resist the reduction of social phenomena to algorithms and models, we need to maintain the tension between metaphors and algorithms, Kairos and Chronos, and ultimately governance and technology. The main purpose of exploratory sandboxes is to preserve this ability to transform technology and governance.

To illustrate this argument, we can use the 1965 'Dining Philosophers' allegory. This thought experiment, formulated by legendary computer scientist Edsger Dijkstra (Dijkstra, 1971), served to challenge students and colleagues to develop original algorithms and solve the time-sharing problem in computing. Dijkstra needed a provocation to inspire a search for different ways for processes and peripherals to 'share' access to a common processor. The dining philosopher allegory helped him define the 'concurrent' programming algorithms that enable all modern computers. It is a trought experiment that influenced all subsequent computing challenges of synchronization and coordination in distributed computing networks. It also defined all governance problems as control over time and the future.

Synchronization and coordination of processes and nodes in a computer or network changed in the 1970s from a problem of sharing food to battles and wars, such as the 1975 gangster scenarios (Akkoyunlu et al., 1975).

After 1975, distributed computing thought experiments included gangster stories and 'two generals' problems (Gray, 1978), leading directly to the most famous 1982 'Byzantine General Problem' (Lamport et al., 1982). These thought experiments led generations of computer scientists to define network challenges as a problem of unreliable and faulty nodes, which also guided the design of blockchain protocols.

While the commensality metaphors of sharing food or drinking in the late 1960s defined the modern personal computer, the battlefield attacks and treacherous behavior of generals and gangsters in the 1970s inspired algorithms for coordinating unreliable nodes in networks. Early computers (mouse, screen, input and output devices and processes) are modeled after philosophers with strange eating habits. They coordinate their talking and eating (communication and processing) in a kind of ritual dinner. Networks then use gangsters and generals to define coordination and communication between unreliable nodes in a distributed computing network or the early Internet.

Should we think of these thought experiments as random ideas, or do they reproduce some Cold War obsessions with game theory in the 1970s and 1980s? Would other aspects of food commensality, such as hospitality to strangers, social bonding, socialization rituals, and hierarchies in ceremonial communion, generate different algorithms for modern computers? What would our networks look like if we used metaphors of dance and choreography instead of battles? Would a close reading of Carl von Clausewitz's themes of chance and uncertainty in war change the way we understand the synchronization of nodes? Do we still need provocative thought experiments and metaphors to foster future technological change? The exploratory and public sandboxes are environments that support such questions and explorations, enabling rich and complex relationships between concepts, metaphors and algorithms, governance, and technology.

Blockchain Governance of Nodes, Users, and Citizens

Metaphors of sharing resources or coordinating attacks influenced the design of early computers and networks, which paradoxically became ideals of governance as automation. Rather than defining new computing challenges, the metaphors at work today use blockchain protocols and machine learning algorithms to reduce the governance to code. As metaphors for governance, algorithms often promise transparency, efficiency, and predictability. However, they reduce governance to a myth of automation and ritual (Chapters 1 and 2) that makes arbitrary phenomena, ideas, and technologies (algorithms) appear as something natural, necessary, and even superior to the political or social process.

Algorithms, which define computer networks and protocols, have paradoxically become standard metaphors for governance, such as the automation over blockchain, artificial intelligence, and other 'smart' technologies. They impose DAOs, smart contracts, consensus mechanisms (Nakamoto, 2008), trustless networks, and distributed ledgers (Filippi & Hassan, 2016; Filippi & Loveluck, 2016; Wright & De Filippi, 2015) as better substitutes for our institutions and political processes. Modern algorithms as metaphors promise automated and decentralized governance (Atzori & Ulieru, 2017; Hassan & De Filippi, 2017) while reducing citizens to unreliable nodes in need of a trustless system to 'synchronize' them:

> Multiparty computation theory, by making possible privy virtual intermediation, has major implications, in theory, for all kinds of contractual relationships. This can be seen most clearly in the area of negotiations. A 'mechanism' in economics is an abstract model of an institution which communicates with its participants via messages and whose rules can be specified algorithmically. These institutions can be auctions, exchanges, voting, etc. They typically implement some kind of negotiation or decision-making process.
>
> (Szabo, 1997b)

Algorithms as metaphors of good governance impose an undemocratic rule on society that reinstates the division between patrons and parasites and reduces politics to cosmology, ontology, and its rituals. It is a rule of automation in a system where citizens are seen as unreliable and untrustworthy actors, prone to betrayal and external attack (the current obsession with disinformation and the use of models in politics). This view of citizens as objects of algorithmic control ignores the importance of dissent or disobedience as expressions of human agency and the ability to transform governance as much as technology.

Human agency is defined by the experience of time as Kairos, an opportunity for success and failure, monopoly, and critique. Opportunity is the essential condition of politics as a matter of open future against any predefined harmony and synchronization (myth of automation).

Consensus mechanisms and smart contracts as metaphors for governance replace the importance of disobedience, dissent, and deliberation in a democratic society with the promise of automation. They reduce the expression of free will and agency to a problem of frictions or 'intermediaries' that slow down the predefined processes that we can program, and even claim that we need to replace political and social processes and institutions with CPU cycles (proof of work, etc.) that embed 'contractual clauses (such as collateral, bonding, delineation of property rights, etc.). ... in hardware and software' (Szabo, 1997a).

Under this myth of automation, the whole of society resembles a complex vending machine or finite automaton, with no independent institutions, no separation of powers, and no possibility of stepping outside the preprogrammed script and transforming anything.

From Metaphors and Thought Experiments to Allegories of Algorithms

The early thought experiments and metaphors that inspired the revolutionary algorithms simulated social interactions without historical or political reference. For example, 'Dining Philosophers' ignores the rich anthropological context of food commensality or the philosophical issues with the senses. Instead, the metaphor offers a comic challenge: we are asked to coordinate philosophers who are unable to eat and think at the same time while seated around a common plate. However, an innovative and groundbreaking algorithm emerged from this extreme and absurd scenario. It solved a problem in concurrent computing, but no one would ever claim that this algorithm will become an actual dining experience. The purpose of the absurd thought experiment was to ground the challenge in an everyday experience and free the imagination. It solved a technical challenge without claiming a superior dining experience.

The original computing metaphors used exaggerated scenarios so that no one confuses technical problems with social and political issues. Although metaphors inspired the algorithms, no one claimed that the algorithms solved or optimized political and social challenges. It is a mystery why the metaphors for algorithms slowly changed their role in the 1980s and 1990s, leading to the current confusion and obsession with algorithmic governance. One possible source of this confusion is the inversion of the metaphor/algorithm relationship in Leslie Lamport's influential 'Byzantine General Problem' in 1982, pretending to refer to a real historical occurrence. With the good intention of coming up with a provocative challenge that would replicate the success of the Dining Philosophers, Lamport blurred the line between a good thought experiment and a real-life, social, and political challenge. Reversing the relationship between algorithms and metaphors reduces the challenges of governance to a problem of automation. In Lamport's later metaphor of a parliament on the Greek island of Paxos, which he used to define a challenge for distributed computing, this lack of distance and confusion is even more evident.

Although the Byzantine generals became something of a literary trope in computing, the Paxos was a complex allegory. It pretended to describe a possible governance even if it was a parody with no intention of reducing the issues of governance to algorithms. The main problem with this thought experiment is that, it blurred the difference between metaphors and algorithms, historical processes and abstractions, and the experience of Kairos with the search for Chronos. This distortion redefined how we think about governance with respect to technology, leading to present promises of a trustless society optimized over blockchain technology and self-learning AIs. Lamport's 1970s algorithms for distributed networks facing faulty, unreliable and even malicious nodes thus played an essential role in modern computing and it is partially responsible for the new myth of automation calling for algorithmic governance.

Lamport's algorithms not only defined modern cryptography (digital signature) and blockchain technologies (consensus mechanisms) but also opened the Pandora's box of algorithms that serve as governance metaphors. According to Lamport's own account, his goal was to popularize algorithmic challenges and amuse the community. He explicitly mentions the popularity of dining philosophers as the reason for inventing the stories:

> I have long felt that, because it was posed as a cute problem about philosophers seated around a table, Dijkstra's dining philosopher's problem received much more attention than it deserves. (For example, it has probably received more attention in the theory community than the readers/writer problem, which illustrates the same principles and has much more practical importance.
>
> (Lamport et al., 1982)

With the Paxos algorithm, Lamport attempted to replicate the success of his Byzantine generals, but failed, and this mixing of fiction and reality created a dangerous precedent for governance and computing. The paper was rejected in 1990 and published only in 1998, and it won a well-deserved prize only in 2012. In the 1990s paper, Lamport describes a lost parliament on an ancient Greek island, even naming the ancient Greek legislators after well-known computer scientists working in the field of distributed computing. He then gave lectures dressed as an Indiana Jones archeologist searching for a new algorithm:

> My attempt at inserting some humor into the subject was a dismal failure. People who attended my lecture remembered Indiana Jones, but not the algorithm. People reading the paper apparently got so distracted by the Greek parable that they didn't understand the algorithm.
>
> (Lamport, 2022)

The reason why Lampert's allegory failed and even slowed down the study of algorithms (not to mention being partly responsible for the later reductionist ideals of algorithmic governance) was precisely the rich details he gave about a possible historical reality and governance challenge. The rich description distracted the readers from solving the puzzle and made the challenge of Paxos Parliament too real. It lacked the simple provocation of earlier thought experiments, which used paradoxical but mundane experiences to provoke researchers to come up with new ideas about computing or networking.

Although the earlier metaphors and thought experiments inspired new ideas for algorithms, the Paxos allegory was a high-fidelity prototype that left no room for imagination or agency. It was too concrete and deceptive in its historical and geographical context, so instead of communicating and provoking, it pretended to be an archeological rather than a computational challenge. Similarly, blockchain algorithms, while solving a technological problem, often claim that they are also solving governance challenges.

The Algorithmic Pamphlet That Announced Algorithmic Governance

The Paxos allegory shows the dangers of algorithms that claim to define imaginary governance. They leave no room for further discussion and development in either computing or governance, reducing both to puzzle solving. The reduction of reality and history to algorithms is the main problem with automation and the ideas of 'governance-by-design' (Mulligan & Bamberger, 2018), which see social and individual decisions as matters of design principles, algorithms, code, and technology. Such reduction of governance challenges to code creates a space for random, arbitrary, hidden, and 'dangerous' decisions and choices made by developers rather than citizens, claiming universality and perfection while retreating 'from the political as they become what 'is' rather than what politics has determined ought to be' (Ibid).

This reduction of the future and agency to predetermined goals expressed in code becomes the norm in the case of blockchain algorithms and 'smart contracts', which take the allegorical genre of possible worlds to its logical conclusion. Since its inception, the Bitcoin protocol has claimed that algorithmic governance is a superior form of governance. Instead of remaining a social and computational challenge, the Bitcoin protocol become the metaphor for a novel form of governance based on automation and decentralization. Instead of a constitution, future governance became the matter of a pamphlet in the original block that mocks traditional forms of governance. The famous Satoshi hidden message in the Bitcoin 0 Genesis block is a newspaper title about the broken financial systems during the economic crisis it claims to solve. It portrays the crisis as a failure of nonalgorithmic governance that will be fixed with the right code – blockchain: 'The Times 03/Jan/2009 Chancellor on brink of second bailout for banks' (Blockchain.Com Explorer | BTC | ETH | BCH, n.d.).

Therefore, the original blockchain algorithm (Bitcoin) is a pamphlet for a new form of automated governance that completely eliminates the divisions between metaphor, allegory, and technology. While the Paxos allegory reversed the logic of the thought experiments that used governance metaphors to discuss new algorithms, the Bitcoin political pamphlet hidden in a code became an explicit call for a change in governance rather than computing. Since then, various algorithms have not only implemented new ideas of computation, but also 'announced' that we are actually 'entering an era of policymaking by "design war"' (Mulligan & Bamberger, 2018).

The idea of governance as an algorithmic and technological 'fix' to social and political problems leads to arbitrary precedents that create power imbalances with unintended consequences. The automation-based governance lacks the 'flexibility to balance equities and adapt to changing circumstances' (Ibid.) and is unable to accommodate complex values and human rights ('privileges one or a few values while excluding other important ones, particularly broad human rights') (Ibid.). There is also a problem with lack of legitimacy and transparency ('Governance-by-design decisions that broadly affect the public are often made in private venues or in processes that make technological choices appear inevitable and apolitical' (Ibid.)). Most importantly, such a reduction of governance to automation closes both the future of governance and technology, including the development of new algorithms or reflection and critique leading to a better society.

Democratic Future-Making in the Sandboxes

The metaphors and allegories that inspired the early computing algorithms are responsible for the resilient networks and infrastructures that we use today. For example, distributed computing and blockchain protocols with fault-tolerant agreements between nodes are a direct result of the 'Byzantine general problem', an allegory of a coordinated attack with potential traitors in the rank of generals. The generals decide when to attack or retreat based on the messages they exchange, but since there are traitors among them who send false messages, they need a mechanism to vote and decide on which messages to trust. To allow loyal generals to coordinate, the algorithm uses data from different nodes to make the decision based on what 50% of them claim.

None of the metaphors and allegories of war used to design the algorithms ever claimed to provide a model for governing a society. They only inspired the algorithm and allowed modern computer networks to be synchronized as an 'army' of nodes (generals) facing unreliable and possibly hacked components. It is surprising that the resulting blockchain protocols became actual metaphors for better governance by design, which claims to embed political and social values in the code. Although the original algorithms of the 1970s and 1980s separated the effects of the metaphors as an experience of Kairos from the effects of the actual algorithms (Chronos), after 2009 we see algorithms, such as the proof-of-work protocol, that claim to be metaphors for better governance.

The separation of Chronos and Kairos, algorithms and metaphors, is essential for understanding the importance of personal and communal agency over time and the future. We discussed this in previous chapters as self-determination and freedom to discover, innovate, and most importantly to make political decisions about the future. Only by separating personal and social life from the experience of ontology or cosmology (discussed as Kairos and Chronos, agency and structure) can we transform both as matters of technology and governance.

Without this separation, governance easily collapses into a technocratic dream of omnipotent technology that closes the future to one project and rule designed by the group of patrons reducing everyone else to parasites (Chapter 3). Such teleological projects of progress and restoration further reduce the possibility of politics, discovery, and innovation (Chapters 6 and 7).

Current ML (machine learning) and DLT (distributed ledger technology) algorithms too often ignore their historical, accidental, and metaphorical origins and claim to offer better governance. They seem completely unaware that the main challenge of governance is not automation, but the division of power and the prevention of arbitrary rules. Fantasies of algorithmic rules modeled on predictive AI, consensus mechanisms, or trustless protocols for synchronizing data on ledgers claim to be an absolute public good. They reduce the governance questions to the management of nodes synchronized by consensus mechanisms and predicted by models. Such reduction of metaphors to algorithms follows the reduction of Kairos to Chronos and governance to ritual and technology that we discussed in Chapters 1–3. It is a reduction that claims that algorithms will solve not only technical challenges but also social and political problems.

The reduction of metaphors to algorithms, or questions of agency to technical infrastructure, is what we call in this book a myth of automation (Chapters 2 and 4). It is a myth that reduces both governance and technology from opportunity (Kairos) to an ideal structure and Chronos (ideal algorithm and technology that solves all political challenges or promises progress and restoration). Everything collapses into a kind of superior synchronization of nodes and actors under a model based on predefined protocols and values with questionable governance of the actual code or parameters and weights. The synchronization under Chronos as time, cycles, patterns, and algorithms leads to a monopoly of one infrastructure and value system that closes the future for the many reduced to mere parasites. Citizens, as users of an infrastructure that manages and predicts their behavior, become nodes that are expected to execute the pre-agreed and preprogrammed code, values, or models, with no agency to change them.

Algorithms that claim to be superior metaphors for governance thus give advantage to the individuals and groups that design the systems and impose the rule of Chronos as a new ontology or cosmology with its rituals. They impose a monopoly that claims to be a public good, as we described in the examples of the early clocks (Chapter 3). Neither better regulation nor code could solve this problem of a monopoly that closes the future to one rule and one goal, even if it is 'decentralized' and supposedly 'ethical'.

The core problem with the myth of automation is that it imposes cosmology or ontology on politics without discussing who 'owns' time and the insight or decides on the future. Instead of agency, justice, self-determination, freedom, etc., politics becomes a problem of design and infrastructure. Governance then becomes a matter of compliance with various regulations, laws, and institutional codes of conduct or industry standards that maintain the status quo and serve the new infrastructure.

To make the processes of designing new infrastructure and policies more democratic and open, we need to involve the public in the entire cycle of innovation and governance, from prototyping to implementation and regulation. We need tools and environments that allow citizens to engage with prototypes and regulations in the early stages of design, implementation, and monitoring. By supporting agency, new metaphors, and the experience of time as Kairos, we can curb the myth of automation and teleology of the future.

Inspired by the liminal environments and the forgotten history of prototyping discussed in Parts II and III, we propose exploratory and public sandboxes that support the design, testing, and iteration of emerging infrastructures and futures. The primary function of a public and exploratory sandbox is to allow citizens to experience agency over the future and time through decision-making about technology and governance. Sandboxes allow stakeholders and participants to articulate diverse expectations and interests about the future, negotiate potential conflicts and values, and define new success metrics.

13 Governance 'Trading Zones'
Exploratory Sandboxes*

The proposal for public and exploratory sandboxes insists on prototypes as a necessary part of any public policy engagement with technology and governance. It extends the function of current regulatory sandboxes in the FinTech space, which pioneered this experimental approach to the governance of emerging blockchain services (Bromberg et al., 2017; Maupin, 2017). As an experimental approach, sandboxes support technological innovation in line with the regulation of 'disruptive' technologies such as peer-to-peer and decentralized insurance schemes, micropayments, land registries, and other industries on the blockchain (Atzori & Ulieru, 2017; Hacker et al., 2019; Hassan & De Filippi, 2017). By creating a controlled environment, regulatory sandboxes already allow the start-ups, financial industry, and public institutions to iterate on design and policy and define common goals.

Regulatory sandboxes help stakeholders negotiate future services and regulations in a safe, controlled, and temporary environment outside of the market or society, but they rarely engage the public. To address this deficit, we argue that the public should be involved not only as users of these future services (as in the case of regulatory sandboxes) but also as citizens deciding on their future. Because of the lack of citizen participation in the regulatory sandboxes, the whole process is in danger of 'algowashing' and further depriving citizens of their agency over the future.

Sandboxes offer an experimental environment to improve not only code but also regulations. They are an alternative to the normative ideals of politics as something driven by theoretical reason, insights, and (good) intentions. Instead of only expressing AI ethics principles and various utopian values in blockchain projects, sandboxes enable participants to test and iterate how such services will work in practice without making irreversible and undemocratic decisions. They enable stakeholders to test the promises of

* This section uses parts of a published article: Reshef Kera, D. (2020). Sandboxes and Testnets as "Trading Zones" for Blockchain Governance. In J. Prieto, A. Pinto, A. K. Das, & S. Ferretti (Eds.), Blockchain and Applications (pp. 3–12). Springer International Publishing. https://doi.org/10.1007/978-3-030-52535-4_1

DOI: 10.4324/9781003189411-17

blockchain applications and services, such as bitcoin cryptocurrency, self-regulating and anonymous decentralized autonomous organizations (DAOs) or smart contracts, that claim to guarantee more efficient, transparent, and decentralized governance (Atzori, 2015; Filippi & Loveluck, 2016). Instead of disrupting the existing institutions with extreme libertarian (Flood & Robb, 2017) and communitarian (Atzori & Ulieru, 2017) aspirations, such as 'credible neutrality' (Buterin, 2020) or 'Ostrom's eight principles for commons stewardship' (Rozas et al., 2021), sandboxes allow tactical and hybrid decisions on values and code. They make the decisions about which values and interests to implement in the code something that has to be negotiated by the stakeholders (rather than only developers) before the implementation of the protocol or smart contract.

Like any software or technology, blockchain requires maintenance and upgrades that respond to security flaws and other challenges related to change, opportunity, and chance (Kairos). Decisions about these changes are often arbitrary and undemocratic, and result in a split of the original 'community' leading to so-called forks. While democratic institutions have a process for negotiating and implementing changes and responding to similar challenges, emerging technical infrastructures claim superior governance, but remain opaque and 'naive'. Instead of coordinating stakeholders such as developers, miners, and users, decisions are often made by a small group of elite developers with power over the source code or digital assets.

This leads to the dangerous paradox: technology that promises to disrupt all governance institutions suffers from a severe governance deficit when it comes to its own maintenance, scaling, or security. The lack of governance over the source code by different stakeholders leads to crises of trust when different factions split off and create their own versions of the ledger or after major breaches of security and frauds.

Many have criticized this lack of blockchain governance and its utopian claims of algorithms and consensus mechanisms that replace existing institutions (Hassan & De Filippi, 2017; Maupin, 2017; Trump et al., 2018). Sandboxes offer a potential solution to the paradox and problems of governance, where both code and institutions matter. It is neither a purist solution, insisting on governance by algorithms and code, nor a resignation upon innovation in the name of the public good. Instead of replacing off-chain regulations and institutions, the sandbox model explores hybrid and experimental arrangements that combine blockchain technology with institutions in temporary and hybrid environments and actively involve stakeholders in decisions about code and regulations.

Sandboxes as liminal environments address the regulatory deficits while resisting the reductionist views of governance-by-design or the calls for moratoria. They offer alternatives to the exaggerated social and political promises and threats of blockchain (and other) technologies, replacing the discourse of disruption with actual experiments that are contained in a supervised environment that supports stakeholder engagement and negotiation

(Allen, 2019; Lim & Low, 2019; Madir, 2019). The experiments integrate technology and governance while avoiding technocratic determinism or equally problematic risk-based approach to regulations that prevent any innovation in the name of 'slow' governance (Hacker et al., 2019; Hassan & De Filippi, 2017).

Although most regulatory sandboxes solve the problems of on-chain infrastructure and off-chain institutions (regulations), they remain closed to public scrutiny and engagement. In this sense, they offer an alternative to the reduction of governance to consensus mechanisms or various libertarian, anarcho-capitalist, or communitarian utopias, but they still support the ideal of experts making decisions in the name of public good without clear rules about representation. They limit the decision-making process about the future and time to invited stakeholders who have the power to influence the adoption and implementation of the technology, while closing the process to the public, NGOs, and citizens.

To prevent arbitrary excesses of power, we need sandboxes that allow direct public engagement with prototypes. We tested such sandbox that allows citizens to reclaim their agency over the future in the Lithopy project, a pilot of what we will call an exploratory and public sandbox (Figure IV.1 – IV.5). The purpose of such environments was to support experience of how metaphors and ideas about governance influence algorithms and vice versa, without reducing one to the other. It supported citizens defined as workshop participants in experiencing how emerging blockchain and satellite infrastructures work (in the case of the Lithopy sandbox) and what types of regulatory mechanisms are available to 'curb' the power of unruly algorithms. Citizens in this fictional village of Lithopy then used emerging satellite and blockchain services to participate in decision-making that integrated code and infrastructure with existing regulatory tools and oversight.

Regulatory Sandboxes for Experimental Governance

The blockchain sandbox model was pioneered in the FinTech domain in 2015 by the UK Financial Conduct Authority as part of its program 'Innovate' (Regulatory Sandbox, 2022). The goal was to create a 'fintech ecosystem' in which stakeholders could negotiate and interact to define their common interests. In the sandbox, innovators, representatives of existing financial institutions, and also government regulators experimented with the new services while combining various agendas: regulatory compliance, innovation, as well as inclusivity and diversity.

In software development and security, a sandbox usually means a virtual server or an isolated and controlled environment, in which we can test how a piece of code interacts with a given operating system and various programs. The regulatory sandbox extended the concept of a testing environment commonly used in software development and computer security to the regulation and governance of emerging services. It supported the interaction between emerging technology and society, regulations, and code, to anticipate potential problems and respond to them. In the regulatory sandbox, multiple regulators thus set up an environment by 'relaxing' the rules to 'live-test' emerging technology on a limited sample of users.

Regulatory sandboxes represent an experimental and pragmatic approach to the dilemmas of code and law well captured in the late 1990s issues with 'invisible regulation' by code (emerging technology platform or 'architecture'). Lawrence Lessig's popularized this as a 'pathetic dot theory' (Lessig, 2006) that discusses the dilemmas of code and regulations (law) as a problem of agency and structure (or what we call here a dichotomy of time as Chronos and Kairos). According to Lessing, people as 'pathetic dots' are subjected to four regulatory forces (law, social norms, market and architecture, or technical infrastructure) that are neither visible nor negotiable. Lessig provided many examples of such regulatory (in)visibility in order to find a way to bridge the divides between code and law. Instead of making a 'better' code or stricter regulations, he proposed a hybrid initiative that connected the four forces and made them visible and negotiable to stakeholders.

While most regulatory sandboxes integrate only two of the regulatory forces defined by Lawrence Lessig (Lessig, 2006) – markets and technology – the exploratory sandboxes, as we proposed them in 2019, attempt to integrate all four regulatory forces: law, social norms, market, and technical infrastructures. The sandbox supports the personal and communal agency over emerging futures as a problem of balancing technology with governance, agency with structure, and the experience of Kairos with Chronos. In this, the proposal continues in Lessig's 2001 work, which resulted in the Creative Commons license suite. Creative Commons (CC) was a simple tool and platform backed by an independent nonprofit organization that supported negotiation between stakeholders over the four regulatory forces while giving flexibility in decision-making regarding licensing.

What makes CC important for the discussion of sandboxes is its hybrid nature of a prototype and regulation: it is a proposal for a regulation of digital content that was also a piece of reusable 'code' included on various websites. It offered a model (and license) for sharing and managing intellectual property. In this sense, the CC license created an alternative to the strict copyright models that could not work for digital content, but it also provided an alternative to the moratoria and lawlessness of powerful rule-breaking code (Napster and torrents at the time). With this elegant hybrid solution of code and license that allows customization, CC created a new market for digital content without a 'middleman' (organization representing copyright owners) and new social norms around the sharing of online content by artists and creators.

The simple but hybrid structure of regulation and code transformed the existing social and legal customs surrounding the use of technology and empowered citizens and stakeholders to engage with regulation, market, culture, and technology over a simple icon that represents the 'code' and defines what is fair use for a particular item, such as an image, text, or data. In this sense, it offered a successful model of engagement with technological governance.

The regulatory sandboxes continue in the hybrid efforts pioneered by Lessig. They make the interaction between the different regulatory forces visible and negotiable to stakeholders involved in the issue of adoption of blockchain services. The value of a sandbox then depends directly on how visible and negotiable it makes all four forces (regulation, market, technology, and culture) to various stakeholders. Rather than reducing the impact to a single domain (better technology or market), exploratory sandboxes support the full spectrum of possibilities, domains, and stakeholders.

The main purpose of a regulatory sandbox is to mitigate and share the risks between different stakeholders, to anticipate challenges and support adoption without disruption or uncertainty. As a hybrid model of governance and development, it connects the work on regulations and code while avoiding the paradoxes of blockchain governance (Lehdonvirta, 2016) or the extreme promises of 'governance by design' (Mulligan & Bamberger, 2018) and regulatory moratoria. What exploratory sandboxes add to this process is the possibility that any organization or group of citizens (and even individuals) could set up such a liminal environment and test the technology to see how it fits their personal needs and how it serves different communities.

Exploratory and Public Sandbox

One main criterion for the success of a regulatory sandbox is its ability to translate the innovation into the market, which the exploratory sandbox also extends to public interests. FCA describes this as an ability to create a 'safe space in which businesses can test innovative products, services, business models, and delivery mechanisms without immediately incurring all the normal regulatory consequences of engaging in the activity in question' (Liao, 2020). The narrow definition of success, the market, reduces the regulatory forces to only two (technology and markets). Instead of solving potential conflicts between various stakeholders, it whitewashes or 'algowashes' the service in a 'safe space' without (or with minimal) regulations.

The emphasis on the market raises a suspicion that a sandbox is not as independent and inclusive as we would expect from a policy tool. To support policy processes that involve all four regulatory forces, we need to insist on an environment that is open to all stakeholders and the public. Therefore, the exploratory and public sandbox is an environment that makes all four regulatory forces visible and remains open to experiments, discussion, and negotiation between stakeholders.

Instead of insisting on code as an absolute law or sacred laws that will curb innovation by blocking a certain code and making it compliant 'by design', the purpose of an exploratory sandbox is to support participation and experiments. As a public environment, it fosters symbiotic relations between code and regulations, platforms and institutions, issues of technology, and governance. As a liminal and hybrid environment, it offers pragmatic alternatives to the ex ante or ex post regulations that come too late to catch up with scandals or misuses of technology (Facebook, Cambridge Analytica, various Google services).

The main difference between the exploratory and regulatory sandbox remains the question of visibility of the four forces shaping the future services and their interactions. The exploratory sandbox invites all direct and indirect stakeholders to be part of the decision-making process and supports their understanding of regulation and technology. Most importantly, the main goal is to enable the agency over the future in a community rather than only market adoption. Instead of offering a final solution or decision about the service, the experimental arrangements support temporary decisions that create additional opportunities for reassessment and negotiation. Instead of 'algowashing' and avoiding regulation, the sandbox generates trust between stakeholders who share risks and opportunities to create a future without monopoly.

Trading Zone for 'Regulation through Dissonance'

To define the evaluation criteria for a public, open, and hybrid sandbox, we used a metaphor of 'trading zones' and 'border crossings' (Galison, 1997; Lewis & Usher, 2016). Trading zones are environments that support the coordination and exchange of knowledge and resources between dissimilar and even antagonistic actors. The exploratory sandboxes for emerging technologies, such as blockchain, AIs, etc., have to function as such trading zones between code and regulation rather than as a safe space for innovation without regulation or a reason to support moratoria stifling any innovation.

The crucial role in the trading zones as captured by Peter Galison's 1997 seminal work, "Image and Logic: A Material Culture of Microphysicc" plays what he calls a 'contact language'. He defines the contact language as a communication system and tool that enables participants to take an 'action' without changing their core 'beliefs' or identity. Galison's classic example of such a sociotechnical space of action without unity is the labs and tools of 20th-century particle physics. He describes how laboratories as such 'trading zones' served the interests and agendas of diverse scientists and other stakeholders to reform particle physics. The resulting achievements were never based on any unified theory, practice, value or institution, but on the 'trade' between often antagonistic groups of scientists and stakeholders forced to work together because they needed access to the equipment.

The trade between antagonistic stakeholders is messy and chaotic, because it is neither organized nor controlled by a single actor, goal, and tool. All exchanges are part of an open process, in which 'pieces of devices, fragments of theories, and bits of language connect disparate groups of practitioners even when these practitioners disagree about their global significance' (Galison, 1997). Particularly important for the success of the open and hybrid process, such as the one described by Galison, is the possibility of reuse ('cannibalization') where tools or ideas evolved rather than simply complied with some ideals:

> Experimenters like to call their extractive moves 'cannibalizing' a device. Televisions, bombs, computers, radios, all are taken apart, rearranged, and welded into the tools of the physicist. and the process can be inverted: instrumentation from physics becomes medical instruments, biological probes, and communication apparatus. Geiger-Miiller counters were cannibalized to make the first electronic logic units for a computer, but pieces of the computer were soon stripped out for use in particle detectors. There is no unique direction, no requirement that the move be a platonic one from technology through experiment and then to the ethereal reaches of theory.
>
> (Ibid.)

The trading zone with a contact language that allows 'cannibalization' of tools and ideas is a good metaphor for an exploratory sandbox because it allows 'innovation through dissonance' (Stark, 2011). We apply this description of innovation to exploratory sandboxes and define them as trading zones that support 'regulation through dissonance'. The sandboxes allow different stakeholders to work in an ad hoc manner and integrate governance issues with new services and algorithms in a temporary manner that creates good enough solutions. As an experimental environment, the sandbox supports 'cannibalization' and reuse of both regulation and code, institutional codes of conduct and algorithms, and creates temporary equilibria to support further negotiations between stakeholders.

The sandbox engages stakeholders who do not share the same goals and beliefs and creates an opportunity to transform the four forces (new market, service, regulation and technology). To illustrate how such 'regulation through dissonance' could look like in a sandbox, we will use the Lithopy project on which we worked as a pilot between 2019 and 2021. It shows the hybrid exchanges between regulation and code as an ad hoc process and improvization that opened the process of decision-making on a future blockchain service that uses satellite and drone data to the public.

Lithopy Sandbox for Extreme Algorithmic Life

Inspired by the concepts of 'innovation through dissonance' and 'trading zone', Lithopy was designed as an exploratory sandbox for emerging blockchain services that use satellite data to automate smart contracts related to becoming a citizen or owning a property. It placed the workshop participants in an imaginary 'smart village' with functional prototypes of smart contracts and templates, and guided the participants through decision-making on a common future as an imaginary community. In the workshops, participants tested how to connect their expectations expressed in natural language with the regulations and code without prioritizing any regulatory force (market, culture, technology, or law). The sandbox supported a playful 'regulation through dissonance' between the different forces and visualized the results of the negotiations on Tableau.[1]

Lithopy started in 2019 as a near-future simulation to explore the anticipatory governance of future blockchain infrastructures that use satellite and drone data to trigger smart contracts. During the workshop in 2019 and 2020, it gradually became a sandbox that emphasized the participation of stakeholders in smart contracts over a method that translated natural language, code, and regulations into each other. The village existed as a simulated ledger on a server (testnet) that the participants inhabited over two- to four-hour workshops, during which they would learn the basics of technology, familiarize themselves with different tools, and also test the possibilities of different regulatory tools.

During the modification of the code for the testnet, the participants made decisions on the type of regulations of the future services by voting and deliberating. In 2019, most participants not only expressed a strong interest in hybrid, on-chain, and off-chain combination of code and regulations but also complained about a lack of skills and tools to do that. The most important outcome of the 2019 workshops became a proposal for an environment or service that supports participants in giving feedback in their natural language about the regulations and also code.

This led to the idea of a hybrid sandbox that uses the model of regulatory sandboxes to support more participatory and public engagements in concrete scenarios of algorithmic services and governance. Rather than a specific set of regulations, values, or codes that make life in Lithopy safe and frictionless, participants demanded respect for their individual social and agency. We describe this demand as a call for 'experimental algorithmic citizenship' that we explored in 2020 in a format that is close to this proposal for an exploratory and public sandbox. The experimental algorithmic citizenship involved continuous deliberation upon and also prototyping and testing of blockchain services.

To show how it feels to live under extreme blockchain automated contracts, we created a design fiction movie about a typical day in the village where people sing with 3D printers, move around their large coins, and perform various actions visible to the satellites and drones. The artistic aspect of the project created an intentional ambiguity to support creative engagements with the code and regulations. Contracts to become a citizen, marry, and own property govern life in the imaginary 'smart village' of a Lithopy as a functional permissioned blockchain platform. After watching a design fiction movie about the life in the village and while interacting with the blockchain services over a dashboard and templates documented on GitHub, the participants witnessed a discriminatory code and had to decide on the future of their community.

As villagers in a sandbox that could be set up anywhere, participants explored the interface to interact with the blockchain infrastructure, a dashboard (Node RED environment), and then used templates of the smart contracts, including the regulatory tools to deliberate on possible regulations of the blockchain and satellite services. Participants explicitly demanded an interface that will translate their opinions, experiences, and knowledge into code or regulation. As one of the participants commented, the simulation made him feel left out of future decision-making processes that were 'outsourced to Silicon Valley code and the regulations of elites of the EU commission'.

Based on this feedback, we redesigned Lithopy in 2020 to become a 'contact language' or a 'trading zone' for programming and regulation through natural language. We made the exchanges between regulation and code more visible and understandable. Through documentation of the process of decision-making and design, we created a possibility of continual reassessment that we believe is what summarizes the sandbox experience. The experience with extreme forms of surveillance and automated governance over satellite and drone data in Lithopy triggered the discussions that led to voting and decision-making processes in the workshops. We used questionnaires that also served as training material to explain the various tools of regulation of emerging technologies (from governance-by-design to market incentives, codes of conduct, ISO norms, provision of service, laws, moratoria, etc.) and the architecture and application level of the blockchain and satellite services.

Rather than deciding on a specific type of on-chain and off-chain regulation or anticipatory governance, Lithopy transformed into a challenge how to design a 'trade zone' and contact language when there is a power asymmetry. Together with the participants, we formulate the following questions: How to enable a contact language between the code and the regulation? How to 'humanize' exchanges with code and regulation that would make possible engagements between different stakeholders? Should there be an interface with explicit rules on how to translate code into regulations, or should natural language be, or should we accept the conflict and insist on the interaction between different stakeholders as a process of negotiations? How to create an environment where we can test a new model connecting the market with everyday life and habits while regulating the protocol?

Contact Language between Code and Law

The frustration with the asymmetry of power between natural language, programming language (code), and bureaucracy (regulations, certification processes, etc.) inspired the idea of a sandbox environment for 'regulation through dissonance'. We used the extreme discrimination scenario in the code to create urgency in the negotiations by introducing a bias that made it impossible for anyone who is Czech to own a property in Lithopy. We tested what types of interventions in the sandbox would make participants with various skills and agenda feel comfortable continuing to live there.

The concrete challenge proved to be an ideal way to induce participation in the 'trade zone' where everyone could preserve their identity, agenda, and even language but still felt comfortable to interact and influence the regulation and code of blockchain and satellite services. The creation of a contact language or environment for learning, exchanging, and interacting proved crucial in this second phase. It was not about designing an interface that translates and formalizes code or rules of satellite smart contracts into natural language, but rather to increase the motivation for interaction and negotiation between the participants. In the sandbox as a trading zone, participants experience not only the conflicts but also the democratic process of negotiation and finding a pragmatic solution instead of forcing anyone to meet one goal (better regulation, better code, or market adoption).

The Lithopy exploratory sandbox helped citizens (villagers) to decide on a collective future outside the decontextualized game theory concepts of various consensus mechanisms (governance by blockchain) or proposals to crowdsource data or attitudes of citizens over technological platforms (Awad et al., 2018). Lithopy became a hybrid and liminal space for experiencing the extremes of algorithmic life and regulations inciting the search for a pragmatic solution. The experience of the asymmetry of power and decision-making would not solve over better communication nor knowledge (learning code, for example, or having the ideal translator), but as an essential political experience of negotiating with others a common future over various available tools.

Instead of anticipatory governance of blockchain futures, which was our starting point, we settled on more modest ad hoc proposal to connect code snippets with regulations as a time-limited experience of 'good enough' solutions in a particular situation. The biased smart contract that prevented the sale of property to anyone who was Czech was the use case and opportunity for a 'contact language' and solution. In the workshops, the majority of the participants preferred more principle-based governance than rule-based governance after witnessing this discrimination. They emphasized the importance of auditing codes and data based on public–private partnerships that will keep the code open source in the future governance infrastructure. Rather than a particular rule, code, tool, or regulation, there was a strong preference for auditing the services. The proposal ranged from an emphasis on independent agency 'reading the code' and cooperating with programmers to more technological testnet to test and communicate the services to everyone (so that everyone can see and test the code before it is implemented).

Participants also emphasized the importance of aspirations and principles in future blockchain services without insisting on 'hardcoding' them in law or software. They embraced the process, or what we call here Kairos, as an opportunity to decide and experience agency and decision-making. The infrastructure and regulations in the village remained open to future interpretation and interventions through the historical and contextual processes of political and stakeholder deliberation and participation rather than being hard coded or over-regulated by experts. The interaction between participants in the sandbox model offered an ideal environment for designing and deciding together upon the future by combining different tools (natural language, regulations, and code) without prioritizing any regulatory force or domain (market, culture, technology, or law).

Note

1 'Future of RegTech: How to Regulate Algorithms?' Tableau visualization: https://public.tableau.com/app/profile/denisa.kera/viz/BookLithopy/FutureofRegTech HowtoRegulateAlgorithms

14 Experimental Algorithmic Citizenship*

There are two main functions of a public and exploratory sandbox as a 'trading zone' for antagonistic stakeholders and citizens that explain the reasons why we need to use prototypes in governance. The first is to support experience and negotiation of common future during the prototyping process, which means understanding what different changes in the code and design decisions mean in terms of values and impacts. The second is to prevent the monopolization of the future by one set of interests and values. In contrast to governance by ritual and machine, which leads to a teleology of progress (Chapters 6 and 7), governance over sandboxes supports temporary and even plural futures for diverse communities. Such temporary, hybrid, and even liminal governance emphasizes the experience of Kairos, agency, and capacity for transformation, and even dissent.

Exploratory sandboxes support the future as something collectively negotiated, experienced, and prototyped, rather than imposed via a teleology of progress and restoration. In the sandbox, stakeholders interact without a final and unified theory, insight, or policy goal that claims to save or doom humanity. They combine code with regulations and values in a pragmatic and iterative way that allows everyone to voice their expectations and concerns as they work together to find provisional solutions. While responding to challenges in this ad hoc way (opportunity as Kairos), participants agree on 'good enough' solutions without insisting on an ideal and final technological intervention or strong regulation.

This is why we describe the process as 'regulation through dissonance,' where dissonance is a necessary condition for the need to regulate at all, to make decisions and reach temporary agreements on how best to proceed until the next iteration. It is an autotelic, even agonistic process that brings the experience of time as Kairos, an opportunity for action without guarantees, to the forefront of governance and technology.

* This section uses parts of a published article: Kera, D. (2021). Algorithmic Sovereignty beyond the Leviathan and the Wicker Man. In Algorithmic Sovereignty beyond the Leviathan and the Wicker Man (pp. 69–90). transcript Verlag. https://doi.org/10.1515/9783839457603-004

Governing technological futures through a sandbox also starts with a contact language or environment, where anyone willing to participate experiences the translation of code into regulation or natural language. To test this approach, we created an imaginary smart village 'Lithopy' and introduced a biased service (smart contract on a blockchain) to confront the villagers, our workshop participants, with the need to make decisions related to both governance and technology. The workshop participants would first become villagers by registering their imaginary name, property, and even partnerships on the proof-of-concept blockchain service we designed on Hyperledger Fabric in a way that allows the use of open satellite data from Sentinel 2A and B EU services.

Upon learning about the layers of technology and different regulatory tools, the Lithopy villagers would make decisions about how to proceed. The workshop as a sandbox experience supported the sharing, experimentation, and negotiation of different solutions and ideas about technology and governance (audits, industry standards, soft and hard regulation, etc.) among the village stakeholders. In the process, they learned about the four domains of regulation (market, culture, technology, and governance), which were presented as different tools and options.

One criterion for the success of this hybrid and liminal form of governance that we were interested in testing was the quality of stakeholder interaction. How many (even antagonistic) stakeholders with different agendas, 'languages', and interests can a sandbox accommodate, and how does this affect the four domains of regulation? We had to abandon this criterion because most participants did not want to take on any role, as they had strong opinions about the issues addressed and remained in their 'role' as ordinary citizens (Reshef Kera, 2020).

However, the main challenge was to reconcile the novelty and efficiency of automated services with democratic values such as separation of powers, political deliberation, or inclusion in decision-making, which we achieved to some extent (Kera & Kalvas, 2022). Based on this limited experience in designing such an environment, we argue that governance of public and exploratory sandboxes means experimenting with and contextualizing the decision-making process, rather than insisting on an ideal regulation or infrastructure. In this respect, exploratory sandboxes are close to the liminal environments of hackerspaces and SEZ described in Chapters 9–11 that inspired our thesis on governance over prototypes.

The exploratory sandbox as an environment offers a pragmatic and iterative alternative to the current attempts to embed predefined cultural, social, and legal norms of ethics, values, etc. into design specifications or machine-readable code, 'by design'. The unexpected outcome of the experimental algorithmic citizenship in the Lithopy sandbox was that most participants preferred to regulate code through audits and industry standards rather than government intervention or free-market mechanisms, and trusted the imperfect process (Kera, 2021). We will first discuss the reasons for choosing the exploratory sandbox over other regulatory tools and then summarize the results of Lithopy pilot in terms of a future research agenda for experimental governance over sandboxes.

Ethical Frameworks and Governance-by-Design Interventions

There is a democratic deficit in most services that support automated decision-making as a basis for future smart cities and algorithmic governance. Rather than supporting democratic institutions and procedures that define our off-line, nondigital institutions (norms, laws, and regulations), the protocols and infrastructures replace legitimacy with efficiency. Reaffirmed biases and injustices translated into algorithms lead to the 'accountability gap' (Crawford & Schultz, 2019) and 'deresponsibilisation of human actors' (Mittelstadt et al., 2016). To challenge this and support legitimacy along efficiency over new infrastructures, we need governance concerns to be embedded in the process of prototyping and allow clashes over issues of power, stakes, interests, and ownership.

The exploratory sandbox balances calls for innovation, disruption, and technological change with participation, deliberation, and legitimacy. It addresses these structural challenges in the use of algorithms and new services for governance and decision-making, different from the various interventions and frameworks that claim to increase transparency (Introna, 2016; Kroll et al., 2016; Lee et al., 2019a), oversight (Burk, 2019; Shneiderman, 2016), accountability (Binns, 2018; Diakopoulos, 2016; Kroll et al., 2016), as well as participation and participation (Lee et al., 2019b; Sloane et al., 2020) with algorithms and data.

Beyond these interventions and frameworks that regulate AI, machine learning (ML) algorithms, and blockchain systems, we can identify two strategies. One strategy reduces and transforms values and regulations into code and data (Hildebrandt, 2018), such as privacy-by-design (Cavoukian, 2009), society-in-the-loop (Rahwan, 2018), and adversarial public AI system proposals (Elkin-Koren, 2020). The 'design for governance' strategy then differs from the ethical frameworks and tactics that try to separate regulations from the code. They insist on oversight by a public institution or independent body outside platforms and infrastructures through laws, regulatory oversight, audits, and industry standards (Edwards & Veale, 2018; Wirtz et al., 2019) or 'social licenses' in cooperation with communities (Aitken et al., 2020) and even 'people's councils' (McQuillan, 2018).

The regulatory sandboxes (Allen, 2019; Arner et al., 2017; Gromova, 2020; Lim & Low, 2019) present a third experimental alternative to aspirational ethical frameworks (Fjeld et al., 2020; Hagendorff, 2020) and popular 'governance-by-design'(Cavoukian, 2009; Mulligan & Bamberger, 2018) or 'value-sensitive design' initiatives (Friedman & Kahn, 2002). Sandboxes address the structural challenges of algorithmic governance and automation (Danaher et al., 2017) by connecting deliberation with experiments that work simultaneously on regulations and code without reducing one to another. Instead of reducing and transforming the various democratic values and regulations to code, such as privacy-by-design (Cavoukian, 2009), society-in-the-loop (Rahwan, 2018), and adversarial public AI system proposals

(Elkin-Koren, 2020), or insisting on the oversight by a public body outside the infrastructure, the sandboxes support hybrid, tactical, and situated engagements with automation and infrastructure over prototypes (Hee-jeong Choi et al., 2020).

Future-Making as Users, Stakeholders, and Citizens

The extremes of 'governance by design' (code) and 'risk-based approach to policy' (via regulations and moratoria) lead to arbitrary exercise of power and loss of legitimacy in governance and technology. To support more transparent decision-making guiding the future services, we created an environment that engages the public with both code and regulations and supports audits while balancing the principles with the implementation of the rules. The Lithopy sandbox in 2019 and 2020 showed public participation that can influence both the governance and the regulation process, as well as the prototyping of the infrastructure.

The current emphasis on ethical frameworks for algorithmic governance often supports only aspirational values and principles, but fails short in implementation and design of the rules in code and regulation. Paradoxically, this leads to technocratic insistence of solving all policy issues on the level of code that reduces everything to emphasis on efficiency and ignores matters of representation and legitimacy. Such a process supports the myth of automation. We believe that sandboxes create an environment that combines the aspirational value and principles with the rules and pragmatic choices we make on the level of code and algorithms.

The future of algorithmic governance is neither about inventing an ideal consensus mechanism, predictive AI, nor about stringent protection laws and never ending risk assessment self-regulation. No consensus mechanism or service will ever prevent a future fork that will defraud some users, nor will predictive AI open the black box of its model. No expensive settlement with some corporation will prevent future algorithmic scandals and excesses. The challenge we identified in our 2019 and 2020 workshops is to create an 'algorithmic' and 'regulatory' public space and environment (described as a sandbox) where citizens can experience, understand, test, and improve such future infrastructure and policy in parallel.

Public and exploratory sandboxes for iterating on policy and design have the potential to improve trust in public institutions but also technical infrastructure by allowing public representatives and NGOs to experience and identify the preferred form of algorithmic citizenship in near-future scenarios. Such environments allow participants to anticipate and prevent problems and excesses instead of applying futile ex post or ex ante regulations.

The main problem in current attempts to combine regulations and code is their democratic deficit and ahistorical narrative (often inspired by game theory concepts, unchecked behaviorism reducing citizens to rational agents, or ideas of crowdsourcing and 'crowd-pleasing' some stable public sentiment). These deficits show the limits of all 'rule-based systems', regardless of whether they use code or law. If our goal is to preserve a free and democratic society, it is not enough to concentrate only on the concrete regulations that fit the existing public sentiments, nor the technological solutions supported by powerful lobbies and platform owners that claim they know how to manipulate behavior or make the agents more rational.

The exploratory and public sandbox as an environment enables stakeholders and citizens to influence how code and regulation are created and implemented. Rather than insisting on more security, penetration testing, or more stringent laws (which are often impossible to implement), we need to increase the direct and public engagement with both regulations and code and find new ways how to impose the division of powers. The purpose of a hybrid public sandbox is to support experimental forms of algorithmic citizenship and to create new forms of division of power. Only when we level the ground for different stakeholders and citizens to participate in codes and regulations can we form a community and a true future 'smart village' where citizens are not users of future services but bit stakeholders in the future.

Algorithmic Governance as Design of Leviathans

What the experimental citizenship in the algorithmic 'hell' of Lithopy revealed was the asymmetry of power in both code and regulation that creates the need for division of powers and oversight impossible to achieve today. We define this as the main challenge of public and exploratory sandboxes that became something of a proposal for the new 'Leviathan(s)'. How to preserve democratic governance under the algorithmic 'Leviathan' formed through ledger, models, and data? Are citizens under the algorithmic Leviathan still members of a society and body politics, or only surpluses and parasites hosted by the new benevolent patrons? How to 'translate' contracts, norms, and laws to algorithms while preserving the agency over the future (and governance)?

The technological 'commonwealth' over various platforms and protocols seems to surpass the original metaphor of Leviathan as absolute sovereignty in terms of the power asymmetries. Emerging infrastructures enforce a governance model that deprives citizens of agency in more radical ways beyond what the social contract theory could ever imagine (Reijers et al., 2016). The original purpose of Hobbes' metaphor of artificial superhuman governance was to serve as an alternative to the redemption model in the Middle Age kingdoms. Instead of a search for spiritual unity with Christ under the eschatological expectations of the second coming that promised to alleviate the suffering of the 'natural condition', war, and chaos, the modern state offered unprecedented security and efficiency (Schmitt, 1996).

Leviathan promised an alternative to the chaos of the Christian kingdoms while still complying with the vision of 'corpus mysticum', a body of believers in Christ waiting for the second coming (Ibid.). Instead of fighting over which states represent the ideal Christian community, Hobbes proposed a solution that replaced the search for a spiritual unity (and constant wars over who is closer to God) with an artificial one. This created the conditions for all later ideas of technocratic and cybernetic governance and management that claim to be able to design stable systems no matter if they are composed of animals, machines, or humans.

Instead of a cosmological or theological embodiment promising historical mission of the second coming, Leviathan was designed by men seeking stability and predictability that paradoxically defines all future aspirations of algorithmic governance. It is a 'command mechanism', a technical apparatus that demands unconditional obedience to work. Inspired by Carl Schmitt's interpretation of the modern state as a 'technical, bureaucratic and 'magical' Leviathan, under which nothing is true but 'everything is a command', we claim that algorithmic governance is a necessary consequence of Leviathan. It is the embodiment of our ideal of absolute control over the future and time over some instrument, knowledge, and mechanism that starts with Thales' monopoly contraption.

Algorithmic governance brings to a conclusion not only the long history of instrument-making and prototyping but also the most critical aspect of Hobbes' social contract theory, the emphasis on automatic authority as the only alternative to the natural condition. Algorithmic 'Leviathans', such as blockchain 'smart contracts' and machine learning algorithms, promise to optimize social phenomena but expect citizens to support, trust, and abide by emerging infrastructures as 'miracles'. We are asked to resign upon our agency, politics, and the experience of time as Kairos because the emerging devil's bridges promise sovereignty as a technical infrastructure and a miracle performed by developers. They promise to provide essential services and absolute protection to citizens who accept their absolute authority (sometimes defined as prediction models, smart cities, intelligent tracking systems during COVID-19 crises, and similar ideas).

Algorithmic 'Leviathans' outsource citizen agency and sovereignty to superhuman institutions, platforms, and protocols that promise peace, stability, health, and efficiency as the only goals of the modern algorithmic state. Resignation upon agency and experience of time as Kairos becomes a necessary condition for all automated systems to function. Paradoxically, we define this as an 'agreement' between rational, free, and equal citizens who resign from their sovereignty to avoid the 'natural' state. Leviathan, as a result of the social contract and algorithms, supports the absolute power of an artificially constructed 'sovereign' that makes citizens not only safe and secure but also redundant, a type of surplus and parasites.

Technological Commonwealth between Leviathan and Wicker Man

The 'rational' agreement between citizens that define the modern state as a sovereign and artificial Leviathan paradoxically supports the myth of automations and reduces citizens to parasites hosted on the table of various patrons. It supports the ideal of irrational and absolute power that is automated and mechanical by default. Leviathan is thus a prototype of algorithmic governance that claims to serve as a tool of automated justice and security possible only when we resign upon the right to question or change the protocol.

Algorithmic governance makes visible the issues with the original metaphor and idea of the Leviathan: that rational beings can agree on an irrational and absolute control to be the only alternative to lawlessness (natural state). In this book, we capture the same paradox in Chapter 3 by using the dichotomies of Kairos and Chronos: we resign upon the agency over the future and time as an experience of time as Kairos to model governance after the structures we discover or prototype (Chronos). Rather than a rational control, such solutions enforce an absolute and arbitrary power.

Algorithmic sovereignty over 'emerging' infrastructures, such as blockchain or ML technologies, thus amplifies an old discussion of whether the Leviathan is an institution that truly protects citizens from chaos or sacrifices them to its evil twin, the Wicker Man. The 1676 image by Aylett Sammes of the Wicker Man summarizes the critique of the Leviathan as a reinforcement of an old pagan ritual of human sacrifices described by Julius Caeser (Duggett, 2007). It summarizes the connection between rituals, machines, and infrastructures that create an image of a superhuman, godlike figure, and power, in which we place living people to burn them.

The image served as a satire of the social contract represented as a pagan belief in magic powers above human agency. It was a visually shocking critique of what the civic body (body politics) does to the individual who resigns upon his or her agency and ability to use time or define the future as an opportunity outside any matter of cosmology or ontology. Politics driven by promises of Leviathans and super- or metahuman structures and algorithms ultimately leads to enslavement. It consumes, imprisons, and destroys the citizen who resigns of the ability to influence the future and preserve agency over his or her time.

The most famous critique of the Leviathan appears in the 1690 Lock's 'Second Treatise of civil government' (Ch VII/93) (Lock, n.d.) where Locke described absolute sovereignty as a catastrophic lack of judgment and governance, rather than a solution. To describe the horrors of such automated and mechanical power, he uses the allegory of a society avoiding attacks by wild cats that lets the lion rule and devour everyone:

> To ask how you may be guarded from harm or injury, on that side where the strongest hand is to do it, is presently the voice of faction and rebellion: as if when men quitting the state of nature entered into society, they agreed that all of them, but one, should be under the restraint of laws, but that he should still retain all the liberty of the state of

nature, increased with power and made licentious by impunity. This is to think, that men are so foolish, that they take care to avoid what mischiefs may be done them by pole-cats or foxes; but are content, nay, think it safety, to be devoured by lions.

(Ibid.)

The issue with law as code in algorithmic governance echoes these discussions about the relationship between might and right, or between sovereignty, power, and law as experiences of agency, ontology, and cosmology, and time as Chronos and Kairos. Although 'absolute authority' in Hobbes is a necessary condition for the law to exist, Lock criticizes it as a dangerous precedent that makes the law impossible. Automated decision-making that is hard-coded without human oversight is an heir to this ideal of absolute authority and mechanical or automated sovereignty. It confronts us with the same problem of unchecked and uncontrolled power that someone ultimately designs without letting the rest participate in it except by resigning on their agency and sovereignty. How to engage with the authority of the code and automated control of the new algorithmic sovereigns (technological platforms as Lockean lions) and contest their power? How to involve citizens in the formation of the algorithmic Leviathan as a lion without letting the algorithmic beasts devour the autonomy while promising to protect us from small dangers (wild cats)?

Political Metaphors as Premonitions of Algorithmic Rule

Governance machines and algorithmic governance as an embodiment of the Leviathan promise efficiency while taking advantage of citizen data, freedom, and agency. These artificial systems (contracts, mechanisms) have absolute authority over the citizens who trade their sovereignty and natural rights for security. In his analysis of the Leviathan, Schmitt explicitly described this as the emergence of the ideal of a 'state as a mechanism' and a 'manmade product' (Schmitt, 1996) that is neither holy nor ideal, but efficient: 'Considering the Leviathan as a great command mechanism of just or unjust states would ultimately be the same as "discrimination" between just or unjust machine' (Ibid.).

For Schmitt, it was this idea of a modern state as an artificial and mechanical rather than spiritual unity that enabled all later forms of industrial state to use new technologies as tools of sovereignty. The idea of a state as a technical apparatus, or what we call algorithmic governance, was born with the metaphor of the Leviathan:

The intrinsic logic of the "state" of a man-made artificial product does not culminate in a person but in a machine. Not the representation by a person, but the factual, current accomplishment of genuine protection is what the state is all about. Representation is nothing if it is not *tutela praesens*. However, this can only be attained by an effectively functioning command mechanism. The state that came into being in the 17th century and prevailed on the continent of Europe is, in fact, a product of men and differs from all earlier kinds of political units [...].

(Ibid.)

The Hobbesian modern state leads directly to the present algorithmic (or technological) governance and governance machines against we are trying to reason for prototypes that democratize governance in the sandboxes. It is the original prototype of absolute and arbitrary power that nothing can resist because everyone will be willing to submit to it: '[T]hat state was created not only an essential intellectual or sociological precondition for the technical-industrial age that followed, but also the typical, even prototypical, work of the new technological era, the development of the state itself' (Ibid.). Schmitt's state as a 'product of human calculation' necessarily leads to automation, a technically perfect mechanism that is synonymous with absolute authority that performs its structure:

> But the idea of the state as a technically completed, manmade magnum-artificium, a machine that realizes 'right' and 'truth' only in itself—namely, in its performance and function—was first grasped by Hobbes and systematically constructed by him into a clear concept. The connection between the highest degree of technical neutrality and the highest authority is, as a matter of fact, not alien to the ingenious thinkers of the [1]7th century. At the end of Campanella's vision of the 'Sun State', there appears a large ship without a rudder and a sail but driven by a mechanism that is commanded and guided by the possessor of 'absolute authority' [...].
>
> (Ibid.)

Algorithmic governance as a modern Leviathan is thus a 'gigantic mechanism in the service of ensuring the physical protection of those governed' that leads directly to cybernetic and military visions of warship in the past (Campanella) and the present. Schmitt quotes Ernst Jünger's vision of warships as to explain how Campanella's vision of the 'Sun state' becomes literal: 'The technically perfect mechanism of a large ship in the hands of an absolute authority who determines its course' (Ibid.).

Exploratory Sandbox Supporting Tactical and Participatory Automation

Is there any alternative to the absolute victory of the modern state as an algorithmic machine, a cybernetic warship that performs sovereignty through its structure and code while claiming to guarantee survival rather than justice or any value? How to rethink algorithmic sovereignty beyond the images of the Leviathan and its shadow, the Wicker Man? Instead of insisting on one or the other mythical figures, we propose multiplying them through sandboxes. In these zoos for 'dangerous' algorithms, participants (stakeholders) can experiment with the gradual process of 'domestication' of algorithms. Simulation of decision-making processes in the sandbox combines smart contracts with existing policy tools for regulation. It balances algorithmic 'wilderness' with domestication through regulations which is also an image we discussed in the case of Plato's demiurge as a model for governance over prototypes discussed in Chapter 11.

This vision of governance over prototypes in the sandboxes engages and supports rather than depriving citizens of agency. Instead of yielding power to one super-platform (Lockean lion or Hobbesian Leviathan), sandboxes teach citizens to live with the wild animals (algorithms) and gradually domesticate them. The exploratory and public sandboxes for algorithmic services offer a model on how to make the automation more 'representational' and participatory, so it is clear at each step what we sacrifice and outsource to the code.

We tested such a gradual process of algorithmic domestication and participation on the example of future services in an imaginary smart village of Lithopy. The format of the workshop enabled participants to understand the technology and influence the design of smart contracts while introducing various forms of regulations. While exploring how to combine technology with existing institutions, participants tested their level of algorithmic sovereignty beyond Leviathan- and Wicker-man-style automation.

The Lithopy sandbox, as a 'fairy tale with code' and design fiction movie, supported the participation in technological futures and algorithmic governance. As a functional prototype of services for a community using satellite data to trigger a transaction, it made clear what is at stake in such futures. Citizens, as participants in the workshop, experienced various degrees of automation and regulation to define the level of personal autonomy under algorithmic governance. The environment helped them investigate the technology while understanding the different possibilities of their agency through regulation to curb the algorithms. In this sense, it served the objective of tactical, situated and 'participatory' automation that embeds social and personal agency in algorithm design processes. The sandbox as a trading zone for 'regulation through dissonance' transformed 'the logic of binary states, yes and no, into fuzzy states of maybes and maybe' (Galison, 1997).

The playful and liminal environment supported the use of regulations and codes as tactics that seek ways to resist the structure of algorithmic governance (de Certeau, 2011). As an environment for 'tactical' and 'situated' automation that is participatory and liminal, the sandbox involved citizens directly as individuals and an ad hoc group:

These workshops support participation in automation by engaging human participants directly in the creation of technologies that are also strategically used to control their daily practices through the dominant sociotechnical order, but with tactical intention in this sense, these participatory workshops make the actual physical production of the

boards, which is tedious part of a community bonding experience that supports peer economy and liberation rather than alienation of labor.
(Hee-jeong Choi et al., 2020)

The exploratory sandbox thus extends the functions of the liminal environments described in Chapter 9 or the workshops in the hackerspaces described in the article on situated and participatory automation (Ibid.). It enables citizens to directly understand what is at stake in the code and regulation while participating in their tweaking and development. In the case of the Lithopy sandbox, participants used the Hyperledger Fabric blockchain as a 'testnet' on a server, where it was possible to check prototypes of smart contracts that use open satellite data (from Sentinel 2A and 2B) for various services and automation. As villagers, they would negotiate interventions and changes after witnessing a discriminatory contract excluding certain nationalities from buying property in the village.

The Lithopy sandbox offered an experience of agency over the code and regulation for a concrete community. It supported the goal of experimental governance as a process of negotiation and consensus building in a power vacuum where individual stakeholders have to define their interests and relations, but also norms and goals on the go (Sabel & Zeitlin, 2012). Although most regulatory sandboxes insist on innovation, the Lithopy sandbox was always a 'trade zone', a productive environment to support coordination and exchanges of knowledge and resources between different and even antagonistic stakeholders. We describe this as tactical and situated automation that preserves personal and social agency.

The type of algorithmic sovereignty explored in the sandbox is tactical and situated and embraces the experience of personal and social agency in time experienced as Kairos. It is plural because it offers a variety of scenarios on how to survive and strive in an algorithmic future while slowly defining a form of social and individual agency and domesticating the algorithms. The result of the Lithopy sandbox was neither an ideal code nor regulation, but an open space for discussion, experience, and decision-making similar to the experience of the city as our original prototype and site of Kairos (Chapter 8). It served citizens who would like to experience what is at stake in their future if a given infrastructure supports automation and algorithmic governance. The exploratory sandbox invited participants to become stakeholders in their future, to 'trade' and define their expectations, desires, and needs in a tactical and situated way ('dissonance').

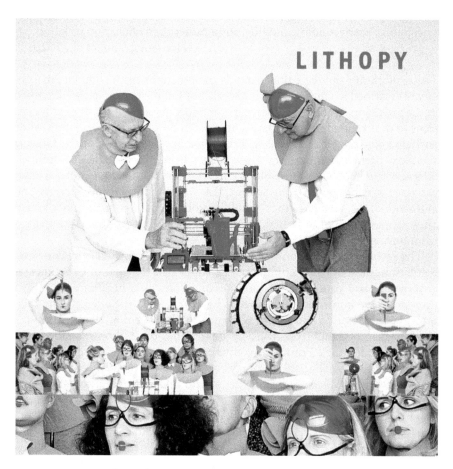

Figure IV.1 Poster for Lithopy Design Fiction movie on the life in a smart village
          where people sing with 3D printers and use satellites and drones to make
          contracts

Credits: Lithopy, a Cartesian multiscreen movie, © 2019: photography Jan Hrdý | visuals, mon-
tage Eva Holá | script, director: Petr Šourek

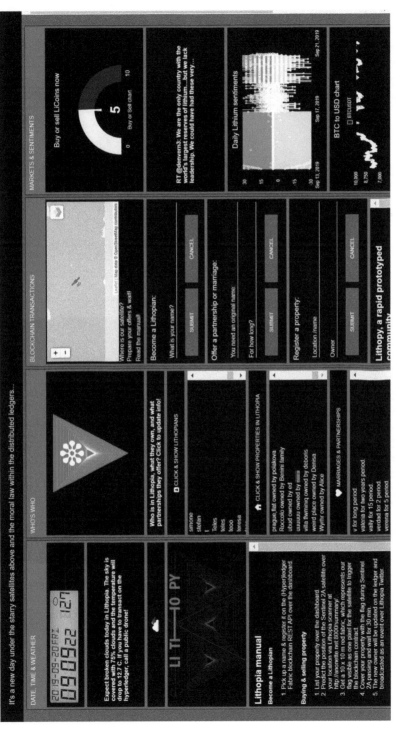

Figure IV.2 Dashboards that Lithopy villagers use to check where the satellites are and what blockchain smart contracts they can trigger —including Twitter real-time data

Figure IV.3–IV.5 Life in the smart village of Lithopy; examples of contracts representing marriage

Credits: Lithopy, a Cartesian multiscreen movie, © 2019: photography Jan Hrdý | visuals, mon-
tage Eva Holá | script, director: Petr Šourek

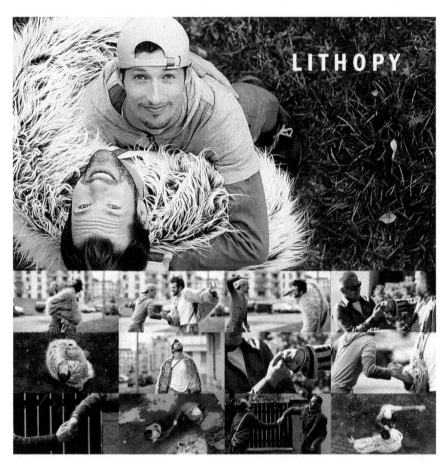

Figure IV.3–IV.5 (Continued) Life in the smart village of Lithopy; examples of contracts representing marriage

15 Conclusions

Prototypes in society mediate the different expectations and experiences of time and agency over the future. On the one hand, they support the open-ended exploration and flourishing of human agency. On the other hand, they promise innovation as control over the future and governance. Examples of ancient clocks, Renaissance visions of scientific instruments that bring light (experimenta lucifera), or infrastructures for automation close the future to predetermined goals of progress and theological restoration. As Renaissance cosmoscopes, living instruments, and examples of the folly of empiricism, including present open science hardware, prototypes open the future to human agency and action with no guarantees. Unlike the teleological expectations of progress and restoration, forgotten and marginal prototyping practices imagine radical transformation on multiple micro, meso, and macro levels.

In previous chapters, we have contrasted the prototypes that reinforce the myth of automation with the possibility of autotelic prototypes that support the experience of time as Kairos (Chapters 6 and 9), opportunity for transformation, and plural future(s). The examples of open science hardware in Chapter 9, along with the living instruments and cosmoscopes of the past (Chapters 6 and 7), demonstrate the personal and social agency as this capacity to transform the human condition and society. Instead of obeying the insights into time as Chronos with its teleology of predetermined goals and futures, the experience of time as Kairos is about the agency over the future and time.

The community-driven and do-it-yourself (DIY) instruments (Chapter 9) revive the practices of artisans and natural philosophers described by critics, such as Francis Bacon, as an anarchistic *folly of empiricism* with fruitful experiments serving no one (*experimenta fructifera* in Chapter 6). Such open-ended, forgotten, and marginal Renaissance projects, including the tinkering of modern artisans, hackers, geeks, and makers define prototyping as a matter of participation and empowerment. Instead of supporting the myth and ideal of automation in governance represented by the figures of the Leviathan and Wicker Man, such prototyping is an opportunity for agency, vision, and experiments beyond any universal solution and absolute rule. In this sense,

DOI: 10.4324/9781003189411-19

prototyping defines a need for democratizing future-making that embraces time as *Kairos*, a public resource and infrastructure for commons preserving the opportunity for our agency.

The marginal and forgotten examples of prototypes supportive of open future make science, technology, and society personal and political rather than a cosmological or ontological project. Prototyping that supports *Kairos* as a personal and social agency over time in Chapters 2 and 3 served as a model for the exploratory governance of emerging infrastructures over sandboxes in Chapter 12. Instead of depending on *homo faber* interventions that always meet predefined targets, the sandboxes support citizens and tinkers as *homo ludens*. Citizens design and prototype together to generate new and temporary visions of a community. They create tools to engage, understand, tinker, customize, and demystify the power behind every scientific and technological disruption.

Science and technology as mundane, accessible, and everyday practices resist the myth of automation as an ideal for governance. Makers, geeks, and tinkerers, modeled after the ambiguous figure of Thales, the prototypical *homo ludens*, cherish their free time as an opportunity to explore and question (even dissent) both governance and technology. Their prototypes are *cosmoscopes*, and living instruments that use scientific insights for social experiments carefully balancing knowledge and power (Chapter 6). In this sense, they embody the hopes of Walter Benjamin, who in his 'One-way street essay' described the connection of metaphysics, cosmology, and technology as crucial to defining personal and social agency in the new century:

'Nothing so distinguishes ancient from modern man as the former's submission to a cosmic experience of which the latter is scarcely aware'.
(Benjamin, 2009)

Benjamin was ambiguous about the reduction of cosmology to new technologies (optical apparati) with their metaphysical automation leading to absolute political unity and mechanical reproduction. He described these experiences as types of intoxication we know from rituals that create a sense of community and politics based on transcendence (aura):

'Intoxication, of course, is the sole experience in which we grasp the utterly immediate and the utterly remote, and never the one without the other. However, this means that communicating ecstatically with the cosmos is something man can only do communally'
(Ibid.)

To neutralize the intoxication, he advocated a more reflective use of cosmology and metaphysics in science and technology. He showed that cosmology, or what we call here the experience of time as *Chronos*, does not liberate but brings the horrors of World War I and *homo faber*: 'new and unprecedented marriage with cosmic powers.... Technology betrayed mankind and turned the marriage bed into a sea of blood'(Ibid.).

Science and technology are not only a matter of control over nature, history, or future but also a search for new relations with the universe, including the formation of new collectives (Benjamin uses the common reference in the 20s and 30s of the 'proletariat'). It is the search for more authentic technology, community, and cosmology over tools in parallel that supports the personal and communal experience of time and agency. We describe such tools as prototypes for governance and propose liminal and exploratory sandboxes as environments, where this could be experiences. To rethink the role of humanity facing various forces and scales mobilized over the new tools and knowledge, we need to prototype and communicate with the external world 'ecstatically', playfully, and creatively. It means embracing the tools of science and technology as probes into new collectives and networks, while remaining skeptical about their use as solutions promising automation that perpetuates the status quo.

The 'new and unprecedented marriage with cosmic powers' (Ibid.) through technologies supports unimaginable control in terms of military and industrial misuses and also playfulness that we see in the hackerspaces or alternative history of instrument-making. The control brings the possibility of a total war, which another of the 20th-century authors brilliantly described in a story about the 'Vietnam project' (Coetzee, 1996). J.M. Coetzee reflected upon the uncanny relation of technology with cosmology in his description of a paranoia that closes the future to one grandiose project.

The beginning of Coetzees' story summarizes the various forms of technology misuse for war propaganda. He explores the extreme views of technology as a military apparatus that breaks the rule and limits of the 'mother earth', bringing echoes of the 'masculine birth of time' imagined by Bacon (Chapter 6). Behind every military technology, Coetzee identifies the cosmic ambitions of Earth's 'celestial sons' (humans and their rockets.) who want to destroy old myths and leave 'mother Earth' to mate with new worlds creating new myths:

> But has the master myth of history not outdated the fiction of earth and heaven? We live no longer by tilling the earth but by devouring her and her waste products. We signed our repudiation of her with flights toward new celestial loves. We have the capacity to breed out of our own head.... In Indo-China we play out the drama of the end of the tellurian age and the marriage of the sky-god with his parthonegene daughter-queen. If the play has been poor, it is because we have stumbled about the stage asleep, not knowing the meaning of our acts. Now I bring their meaning to light in that blinding moment of ascending meta-historical consciousness in which we begin to shape our own myths.
>
> (Ibid.)

Coetzees' 'Vietnam project' captures how the interests in automation and technology are intimately connected to fantasies of war as the ultimate control over time, future, and world. The image of leaving 'mother earth' and mating with new celestial lovers celebrates the technological and military power that is able to subdue and rule all humans, even the whole universe. It is a fetishistic fantasy of an absolute power that nothing can resist. To avoid these extremes of the myth of automation leading to destruction, war, and annihilation, we need prototypes and environments that resist the teleology of progress, restoration, or apocalypse. We need prototypes that serve playful tinkerers instead of *homo faber* with its grandiose plans about the masculine birth of time, *Instauratio*, or future that belongs to the stars:

> For years now we have attacked the earth, explicitly in the defoliation of crops and jungle, implicitly in aleatoric shelling and bombing. Let us, in the act of ascending consciousness mentioned above, admit the meaning of our acts.... They know our guilt at devastating the earth and know that our fiction of aiming at the 0.058% of a man crossing the spot we strike at the moment we strike it is a guilty lie. Press back such atavistic guilt! Our future belongs not to the Earth but to the stars. Let us show the enemy that he stands naked in a dying landscape.
>
> (Ibid.)

Governance over prototypes is an attempt to rethink the engagement with science and technology beyond the myth of automation that leads to such teleological fantasies of absolute control and destruction. Instead of monopolies, war, and annihilation, prototyping described in this book supports the experience of time and future as Kairos, mundane opportunities for change, but also uncontrollable chance. It means time as expression of personal agency against the totalitarian ideals of 'meta-historical consciousness' with its teleological projects, celestial sons, and apocalyptic futures. To support personal and collective agency over prototyping, we propose sandboxes as public spaces for experimental governance that will help citizens define their stakes and negotiate a common future.

Exploratory sandboxes support the participation of citizens in the whole process of designing and deciding on the future 'Leviathans'. They support tactical and situated automation that balances the power of the code with personal and social agency. At every step, citizens have the power to decide how much agency they are willing to sacrifice for automation that promises frictionless and more efficient futures and how they wish to 'domesticate' algorithms and code. Such tactical and experimental engagements help us avoid the extreme scenarios of future governance reduced to the metaphor of the Wicker Man (Chapter 14). Instead of an idealized state that makes citizens and their agency obsolete (Leviathan) or even sacrifices them to optimize the system (Wicker Man), the sandboxes offer a trading zone for making decisions on the common future. More importantly, they challenge the narrative of disruptive technology with an emphasis on everyday experience with prototyping, deliberating, and working together.

The proposal for exploratory and public sandboxes as 'trading zones' (Chapters 13 and 14) was inspired by Peter Galison's metaphor describing how innovation, discovery, and regulation occur in the case of particle physics in the 20th century (Galison, 1997). Galison was able to show how successful exchanges between various stakeholders (scientists, as well as policymakers and businesses) depends on preserving their identity and diversity, even potential conflicts. Instead of finding a single unified theory, practice, value or institution, innovation (and we claim also regulation) depends on the plurality and dissent as experiences of *Kairos*. Neither the absolute power of the code nor some predefined values define the common algorithmic and automated future, but the ability to 'trade' with groups and stakeholders we do not understand or agree on:

> But here we can learn from the anthropologists who regularly study unlike cultures that do interact, most notably by trade. Two groups can agree on rules of exchange even if they ascribe utterly different significance to the objects being exchanged; they may even disagree on the meaning of the exchange process itself. Nonetheless, the trading partners can hammer out a local coordination despite vast global differences. In an even more sophisticated way, cultures in interaction frequently establish contact languages, systems of discourse that can vary from the most function-specific jargons, through semispecific pidgins, to full-fledged creoles rich enough to support activities as complex as poetry and metalinguistic reflection.
>
> (Ibid.)

In the exploratory sandboxes as trading zones, we can create a contact language between programming and natural language, code and regulation, current institutions and future infrastructures, present experiences and future visions. Instead of expecting redemption, singularity of some catastrophe, we can collaboratively design new Leviathans that enable tactical and situated decisions with the main goal of preserving personal and social agency over time and the future.

Afterword

In loving memory of David Conz and Tommy Surya, makers, brewers, and friends of the tenth or eleventh muse of tinkering.

'We think of futurism, constructivism, and modernism as part of Western culture, but in the 1930s Indonesia and other former colonies you will find more radical examples of utopian futures of science, technology, and society. Start learning Bahasa while you are here. It will open your eyes'. This casual remark, addressed to me in Czech during a conference break in 2008, turned out to be a prophecy that has not come to pass, but holds a deeper truth. I thought that Rudolf Mrázek, an eminent historian of science and technology and an expert on Indonesia, was teasing me about my lack of knowledge of Southeast Asia, where I just moved to join National University of Singapore. I never expected that Indonesia, where I knew few artists, would profoundly change my views on philosophy, science, and technology.

I never learned Bahasa to fulfill the prophecy, but Yogyakarta became my intellectual and spiritual home between 2009 and 2015. I went there every time I needed clarity on the emerging hackspaces, makerspaces, and citizen labs around the world that I started to follow. Prototyping in these alternative R&D communities made me realize that patented science, university ranking systems, and journal publications make little real impact. They inspired me to imagine different futures for science and technology that I found in Yogyakarta. Indonesia made me mourn the loss of freedom, beauty, and passion in science and technology that I could still find in the descriptions of Renaissance science by a historian of scientist who deeply influenced my views, Professor Vera Keller from the University of Oregon.

When I visited the United States in 2010 to research consumer genomic and the do-it-yourself biology (DIYbio) movement, the hackerspaces reminded me of the citizen science and art projects I knew from Yogyakarta. While the world was admiring the MIT fablabs, the Berlin hackerspaces, and the emerging Maker Fairs, my mission became to show that do-it-yourself culture and community science in Indonesia actually precede the attempts to democratize science in the West. Was Mrázek right? Will it take another century to realize that something more radical and experimental was happening in unexpected places? For almost a decade, I was exploring his insight about Indonesia in various research projects.

Yogyakarta, as the cultural and spiritual center of Southeast Asia, always combined art, science, technology, and crafts, erasing the divisions between science and 'nonscience' (values, culture), between knowledge and action, disciplines and friendships. In this place where the DIY logo can be seen on every street because it indicates the logo of the region describing its special status of Daerah Istimewa Yogyakarta, prototyping with friends challenges the narratives of disruptive innovation, start-up nations, and solutions saving humanity from the next human-made apocalypse.

Science and technology in Yogyakarta remain a unique experiences of flow, time, and agency revealing something essential about the human condition. While in the West, prototypes and design thinking embraced the hollow rhetoric of start-up disruption and technological progress, in Yogyakarta I experienced the freedom to explore and imagine different relations of science and technology to the world. Instead of narratives of salvation, disruption, and progress, working on the future was more like having a dinner with friends or a family gathering, an opportunity to enjoy the full presence and freedom.

I have only scratched the surface of these unique experiences of community science and creative technology in Indonesia. The generation of academics that came after me, such as Dr. Stefanie Wuschitz and Dr. Cindy Lin, capture the full extent of the interactions over science, technology, and community. Their dictionary of words that connect tinkering, technology, and science with everyday activities define these experiences as a form of collective and creative 'hanging out' or 'gotong-royong', an informal work that includes tools, new ideas, and infrastructures.

Science and technology as an experience of hanging out and gathering makes the flow and opportunity more important than the telos (goal) of various projects and explorations. These gatherings inspired not only hacktivist fantasies of independent infrastructure and capacity building via open science hardware but also numerous other visions of community science.

Prototyping in Yogyakarta was always an ongoing collective experimentation with open future rather than 'social action' or preparation for a start-up pitch. Tinkering, discussing, and weighing different social, political, and technological issues meant playing with artistic ideas. It was always concrete, serving concrete individuals and collectives to engage and integrate new technologies and ideas in their lives, rather than to fulfill predefined goals of social or technological progress or abstract calls to bridge different divides.

Surrounded by friends who became my global family, I experienced prototyping as an open-ended, even transgressive process that easily incorporates crafts, art, pop culture, myths. The experience of friendship, tinkering, exploration, and literal cooking in various maker and hacker communities thus led me to the main thesis of this book, that prototyping is a form of 'doing' philosophy and politics; it is an activity of creating community and governing society that I am trying to recreate over the exploratory sandboxes. Prototyping makes us realize the importance of our agency over the future and time as crucial for politics.

The art and citizen science activities initiated by House of Natural Fiber (HONF) and later by Lifepatch (Citizens Initiative for Arts, Science, and Technology), as well as interactions with numerous collectives around the world, changed my view of how we integrate new technologies and knowledge into our lives, culture and society. I was inspired by the work of fellow researchers and academics from the Gadjah Mada University, especially Professor Irfan D. Prijambada, for whom community outreach was always part of research, and Professor Mohan Dutta and his Center for Culture-Centered Approach to Research and Evaluation (CARE), who made me realize that this research is part of a larger movement for empowerment. They inspired me to imagine a future of science, technology, and society that supports personal and social action beyond any teleology of progress and exaggerated expectations of final and idealized goals.

Prototyping in the informal networks of geeks, makers, and hackers around the world rarely results in a finished product. It always remains a community work, fostering personal relationships and visions of the world. The flows and processes of prototyping erase cultural and geopolitical divisions by emphasizing the unique experience of time as Kairos, leaving the future open to new engagements rather than obsessing over outcomes and products. As Yair Reshef, my 'partner in (prototyping) crimes' and founder of Tel Aviv hackerspace summed up in a 2014 chat:

> I tell ppl that in hackerspaces we don't *start* anything. we are here to fail. gracefully if possible. completed projects tend to become a show-off. people always look for the product. a goal embodied in an object. It should be effortless. effortless technology.

It was the first Asia-Pacific DIYbio and Bioart Meeting 'Democratizing the Laboratory' in 2011 that inspired me to understand that the pace of our technological and scientific progress does not have to exceed our moral and social maturity, as we are always told. Hackerspace and makerspace demonstrate the opposite. Tinkering with science and technology is a direct way to define our values, negotiate visions, and shape a future that meets our needs and desires.

The geeks, artists, designers, and academics who participate in these gatherings combine in often unexpected ways their scientific, artistic, personal and social practices, values, and ideas. Furthermore, Yogyakarta universities were always connected to local communities, villages, artists' organizations, and various other collectives, where they use prototypes to strengthen the relations and negotiate new ideas about common futures.

The rich cultural traditions as well as the environmental and economic challenges create conditions for radical visions that Professor Mrázek pointed at in that casual remark. Only after 2010 I realized that he was right. We do not have to visit Silicon Valley, NASA, or a Mars colony to experience future communities that are resilient to extreme conditions by embracing new technologies. Groups of artists, scientists, and farmers around Yogyakarta have been using prototypes to study climate change around the Merapi volcano in Java at least since 2012, when the HONF Foundation launched its Micro/ Macro Nation project. They connected a prototype of ethanol reactor that ferments waste to farm aquaponics systems and collected data from these experiments for an artistic performance. They even hacked an Indonesian government satellite to get the environmental data they needed to predict the effects of climate change, setting a precedent in governance with open data for future scenarios. None of this was part of any official plan, ideology or project but a work of an opportunity that expresses the agency over the future as open, radical, and experimental.

Prototyping was always at the heart of these activities that explore personal and social agency over the future. It combines research with community activism, hacktivism, artistic sensibility, and visions that question the dichotomies between theory and practice, community and tools (infrastructure), science, technology, and art. Whether as Hackteria's hacked webcams with a stage for a microscope made by Indonesian artisans, or gel electrophoresis chamber made from IKEA Tupperware for playing with food dyes, even the optical density and turbidity sensors made from 'tick-tock' boxes, these prototypes combine esthetic, critical, and philosophical engagements similar to 16th-century instruments.

While working and living between Indonesia, Switzerland, and Singapore, I engaged with similar instruments, kits, and prototypes that serve scientific education and research and also as VJing and DJing or even science (geek) diplomacy. These tools created an 'imagined community' or transglobal and interdisciplinary collaborations that define a whole new geopolitical order and vision for the future. The prototypes fostered not only creative appropriations of scientific protocols and open-source technologies but also unique collaborations between universities, arts organizations, and local communities, and between science and indigenous knowledge, design, and craft.

I never expected Yogyakarta to play such an important role in my identity as a scientist, designer, and philosopher, and I think Professor Mrázek predicted something more universal. The DIY capital of the world inspire us to rethink our cultural and disciplinary boundaries, even ideas about who is family and what is friendship. I still feel part of this nomadic family, formed while prototyping around the world with friends from different continents, cultures, and ideas.

Rudolf Mrázek's prophecy is true because it expresses a provocation relevant to all of us. Indonesia and other places outside the established cultural and technological centers, as well as forgotten crafts from older periods in different cultures, define new and unexpected connections between social, cultural, and technological practices. We need to explore these unique networks, connections, and histories because they define our agency and power over time and the future, which is crucial at a moment when models and algorithms with their extractive data are once again trying to close the future and divide us into parasites and patrons.

References

Ackermann, R. J. (2014). *Data, Instruments, and Theory: A Dialectical Approach to Understanding Science*. Princeton University Press.

Adam, B. (2000). The temporal gaze: The challenge for social theory in the context of GM food. *The British Journal of Sociology, 51*(1), 125–142. https://doi.org/10.1111/j.1468-4446.2000.00125.x

Agamben, G. (2009a). What is a paradigm? *Filozofski Vestnik, 30*(1), 107–125.

Agamben, G. (2009b). *The Signature of All Things*. Zone Books. ISBN 1890951986.

Aitken, M., Toreini, E., Carmichael, P., Coopamootoo, K., Elliott, K., & van Moorsel, A. (2020). Establishing a social licence for financial technology: Reflections on the role of the private sector in pursuing ethical data practices. *Big Data & Society, 7*(1), 2053951720908892. https://doi.org/10.1177/2053951720908892

Akiba. (2011). *Kimono Lantern and Humanitarian Open Source Hardware*. http://www.freaklabs.org/index.php/Blog/Misc/Kimono-Lantern-and-Humanitarian-Open-Source-Hardware.html

Akkoyunlu, E. A., Ekanadham, K., & Huber, R. V. (1975). Some constraints and tradeoffs in the design of network communications. *ACM SIGOPS Operating Systems Review, 9*(5), 67–74. https://doi.org/10.1145/1067629.806523

Allen, H. J. (2019). *Regulatory Sandboxes*. https://ssrn.com/abstract=3056993

Ames, M. G., Bardzell, J., Bardzell, S., Lindtner, S., Mellis, D. A., Rosner, D. K., Ames, M. G., Bardzell, J., Bardzell, S., Lindtner, S., Mellis, D. A., & Rosner, D. K. (2014). Making cultures. *Proceedings of the Extended Abstracts of the 32nd Annual ACM Conference on Human Factors in Computing Systems - CHI EA '14*, 1087–1092. https://doi.org/10.1145/2559206.2579405

Ananny, M. (2016). Toward an ethics of algorithms: Convening, observation, probability, and timeliness. *Science Technology and Human Values, 41*(1), 93–117. https://doi.org/10.1177/0162243915606523

Ananny, M., & Crawford, K. (2018). Seeing without knowing: Limitations of the transparency ideal and its application to algorithmic accountability. *New Media and Society, 20*(3). https://doi.org/10.1177/1461444816676645

Arendt, H. (2013). *The Human Condition*. University of Chicago Press.

Aristophanes, Acharnians, line 692. (n.d.). Retrieved July 6, 2022, from https://www.perseus.tufts.edu/hopper/text?doc=Perseus%3Atext%3A1999.01.0240%3Acard%3D692

Aristotle. (1933). Book I., section 981a. In *Metaphysics*. Aristotle in 23 Volumes, Vols.17, 18, translated by Hugh Tredennick. Cambridge, MA, Harvard University

Press; London, William Heinemann Ltd. 1933, 1989. Retrieved June 26, 2022, from https://www.perseus.tufts.edu/hopper/text?doc=Perseus%3Atext%3A1999. 01.0052%3Abook%3D1%3Asection%3D981a#:~:text=%5B981a%5D%20% 5B1%5D%20Experience,is%20formed%20with%20regard%20to

Aristotle. (1944a). Book I., section 1259a and 1260a. In *Politics*. Aristotle in 23 Volumes, Vol. 21, translated by H. Rackham. Cambridge, MA, Harvard University Press. Retrieved June 26, 2022, *from* niversity Press; London, William Heinemann Ltd. 1944. http://www.perseus.tufts.edu/hopper/text?doc=Perseus%3 Atext%3A1999.01.0058%3Abook%3D1%3Asection%3D1260a

Aristotle. (1944b). Book VII. In *Politics*. Aristotle. Aristotle in 23 Volumes, Vol. 21, translated by H. Rackham. Cambridge, MA, Harvard University Press; London, William Heinemann Ltd. 1944. Retrieved June 26, 2022, from http://www.perseus.tufts.edu/hopper/text?doc=Perseus%3Atext%3A1999.01.0058%3Abook%3D1%3Asection%3D1260a

Arner, D. W., Barberis, J. N., & Buckley, R. P. (2017). FinTech and RegTech in a nutshell, and the future in a sandbox. *SSRN Electronic Journal*. https://doi.org/10.2139/ssrn.3088303

Atlas, R. M., & Dando, M. (2006). The dual-use dilemma for the life sciences: Perspectives, conundrums, and global solutions. *Biosecurity and Bioterrorism: Biodefense Strategy, Practice, and Science*, 4(3), 276–286. https://doi.org/10.1089/bsp.2006.4.276

Atzori, M. (2015). *Blockchain Technology and Decentralized Governance: Is the State Still Necessary?* (SSRN Scholarly Paper No. 2709713). https://doi.org/10.2139/ssrn.2709713

Atzori, M., & Ulieru, M. (2017). Architecting the eSociety on blockchain: A provocation to human nature. *Social Science Research Network*. https://papers.ssrn.com/abstract,2999715

Ausareny, J., Kera, D., Druga, S., & Reshef, Y. (2014). Open source hardware (OSHW) supporting interaction between traditional crafts and emergent science. *SIGGRAPH Asia 2014 Designing Tools For Crafting Interactive Artifacts on - SIGGRAPH ASIA '14*, 1–4. https://doi.org/10.1145/2668947.2668955

Awad, E., Dsouza, S., Kim, R., Schulz, J., Henrich, J., Shariff, A., Bonnefon, J.-F., & Rahwan, I. (2018). The Moral Machine experiment. *Nature*, 563(7729), Article 7729. https://doi.org/10.1038/s41586-018-0637-6

Bacon, Francis. Novum Organum. (n.d.). *Novum Organum; Or, True Suggestions for the Interpretation of Nature*. Retrieved August 14, 2023, from https://www.gutenberg.org/ebooks/45988/pg45988-images.html.utf8

Barbiero, E. A. (2018). *Time to Eat: Chronological Connections in Alciphron's Letters of Parasites* (pp. 42–58). Brill. https://doi.org/10.1163/9789004383388_004

Barthes, R. (1993). *Mythologies*. Vintage.

Bassett, C., & Roberts, B. (2020). Automation now and then: Automation fevers, Anxieties and Utopias. *New Formations*, 98(98), 9–28. https://doi.org/10.3898/newf:98.02.2019

Bastani, A. (2020). *Fully Automated Luxury Communism a Manifesto*. Verso.

Baudot, L. (2012). An air of history: Joseph wright's and Robert Boyle's air pump narratives. *Eighteenth-Century Studies*, 46(1), 1–28. https://doi.org/10.1353/ecs.2012.0075

Bénatouïl, T., & Bonazzi, M. (2012). Θεωρια and Βιοσ Θεωρητικοσ from the presocratics to the end of antiquity: An overview. In T. Bénatouïl & M. Bonazzi (Eds.),

Theoria, Praxis, and the Contemplative Life after Plato and Aristotle. BRILL. https://doi.org/10.1163/9789004230040

Benjamin, W. (2009). *One-way Street and Other Writings*. (p. 278).

Benjamin, W. (2018). The work of art in the age of mechanical reproduction. In *A Museum Studies Approach to Heritage* (pp. 226–243). Fontana. https://doi.org/10.4324/9781351226387-29

Bigger, C. P. (2004). Between chora and the good: Metaphor's metaphysical neighborhood. In *Between Chora and the Good: Metaphor's Metaphysical Neighborhood*. Fordham University Press.

Binns, R. (2018). Algorithmic accountability and public reason. *Philosophy & Technology, 31*(4), 543–556. https://doi.org/10.1007/s13347-017-0263-5

Blockchain.com Explorer | BTC | ETH | BCH. (n.d.). Retrieved July 6, 2022, from https://www.blockchain.com/explorer

Boyd, D., & Crawford, K. (2012). Critical questions for big data: Provocations for a cultural, technological, and scholarly phenomenon. *Information Communication and Society, 15*(5), 662–679. https://doi.org/10.1080/1369118X.2012.678878

Brantley, B. (2014). *Lean Startup: Changing Government Services and Agencies to Better Serve the Citizens*. Digital.Gov. https://digital.gov/2014/07/11/lean-startup-changing-government-services-and-agencies-to-better-serve-the-citizens/

Brennan, N. M., Subramaniam, N., & van Staden, C. J. (2019). Corporate governance implications of disruptive technology: An overview. *British Accounting Review, 51*(6). https://doi.org/10.1016/j.bar.2019.100860

Bromberg, L., Godwin, A., & Ramsay, I. (2017). *Fintech Sandboxes: Achieving a Balance between Regulation and Innovation* (SSRN Scholarly Paper No. 3090844). https://papers.ssrn.com/abstract=3090844

Brundtland, T. (2011). After Boyle and the Leviathan: The Second Generation of British Air Pumps. *Annals of Science, 68*(1), 93–124.

Burk, D. L. (2019). Algorithmic fair use. *University of Chicago Law Review, 86*, 283.

Burns, W. (2013). *The Potential of Science Diasporas | Science & Diplomacy*. Science Diplomacy Blog. Retrieved December 15, 2014, from http://www.sciencediplomacy.org/perspective/2013/potential-science-diasporas

Buterin, V. (2014). *An Introduction to Futarchy*.

Buterin, V. (2020). *Credible Neutrality As A Guiding Principle*. https://messari.io

Buterin, Vitalik E. (2015). *Superrationality and DAOs*. https://blog.ethereum.org/2015/01/23/superrationality-daos/

Caragliu, A., Del Bo, C., & Nijkamp, P. (2011). Smart cities in Europe. *Journal of Urban Technology, 18*(2), 65–82.

Carmona, M. (2015). Re-theorising contemporary public space: A new narrative and a new normative. *Journal of Urbanism, 8*(4), 373–405. https://doi.org/10.1080/17549175.2014.909518

Cassin, B. (2014). *Sophistical Practice: Toward a Consistent Relativism*. Fordham University Press. https://doi.org/10.1515/9780823256426

Cavoukian, A. (2009). Privacy by design: The 7 foundational principles. *Information and Privacy Commissioner of Ontario, Canada, 5*, 2009.

Coetzee, J. M. (1996). *Dusklands*. Penguin Books.

Colburn, T. R., & Shute, G. M. (2008). Metaphor in computer science. *Journal of Applied Logic, 6*(4). https://doi.org/10.1016/j.jal.2008.09.005

Coleman, E. G. (2013). *Coding Freedom: The Ethics and Aesthetics of Hacking*. Princeton University Press.

Colie, R. L. (1955). Cornelis Drebbel and Salomon de Caus: Two Jacobean models for Salomon's house. *Huntington Library Quarterly*, *18*(3), 245–260. https://doi.org/10.2307/3816455

Crawford, K. (2013). The Atlas of AI - Power, politics, and the planetary costs of artificial intelligence. In *The Atlas of AI* (Vol. 53, Issue 9, pp. 1689–1699). Yale University Press.

Crawford, K. (2016). Can an algorithm be agonistic? Ten Scenes from life in calculated publics. *Science, Technology, & Human Values*, *41*(1), 77–92. https://doi.org/10.1177/0162243915589635

Crawford, K., & Schultz, J. (2019). AI systems as state actors. *Columbia Law Review*, *119*(7), 1941–1972.

Cugurullo, F. (2020). Urban artificial intelligence: From automation to autonomy in the smart city. *Frontiers in Sustainable Cities*, *2*. https://www.frontiersin.org/articles/10.3389/frsc.2020.00038

Cummings, D. (2019). *High performance government, 'cognitive technologies'*. Blog. https://dominiccummings.com/2019/06/26/on-the-referendum-33-high-performance-government-cognitive-technologies-michael-nielsen-bret-victor-seeing-rooms/

Danaher, J. (2016). The threat of algocracy: Reality, resistance and accommodation. *Philosophy and Technology*, *29*(3), 245–268. https://doi.org/10.1007/s13347-015-0211-1

Danaher, J., Hogan, M. J., Noone, C., Kennedy, R., Behan, A., De Paor, A., Felzmann, H., Haklay, M., Khoo, S.-M., Morison, J., Murphy, M. H., O'Brolchain, N., Schafer, B., & Shankar, K. (2017). Algorithmic governance: Developing a research agenda through the power of collective intelligence. *Big Data & Society*, *4*(2), 2053951717726554. https://doi.org/10.1177/2053951717726554

Dantec, C. A. L., & DiSalvo, C. (2013). Infrastructuring and the formation of publics in participatory design. *Social Studies of Science*, *43*(2), 241–264. https://doi.org/10.1177/0306312712471581

Davies, S. R. (2017). *Hackerspaces: Making the maker movement*. Polity

Davies, S. R., Tybjerg, K., Whiteley, L., & Söderqvist, T. (2015). Co-curation as hacking: Biohackers in Copenhagen's medical museion. *Curator: The Museum Journal*, *58*(1), 117–131. https://doi.org/10.1111/cura.12102

de Certeau, M. (2011). *The Practice of Everyday Life* (S. Rendall, Trans.; 3rd ed.). University of California Press.

de Price, D. J. S. (Derek J. de S.) (1986). *Little Science, Big Science—And Beyond*. Columbia University Press.

Delfanti, A. (2013). *Biohackers: The Politics of Open Science, Delfanti*. Pluto Press.

Delgado, A. (2013). DIYbio: Making things and making futures. *Futures*, *48*, 65–73.

Devellennes, C. (2017). Atheism, secularism and toleration: Towards a political atheology. *Contemporary Political Theory*, *16*(2), 228–247. https://doi.org/10.1057/cpt.2016.13

Devellennes, C. (2021). Introduction. *Positive Atheism*, 1–28.

Diakopoulos, N. (2016). Accountability in algorithmic decision making. *Communications of the ACM*, *59*(2), 56–62. https://doi.org/10.1145/2844110

Dickel, S., Ferdinand, J.-P., & Petschow, U. (2014). Shared machine shops as real-life Laboratories. *Journal of Peer Production*. http://peerproduction.net/issues/issue-5-

shared-machine-shops/peer-reviewed-articles/shared-machine-shops-as-real-life-laboratories/

Dijkstra, E. W. (1971). Hierarchical ordering of sequential processes. *Acta Informatica*, *1*(2), 115–138. https://doi.org/10.1007/BF00289519

DiSalvo, C. (2012). *Adversarial Design*. MIT Press.

DiSalvo, C. (2014). Critical making as materializing the politics of design. *The Information Society*, *30*(2), 96–105. https://doi.org/10.1080/01972243.2014.875770

Dolejšová, M., & Kera, D. (2016). Fermentation GutHub: Designing for food sustainability in Singapore. *Proceedings of the 2nd International Conference in HCI and UX Indonesia 2016*, 69–76. https://doi.org/10.1145/2898459.2898470

Dolejšová, M., & Kera, D. (2017). Soylent diet self-experimentation. *Proceedings of the 2017 ACM Conference on Computer Supported Cooperative Work and Social Computing - CSCW '17*, 2112–2123. https://doi.org/10.1145/2998181.2998365

Duggett, T. (2007). Celtic night and gothic grandeur: Politics and antiquarianism in Wordsworth's salisbury plain. *Romanticism*, *13*, 164–176. https://doi.org/10.3366/rom.2007.13.2.164

Dunne, A. (2008). *Hertzian Tales: Electronic Products, Aesthetic Experience, and Critical Design*. The MIT Press.

Dunne, A., & Raby, F. (2013). *Speculative Everything: Design, Fiction, and Social Dreaming* (Vol. 22). MIT Press.

Edwards, L., & Veale, M. (2018). Enslaving the algorithm: From a "right to an explanation" to a "right to better decisions"? *IEEE Security & Privacy*, *16*(3), 46–54. https://doi.org/10.1109/MSP.2018.2701152

Elkin-Koren, N. (2020). Contesting algorithms: Restoring the public interest in content filtering by artificial intelligence. *Big Data & Society*, *7*(2), 2053951720932296. https://doi.org/10.1177/2053951720932296

Esses, D. (2018). *Images of the World: Cosmology and Rhetoric in Plato's Timaeus and Laws*. Dissertation University of California. https://escholarship.org/uc/item/4pj0j15s

Faulkner, R. K. (1993). *Francis Bacon and the Project of Progress*. Rowman & Littlefield Publishers.

Feenberg, A. (1991). *Critical Theory of Technology*. Oxford University Press.

Feenberg, A. (1994). The technocracy thesis revisited: On the critique of power*. *Inquiry*, *37*(1), 85–102. https://doi.org/10.1080/00201749408602341

Filippi, P. D., & Hassan, S. (2016). Blockchain technology as a regulatory technology: From code is law to law is code. *First Monday*. https://doi.org/10.5210/fm.v21i12.7113

Filippi, P. D., & Loveluck, B. (2016). The invisible politics of Bitcoin: Governance crisis of a decentralised infrastructure. *Internet Policy Review*, *5*(3). https://policyreview.info/articles/analysis/invisible-politics-bitcoin-governance-crisis-decentralised-infrastructure

Fjeld, J., Achten, N., Hilligoss, H., Nagy, A., & Srikumar, M. (2020). Principled artificial intelligence: Mapping consensus in ethical and rights-based approaches to principles for AI. *Berkman Klein Center Research Publication*, *2020–1*.

Flood, J., & Robb, L. (2017). Trust, anarcho-capitalism, blockchain and initial coin offerings. *Griffith University Law School Research Paper*, 17–23. https://doi.org/10.2139/ssrn.3074263

Foucault, M. (1977). Power and sex: An interview with Michel Foucault. *Telos: Critical Theory of the Contemporary, 32*, 154–161. http://journal.telospress.com/content/1974/19/154.full.pdf+html

Foucault, M. (2000). *Ethics Subjectivity and Truth; the Essential Works of Michael Foucault, 1954–1984*. Penguin Classics.

Frayne, S. (n.d.). *Mantis Shrimp Invention – confluence*. Mantis Shrimp Invention Blog. Retrieved December 15, 2014, from https://web.archive.org/web/20130210092328/http://manilamantis.com/tag/confluence/

Friedman, B., & Kahn, P. (2002). Value sensitive design: Theory and methods. *University of Washington Technical, December*, 1–8. https://doi.org/10.1016/j.neuropharm.2007.08.009

Fuchs, C., & Dyer-Witheford, N. (2012). Karl Marx @ Internet studies. *New Media & Society, 15*(5), 782–796.

Gabrys, J. (2020). Smart forests and data practices: From the Internet of Trees to planetary governance. *Big Data & Society, 7*(1), 205395172090487. https://doi.org/10.1177/2053951720904871

Galison, P. (1987). *How Experiments End*. University of Chicago Press.

Galison, P. (1988). Philosophy in the laboratory. *The Journal of Philosophy, 85*(10), 525–527.

Galison, P. (1997). *Image and Logic: A Material Culture of Microphysics*. University of Chicago Press.

Gardiner, M. E. (2017). Critique of accelerationism. *Theory, Culture and Society, 34*(1). https://doi.org/10.1177/0263276416656760

Gardiner, M. E. (2020). Automatic for the people? cybernetics and left-accelerationism. *Constellations*. https://doi.org/10.1111/1467-8675.12528

Gershenfeld, N., Krikorian, R., & Cohen, D. (2004). The internet of things. *Scientific American, 291*(4), 76–81. https://doi.org/10.1038/scientificamerican1004-76

Global Open Science Hardware (GOSH) Manifesto. (2016).

Gomba, D. (2013). *Arduino Blog » Blog Archive » Arduino goes to Shenzhen: The Hollywood of hardware products*. Retrieved December 15, 2014, from http://blog.arduino.cc/2013/04/11/arduino-goes-shenzen/

Gopinath, D. (2009). Contemporary approaches to economic development: The special economic zone programme. *Local Economy, 24*(6), 448–455. https://doi.org/10.1080/02690940903319018

Gratwick, A. S. (1979). Sundials, parasites, and girls from Boeotia. In A. Long and R.M. Ogilvie (Eds.), *The Classical Quarterly* (Vol. 29, pp. 308–323). Cambridge University Press. The Classical Association. https://doi.org/10.2307/638098

Grau, Oliver. (Editor). (2007). Media art histories. In O. Grau (Ed.), *Media Art Histories*. MIT press,.

Gray, J. N. (1978). Notes on data base operating systems. In R. Bayer, R. M. Graham, & G. Seegmüller (Eds.), *Operating Systems* (Vol. 60, pp. 393–481). Springer Berlin Heidelberg. https://doi.org/10.1007/3-540-08755-9_9

Gromova, E. (2020). *Regulatory Sandboxes (Experimental Legal Regimes) for Digital Innovations in BRICS* (SSRN Scholarly Paper No. 3700256). https://papers.ssrn.com/abstract=3700256

Habermas, J. (1989). *The Structural Transformation of the Public Sphere: An Inquiry into a Category of Bourgeois Society* (T. Burger, Trans.). MIT Press.

Hacker, P., Lianos, I., Dimitropoulos, G., & Eich, S. (Eds.). (2019). *Regulating Blockchain: Techno-Social and Legal Challenges*. Oxford University Press. https://doi.org/10.1093/oso/9780198842187.001.0001

Hagendorff, T. (2020). The ethics of AI ethics: An evaluation of guidelines. *Minds and Machines*, 30(1), 99–120. https://doi.org/10.1007/s11023-020-09517-8

Harvey, A. D. (2007). *Body Politic: Political Metaphor and Political Violence*. Cambridge scholars Publishing.

Hassan, S., & De Filippi, P. (2017). The expansion of algorithmic governance: From code is law to law is code. *Field Actions Science Reports. The Journal of Field Actions, Special Issue, 17*, 88–90.

Hee-Jeong Choi, J., Forlano, L., & Kera, D. (2020). Situated automation: Algorithmic creatures in participatory design. *Proceedings of the 16th Participatory Design Conference 2020 - Participation(s) Otherwise - Volume 2*, 5–9. https://doi.org/10.1145/3384772.3385153

Heidegger, M. (1977). *The Question Concerning Technology, and Other Essays*. Harper & Row.

Heilbron, J. L. (1989). Leviathan and the air-pump. Hobbes, Boyle, and the experimental life. *Medical History, 33*(2), 256–257.

Henderson, J. (n.d.-a). *Book III: Letter 24*. Loeb Classical Library. Retrieved July 6, 2022, from https://www.loebclassics.com/view/alciphron-letters_book_iii_letters_parasites/1949/pb_LCL383.209.xml

Henderson, J. (n.d.-b). *PLAUTUS, amphitryon. The comedy of asses. The pot of gold. The two bacchises. The Captives*. Loeb Classical Library. Retrieved July 6, 2022, from https://www.loebclassics.com/view/LCL060/2011/pb_LCL060.i.xml

Hildebrandt, M. (2018). Algorithmic regulation and the rule of law. *Philosophical Transactions of the Royal Society A: Mathematical, Physical and Engineering Sciences, 376*(2128), 20170355. https://doi.org/10.1098/rsta.2017.0355

Hirosue, S., Kera, D., & Huang, H. (2015). Promises and perils of open source technologies for development: Can the "Subaltern" research and innovate? In S. Hostettler, E. Hazboun, & J.-C. Bolay (Eds.), *Technologies for Development SE - 7* (pp. 73–80). Springer International Publishing. https://doi.org/10.1007/978-3-319-16247-8_7

Hong, D. (2020, November 28). *On Decentralized Clocks: How Time Became the Biggest Security Threat on blockchain Systems*. Medium. https://blog.unifiedh.com/on-decentralized-clocks-how-time-became-the-biggest-security-threat-on-blockchain-systems-8a7e13622bb0

Hornstein, A. (n.d.). *Kickstarter >> The Solar Pocket Factory: An Invention Adventure by Alex Hornstein*. The Solar Pocket Factory: An Invention Adventure Blog. Retrieved December 15, 2014, from https://www.kickstarter.com/projects/alex9000/the-solar-pocket-factory-an-invention-adventure/posts?page=3

Huang, B. (2012). *Safecast Geiger Counter Reference Design « bunnie's blog*. http://www.bunniestudios.com/blog/?p=2218

Huang, B. (2013). *The $12 Gongkai Phone « bunnie's blog*. http://www.bunniestudios.com/blog/?p=3040

Huang, B. (2014). *Novena « bunnie's blog*. http://www.bunniestudios.com/blog/?tag=novena

Huang, H. (2015). *Networks of Practice Around Open Science: A Case Study on The House of Natural Fiber Foundation in Yogyakarta, Indonesia*. Chulalongkorn University, Bangkok, Thailand.

Hurley, D. (2016, April). Artificial pancreas makers race to market. *Discovery Magazine.* https://www.discovermagazine.com/technology/artificial-pancreas-makers-race-to-market

Husserl, E. (1970). *The Crisis of European Sciences and Transcendental Phenomenology an Introduction to Phenomenological Philosophy.* Northwestern University Press.

Iliffe, R. (2000). The masculine birth of time: Temporal frameworks of early modern natural philosophy. *The British Journal for the History of Science, 33*(4), 427–453.

Introna, L. D. (2016). Algorithms, governance, and governmentality: On governing academic writing. *Science, Technology, & Human Values, 41*(1), 17–49. https://doi.org/10.1177/0162243915587360

Izwaini, S. (2003). *A corpus-based study of metaphor in information technology.* https://www.researchgate.net/publication/228576452_A_corpus-based_study_of_metaphor_in_information_technology

Jacobs, J. (1962). *The Death and Life of Great American Cities: Vol. null.* (null, Ed.). (Modern Library (hardcover) ed.). New York: Random House.

Jacobus, H. R. (2014). *4 The 'Enoch Zodiac' and Greco-Roman Zodiac Sundials* (pp. 344–388). Brill. https://doi.org/10.1163/9789004284067_006

Jagendorf, Z. (1990). Coriolanus: Body politic and private parts. *Shakespeare Quarterly, 41*(4), 455–469. https://doi.org/10.2307/2870776

Jardine, L. (1974). *Francis Bacon: Discovery and the Art of Discourse.* Cambridge University Press.

Jingfang, W., & Rong, C. (2013). Metaphors ubiquitous in computer and internet terminologies. *Journal of Arts and Humanities, 2*(10), Article 10. https://doi.org/10.18533/journal.v2i10.261

Johnson, M. W., Christensen, C. M., & Kagermann, H. (2008, December 1). Reinventing your business model. *Harvard Business Review.* https://hbr.org/2008/12/reinventing-your-business-model

Just, N., & Latzer, M. (2017). Governance by algorithms: Reality construction by algorithmic selection on the Internet. *Media, Culture & Society, 39*(2), 238–258. https://doi.org/10.1177/0163443716643157

Kahn, P. W. (2012). *Political Theology Four New Chapters on the Concept of Sovereignty.* Columbia University Press.

Kahn, P. W. (2019). *Origins of Order.* Yale University Press.

Kaiying, C. L., & Lindtner, S. (2016). Legitimacy, boundary objects & participation in transnational DIY biology. *Proceedings of the 14th Participatory Design Conference on Full Papers - PDC '16,* 171–180. https://doi.org/10.1145/2940299.2940307

Karvonen, A., Cugurullo, F., & Caprotti, F. (2018). *Inside Smart Cities: Place, Politics and Urban Innovation.* https://doi.org/10.4324/9781351166201

Keller, V. (2010). Drebbel's living instruments, Hartmann's microcosm, and libavius' thelesmos: Epistemic machines before descartes. *History of Science, 48,* 39–74.

Keller, V. (2011). How to become a seventeenth-century natural philosopher: The case of Cornelis Drebbel. In *Silent Messengers the Circulation of Material Objects of Knowledge in the Early Modern Low Countries.* (Low Countries Studies on the Circulation of Natural Knowledge, 1.) volume 1.

Keller, V. (2012). The "New World of Sciences". The temporality of the research agenda and the unending ambitions of science. *Isis; An International Review Devoted to the History of Science and Its Cultural Influences, 103*(4), 727–734. https://doi.org/10.1086/669047

Keller, V. (2013). Re-entangling the thermometer: Cornelis Drebbel's description of his self-regulating oven, the regiment of fire, and the early history of temperature. *Nuncius, 28*(2), 243–275. https://doi.org/10.1163/18253911-02802001

Keller, V. (2015). *Knowledge and the Public Interest, 1575–1725*. Cambridge University Press.

Keller, V. (2018). Deprogramming Baconianism: The meaning of desiderata in the eighteenth century. *Notes and Records: The Royal Society Journal of the History of Science, 72*(2), 119–137. https://doi.org/10.1098/rsnr.2018.0008

Kelty, C. M. (2008). *Two Bits: The Cultural Significance of Free Software*. Duke University Press.

Kera, D. (2011). Entrepreneurs, squatters and low-tech artisans: DIYbio and Hackerspace models of citizen science between EU, Asia and USA. In L. Aceti (Ed.), *17th International Symposium on Electronic Art ISEA2011 Istanbul*. Sabanci University.

Kera, D. (2012a). Design probes into nutrigenomics: From data to user experiences. In T. Kido & K. Takadama (Eds.), *Self-tracking and Collective Intelligence for Personal Wellness: Papers from the AAAI Spring Symposium* (pp. 26–30). AAAI Press.

Kera, D. (2012b). Hackerspaces and DIYbio in Asia: Connecting science and community with open data, kits and protocols. *Journal of Peer Production*, June, 1–8. http://peerproduction.net/issues/issue-2/peer-reviewed-papers/

Kera, D. (2012c). NanoŠmano Lab in Ljubljana: Disruptive prototypes and experimental governance of nanotechnologies in the hackerspaces. *Journal of Science Communication, 11*(04). http://peerproduction.net/issues/issue-2/peer-reviewed-papers/

Kera, D. (2013). *Can There Be a Republic of Coders? The Aesthetics, Ethics, and Metaphysics of Coding Freedom | Mobilizing Ideas*. Mobilizing ideas. https://mobilizingideas.wordpress.com/2013/07/01/can-there-be-a-republic-of-coders-the-aesthetics-ethics-and-metaphysics-of-coding-freedom/

Kera, D. (2014a). Innovation regimes based on collaborative and global tinkering: Synthetic biology and nanotechnology in the hackerspaces. *Technology in Society, 37*(1), 28–37. https://doi.org/10.1016/j.techsoc.2013.07.004

Kera, D. (2014b). Uncanny Microelectronics: Intaglio & the Aesthetics of Circuit Boards. *Das SUPER PAPER*. https://swarmmag.com/words/eternal-circuits/

Kera, D. (2015). Open Source Hardware (OSHW) for open science in the global south: Geek diplomacy? In S. Albagli, L. Maciel, & H. A. Abdo (Eds.), *Open Science, Open Issues* (pp. 133–157). Instituto Brasileiro de Informação em Ciência e Tecnologia (IBICT).

Kera, D. (2017). Maker culture liminality and open source (science) hardware: Instead of making anything great again, keep experimenting! | A liminaridade da cultura maker e o hardware de fonte (na ciência): Em vez de fazer algo ser grande de novo, continue experimentando. *Liinc Em Revista, 13*(1). https://doi.org/10.18617/LIINC.V13I1.3875

Kera, D., Huang, H., Agrivine, I., & Surya, T. (2019). Open Science Hardware (OSH) for development: Transnational networks and local tinkering in Southeast Asia. In L. Chan, A. Okune, B. Hillyer, D. Albornoz, & A. Posada (Eds.), *Contextualizing Openness: Situating Open Science*. University of Ottawa Press. https://doi.org/10.1007/978-3-319-00026-8

Kera, D., Rod, J., & Peterova, R. (2013). Post-apocalyptic citizenship and humanitarian hardware. In Hindmarsh, R. A. (Ed.), *Nuclear Disaster at Fukushima Daiichi: Social, Political and Environmental Issues* (pp. 97–116). Routledge.

Kera, D., & Storni, C. (2011). Interfaces for nutrigenomics and nutrigenetics: Connecting participatory design with citizen science projects. In K. Rocker, M.

Ziefle, A. Holzinger, S. Hansen, & K. McGee (Eds.), *SmartHealth'11: Extended Abstracts of the Third International Workshop on Smart Healthcare Applications, OzCHI2011* (pp. 14–22). Aachen University.

Kera, D., & Sulaiman, N. L. (2014). FridgeMatch: Design probe into the future of urban food commensality. *Futures*, 62, 194–201. https://doi.org/10.1016/j.futures.2014.04.007

Kera, D. R. (2021). Exploratory RegTech: Sandboxes supporting trust by balancing regulation of algorithms with automation of regulations. In M. H. Ur Rehman, D. Svetinovic, K. Salah, & E. Damiani (Eds.), *Trust Models for Next-Generation Blockchain Ecosystems* (pp. 67–84). Springer International Publishing. https://doi.org/10.1007/978-3-030-75107-4_3

Kera, D. R., & Kalvas, F. (2022). No algorithmization without representation: Pilot study on regulatory experiments in an exploratory Sandbox. *Digital Society*, 1(2), 8. https://doi.org/10.1007/s44206-022-00002-6

Kirby, D. (2009). The future is now: Diegetic prototypes and the role of popular films in generating real-world technological development. *Social Studies of Science*, 40(1), 41–70. https://doi.org/10.1177/0306312709338325

Kitchin, R. (2017). Thinking critically about and researching algorithms. *Information Communication and Society*, 20(1), 14–29. https://doi.org/10.1080/1369118X.2016.1154087

Kluitenberg, Eric. (2006). *The book of imaginary media: Excavating the dream of the ultimate communication medium*. De Balie.

Knorr-Cetina, K. (1995). Laboratory studies: The cultural approach to the study of science. In *The Handbook of Science and Technology Studies* (pp. 140–166). SAGE Publications, Inc. https://doi.org/10.4135/9781412990127.n7

Knorr-Cetina, K. D. (1983). The ethnographic study of a scientific work: Towards a constructivist interpretation of science. *Science Observed: Perspectives of the Social Study of Science*, 1913, 115–140.

Krohn, R., Latour, B., & Woolgar, S. (1981). Laboratory life. *Contemporary Sociology*, 10(3), 433). https://doi.org/10.2307/2067378

Kroll, J. A., Huey, J., Barocas, S., Felten, E. W., Reidenberg, J. R., Robinson, D. G., & Yu, H. (2016). *Accountable Algorithms* (SSRN Scholarly Paper No. 2765268). https://papers.ssrn.com/abstract=2765268

Lamport, L. (2022). *My writtings*. https://lamport.azurewebsites.net/pubs/pubs.html

Lamport, L., Shostak, R., & Pease, M. (1982). The Byzantine generals problem. *ACM Transactions on Programming Languages and Systems*, 4(3), 20.

Landels, J. G. (1979). Water-clocks and time measurement in classical antiquity. *Endeavour*, 3(1), 32–37. https://doi.org/10.1016/0160-9327(79)90007-3

Landrain, T., Meyer, M., Perez, A. M., & Sussan, R. (2013). Do-it-yourself biology: Challenges and promises for an open science and technology movement. *Systems and Synthetic Biology*, 7(3), 115–126. https://doi.org/10.1007/s11693-013-9116-4

Larsson, S. (2018). Algorithmic governance and the need for consumer empowerment in data-driven markets. *Internet Policy Review*, 7(2), 1–13. https://doi.org/10.14763/2018.2.791

Latour, B. (1993). *We Have Never Been Modern*. Harvard University Press.

Latour, B., & Woolgar, S. (1986). *Laboratory Life: The Construction of Scientific Facts*. Princeton University Press.

Lebniz, Gottfried Wilhelm. (1898). *Monadology*. https://www.plato-philosophy.org/wp-content/uploads/2016/07/The-Monadology-1714-by-Gottfried-Wilhelm-LEIBNIZ-1646-1716.pdf

LeCompte, C. (2013). *Introducing the Ocean Invention Network, a super lab trying to save the world—Tech News and Analysis*. Gigaom. Retrieved December 15, 2014, from https://gigaom.com/2013/01/07/introducing-the-ocean-invention-network-a-super-lab-trying-to-save-the-world/

Ledford, H. (2010). Garage biology: Life hackers. *Nature*.

Lee, M. K., Jain, A., Cha, H. J., Ojha, S., & Kusbit, D. (2019a). Procedural justice in algorithmic fairness: Leveraging transparency and outcome control for fair algorithmic mediation. *Proceedings of the ACM on Human-Computer Interaction*, 3(CSCW), 1–26. https://dl.acm.org/doi/10.1145/3359284

Lee, M. K., Kusbit, D., Kahng, A., Kim, J. T., Yuan, X., Chan, A., See, D., Noothigattu, R., Lee, S., Psomas, A., & Procaccia, A. D. (2019b). WeBuildAI: Participatory framework for algorithmic governance. *Proceedings of the ACM on Human-Computer Interaction*, 3(CSCW), 1–35. https://doi.org/10.1145/3359283

Lehdonvirta, V. (2016). *The blockchain paradox: Why distributed ledger technologies may do little to transform the economy*. https://www.oii.ox.ac.uk/news-events/news/the-blockchain-paradox-why-distributed-ledger-technologies-may-do-little-to-transform-the-economy

Leppälä, K. (2007). *Diffusion of parallel computing and transputing concepts. A trial for unifying metaphors*. https://www.researchgate.net/publication/228894045_Diffusion_of_parallel_computing_and_transputing_concepts_A_trial_for_unifying_metaphors

Lessig, L. (2006). *Code* (Version 2.0). Basic Books.

Lewenstein, B. V. (2003). Models of public communication of science and tecnhology. In B. Schiele (Ed.), *Public Understanding of Science* (Vol. 25, Issue 3, pp. 288–293). Department of Communication and of Science and Technology Studies http://www.dgdc.unam.mx/Assets/pdfs/sem_feb04.pdf

Lewis, S. C., & Usher, N. (2016). Trading zones, boundary objects, and the pursuit of news innovation: A case study of journalists and programmers. *Convergence*, 22(5), 543–560. https://doi.org/10.1177/1354856515623865

Liao, F. (2020). Does China need the regulatory sandbox? A preliminary analysis of its desirability as an appropriate mechanism for regulating fintech in China. In *Perspectives in Law, Business and Innovation* (pp. 81–95). Springer. https://ideas.repec.org/h/spr/perchp/978-981-15-5819-1_5.html

Lim, B., & Low, C. (2019). Regulatory sandboxes. In Madir, J (Ed), *FINTECH: Law and Regulation* (pp. 302–325). EE Publishing. https://www.elgaronline.com/display/edcoll/9781788979016/27_chapter14.xhtml

Lindtner, S. (2014). Hackerspaces and the Internet of Things in China: How makers are reinventing industrial production, innovation, and the self. *China Information*, 28(2), 145–167.

Lindtner, S., Bardzell, S., & Bardzell, J. (2016). Reconstituting the Utopian Vision of Making. *Proceedings of the 2016 CHI Conference on Human Factors in Computing Systems - CHI '16*, 1390–1402. https://doi.org/10.1145/2858036.2858506

Lindtner, S., & Lee, D. (2012). Created in China. *Interactions*, 19(6), 18. https://doi.org/10.1145/2377783.2377789

Lindtner, S. M. (2020). Prototype nation. In *Prototype Nation*. Princeton University Press. https://doi.org/10.2307/j.ctvz938ps

Liu, H. (2010). Open innovation in China. *Economy, Culture & History Japan Spotlight Bimonthly, 29*(1), 16–17.

Liu, X., Heilig, G. K., Chen, J., & Heino, M. (2007). Interactions between economic growth and environmental quality in Shenzhen, China's first special economic zone. *Ecological Economics, 62*(3–4), 559–570.

Lock, J. (n.d.). *Constitutional Government: John Locke, Second Treatise, §§ 89—94, 134—42, 212*. Retrieved July 8, 2022, from https://press-pubs.uchicago.edu/founders/documents/v1ch17s5.html

Lombard, C. G. (2005). Conceptual metaphors in computer networking terminology. *Southern African Linguistics and Applied Language Studies, 23*(2), 177–185. https://doi.org/10.2989/16073610509486382

Long, P. O. (2015). Trading zones in early modern Europe. *Isis, 106*(4), 840–847.

Longyi, L., & Lihua, T. (2009). Study of open innovation on electronic information industry in Shenzhen of China. *Proceedings - International Conference on Management and Service Science, MASS 2009.*

Mac Síthigh, D. (2012). Virtual walls? The law of pseudo-public spaces. *International Journal of Law in Context, 8*(3), 394–412. https://doi.org/10.1017/S1744552312000262

Macbain, B. (1980). Appius claudius caecus and the via appia. *The Classical Quarterly, 30*(2). https://doi.org/10.1017/S0009838800042294

MacDowell, D. M. (1985). The length of the speeches on the assessment of the penalty in athenian courts. *Classical Quarterly, 35*(02), 525. https://doi.org/10.1017/S0009838800040386

Madir, J. (2019). *FINTECH: Law and regulation*. EE Publishing. https://search.ebscohost.com/login.aspx?direct=true&scope=site&db=nlebk&db=nlabk&AN=2248595

Mansfeld, J. (1985). Aristotle and others on thales, or the beginnings of natural philosophy. *Mnemosyne, 38*(1–2), 109–129. https://doi.org/10.1163/156852585X00041

Marres, N. (2012). *Material Participation: Technology, the Environment and Everyday Publics*. Palgrave Macmillian.

Marres, N., & Lezaun, J. (2011). Materials and devices of the public: An introduction. *Economy and Society*. https://www.tandfonline.com/doi/abs/10.1080/03085147.2011.602293

Marx, K., & Engels, F. (1998). The German ideology: Including theses on Feuerbach and introduction to the critique of political economy. Prometheus Books.

Maupin, J. (2017). *Mapping the Global Legal Landscape of Blockchain and Other Distributed Ledger Technologies. 149*, 28.

McCarthy, J. C. (1995). Francis Bacon and the project of progress. *Review of Metaphysics, 49*(1), 129–131. https://doi.org/revmetaph1995491110

McClintock, A. (2019). Appius Claudius Caecus and Roman law. *The Encyclopedia of Ancient History*. https://doi.org/10.1002/9781444338386.wbeah30650

McQuillan, D. (2018). People's councils for ethical machine learning. *Social Media + Society, 4*(2), 2056305118768303. https://doi.org/10.1177/2056305118768303

Mellis, D. A., & Buechley, L. (2011). Scaffolding creativity with open-source hardware. *Proceedings of the 8th ACM Conference on Creativity and Cognition - C&C '11*, 373. https://doi.org/10.1145/2069618.2069702

Mennicken, A., & Espeland, W. (2019). What's new with numbers? Sociological approaches to the study of quantification. *Annual Review of Sociology, 45*. https://doi.org/10.1146/annurev-soc-073117-041343

Meyer, M. (2015). Amateurization and re-materialization in biology: Opening up scientific equipment. In Wienroth M. and Rodrigues E. (Ed.), *Knowing New Biotechnologies. Social Aspects of Technological Convergence* (pp. 142–157). Routledge.

Micheli, M., Ponti, M., Craglia, M., & Berti Suman, A. (2020). Emerging models of data governance in the age of datafication. *Big Data & Society*, 7(2), 205395172094808. https://doi.org/10.1177/2053951720948087

Mitchell, D. (1995). The end of public space? people's park, definitions of the public, and democracy. *Annals of the Association of American Geographers*, 85(1), 108–133. https://doi.org/10.1111/j.1467-8306.1995.tb01797.xa

Mittelstadt, B. D., Allo, P., Taddeo, M., Wachter, S., & Floridi, L. (2016). The ethics of algorithms: Mapping the debate. *Big Data & Society*, 3(2), 205395171667967. https://doi.org/10.1177/2053951716679679

Moilanen, J. (2012). Emerging hackerspaces—Peer-production generation. *IFIP Advances in Information and Communication Technology*, 378 AICT, 94–111. https://link.springer.com/chapter/10.1007/978-3-642-33442-9_7

Molitch-Hou, M. (2014). *Has MakerBot Become TakerBot? - 3D Printing Industry*. 3D Printing Industry. http://3dprintingindustry.com/2014/05/28/makerbot-become-takerbot/

Morozov, E. (2014a). *To Save Everything, Click Here* (Reprint edition). PublicAffairs.

Morozov, E. (2014b, July). The rise of data and the death of politics. *Guardian*. https://www.theguardian.com/technology/2014/jul/20/rise-of-data-death-of-politics-evgeny-morozov-algorithmic-regulation

Mulligan, D. K., & Bamberger, K. A. (Eds.). (2018). Saving governance-by-design. *California Law Review*. https://doi.org/10.15779/Z38QN5ZB5H

Nakamoto, S. (2008). *Bitcoin: A Peer-to-Peer Electronic Cash System*. https://bitcoin.org/bitcoin.pdf

Newman, W. R. (2005). Promethean ambitions: Alchemy and the quest to perfect nature. In *Promethean Ambitions*. University of Chicago Press. https://doi.org/10.7208/9780226577135

Ng, M. K. (2003). Shenzhen. *Cities*, 20(6), 429–441.

Nummedal, T. E. (2011). Words and works in the history of Alchemy. *Isis*, 102(2), 330–337. https://doi.org/10.1086/660142

O'Dwyer, R. (n.d.). *Code != Law: Explorations of the Blockchain as a Mode of Algorithmic Governance*. Retrieved July 6, 2022, from https://www.academia.edu/34734732/Code_Law_Explorations_of_the_Blockchain_as_a_Mode_of_Algorithmic_Governance

Oliver, J., Savičić, G., & Vasiliev, D. (n.d.). *The Critical Engineering Manifesto*. 2011. Retrieved December 5, 2014, from http://criticalengineering.org/

Parikka, J. (2012). *What is Media Archaeology?* Polity Press.

Parikka, J. (2015). A geology of media. In *A Geology of Media*. University of Minnesota Press. https://doi.org/10.1080/17460654.2015.1134150

Parry, R. (2020). Episteme and Techne—Stanford encyclopedia of philosophy. In *The Stanford Encyclopedia of Philosophy (Fall 2010 Edition)*.

Patočka, J. (1996). *Heretical Essays in the Philosophy of History*. Open Court Publishing Company.

Pearce, J. M. (2012). Building research equipment with free, open-source hardware. *Science*, 337(6100), 1303–1304.

Pearce, J. M. (2014). Open-source lab. In *Open-Source Lab*. Elsevier. https://doi.org/10.1016/B978-0-12-410462-4.00006-8

Perez-Ramos, A. (1988). *Francis Bacon's Idea of Science and the Maker's Knowledge Tradition*. Oxford University Press.

Demosthenes. (n.d.). Speeches. *Dem. 53.4*. Retrieved July 6, 2022, https://anastrophe.uchicago.edu/cgi-bin/perseus/citequery3.pl?dbname=GreekNov21&getid=1&query=Dem.%2053.4

Pettis, B. (2014). *Let's Try that Again*. MakerBot Blog. http://www.makerbot.com/blog/2012/09/24/lets-try-that-again/

Plato. (1871). *Timaeus*. Retrieved July 6, 2022, from https://www.gutenberg.org/files/1572/1572-h/1572-h.htm

Plato. (1925). Section 236d-e. In *Menexenus*. Plato in Twelve Volumes, Vol. 9 translated by W.R.M. Lamb. Cambridge, MA, Harvard University Press; London, William Heinemann Ltd. 1925. Retrieved June 26, 2022, from http://www.perseus.tufts.edu/hopper/text?doc=Perseus%3Atext%3A1999.01.0180%3Atext%3DMenex.%3Asection%3D236d

Plato, Theaetetus, section 174a. (n.d.). Plato in Twelve Volumes, Vol. 12 translated by Harold N. Fowler. Cambridge, MA, Harvard University Press; London, William Heinemann Ltd. 1921. Retrieved June 26, 2022, from http://www.perseus.tufts.edu/hopper/text?doc=plat.+theaet.+174a

Polanyi, M. (2009). *The Tacit Dimension*. University of Chicago Press.

Rahwan, I. (2018). Society-in-the-loop: Programming the algorithmic social contract. *Ethics and Information Technology*, 20(1), 5–14. https://doi.org/10.1007/s10676-017-9430-8

Ratcliff, J. R. (2007). Samuel Morland and his calculating machines c.1666: The early career of a courtier–inventor in Restoration London. *The British Journal for the History of Science*, 40(02), 159. https://doi.org/10.1017/S0007087407009466

Ratto, M. (2011). Critical making: Conceptual and material studies in technology and social life. *The Information Society*, 27(4), 252–260. https://doi.org/10.1080/01972243.2011.583819

Ratto, M., & Boler, M. (2014). *DIY Citizenship: Critical Making and Social Media* (M. Ratto & M. Boler, Eds.). MIT Press.

Ratto, M., & Ree, R. (2012). Materializing information: 3D printing and social change. *First Monday*, 17(7). https://firstmonday.org/ojs/index.php/fm/article/view/3968

Ratzan, L. (n.d.). *Making Sense of the Web: A Metaphorical Approach*. Information Research. Retrieved July 6, 2022, from http://informationr.net/ir/6-1/paper85.html

Regulatory Sandbox. (2022, March 1). FCA. https://www.fca.org.uk/firms/innovation/regulatory-sandbox

Reijers, W., O'Brolcháin, F., & Haynes, P. (2016). Governance in blockchain technologies & social contract theories. *Ledger*, 1, 134–151. https://doi.org/10.5195/ledger.2016.62

Reshef Kera, D. (2020). Sandboxes and testnets as "trading zones" for blockchain governance. In J. Prieto, A. Pinto, A. K. Das, & S. Ferretti (Eds.), *Blockchain and Applications* (pp. 3–12). Springer International Publishing. https://doi.org/10.1007/978-3-030-52535-4_1

Rheinberger, H.-J. (2010). *An Epistemology of the Concrete: Twentieth-century Histories of Life*. Duke University Press.

Roio, D. (2018). *Algorithmic Sovereignty* [Thesis, University of Plymouth]. https://pearl.plymouth.ac.uk/handle/10026.1/11101

Rosen, S. (2005). *Plato's Republic: A Study*. In *Library*. Yale University Press.

Rouvroy, A. (n.d.). Technology, virtuality and Utopia: Governmentality in an age of autonomic computing. In Mireille Hildebrandt and A. Rouvroy (Eds.), *Autonomic Computing and Transformations of Human Agency*. Routledge, 2011. Retrieved August 17, 2022, from https://www.academia.edu/7815966/Technology_Virtuality_and_Utopia_Governmentality_in_an_Age_of_Autonomic_Computing

Rozas, D., Tenorio-Fornés, A., Díaz-Molina, S., & Hassan, S. (2021). When ostrom meets blockchain: Exploring the potentials of blockchain for commons governance. *Sage Open, 11*(1), https://journals.sagepub.com/doi/full/10.1177/2158244021100 2526

Sabel, C. F., & Zeitlin, J. (2012, March 29). *Experimentalist Governance*. The Oxford Handbook of Governance. https://doi.org/10.1093/oxfordhb/9780199560530.013.0012

Salkever, S. G. (1992). Plato on practices: The "Technai" and the socratic question in republic I. *Proc Boston Colloq Anc Phil, 8*, 243–267.

Sanders, Carol. (2004). The Cambridge companion to Saussure. *The Cambridge Companion to Saussure.* https://doi.org/10.1017/CCOL052180051X

Sandoval, M. (2019). Entrepreneurial activism? Platform cooperativism between subversion and co-optation. *Critical Sociology*. https://doi.org/10.1177/08969205198 70577

Saurwein, F., Just, N., & Latzer, M. (2015). Governance of algorithms: Options and limitations. *Info, 17*(6), 35–49. https://doi.org/10.1108/info-05-2015-0025

Savransky, M., Wilkie, A., & Rosengarten, M. (2017). *The Lure of Possible Futures: On Speculative Research* (A. Wilkie, M. Savransky, & M. Rosengarten, Eds.). Routledge.

Schaffer, S. (1987). Godly men and mechanical philosophers: Souls and spirits in restoration natural philosophy. *Science in Context, 1*(01), 53–85. https://doi.org/10.1017/S0269889700000053

Schmitt, C. (1996). *The Leviathan in the State Theory of Thomas Hobbes: Meaning and Failure of a Political Symbol*. Greenwood Press.

Schneider, N., & Scholz, T. (2016). Ours to hack and to own: The rise of platform cooperativism, a new vision for the future of work and a Fairer internet. OR Books. https://worldpece.org/sites/default/files/artifacts/media/pdf/ourstohackandown.pdf

Schulman, A. (2009). The twilight of probability: Locke, Bayle, and the toleration of atheism. *Journal of Religion, 89*(3), 328–360). https://doi.org/10.1086/597819

Selin, C. (2015). Merging art and design in foresight: Making sense of emerge. *Futures, 70*, 24–35. https://doi.org/10.1016/j.futures.2014.12.006

Selin, C., Rawlings, K. C., de Ridder-Vignone, K., Sadowski, J., Altamirano Allende, C., Gano, G., Davies, S. R., & Guston, D. H. (2016). Experiments in engagement: Designing public engagement with science and technology for capacity building. *Public Understanding of Science*, 0963662515620970. https://doi.org/10.1177/0963662515620970

Sennett, A. (2009). Play it again, uncle Sam: Casablanca & US foreign policy. *Journal of Popular Film and Television, 37*(1), 2–8.

Seyfried, G., Pei, L., & Schmidt, M. (2014). European do-it-yourself (DIY) biology: Beyond the hope, hype and horror. *BioEssays, 36*(6), 548–551. https://doi.org/10.1002/bies.201300149

Shapin, Steven., & Schaffer, S. (2011). *Leviathan and the Air-Pump Hobbes, Boyle, and the Experimental Life: With a New Introduction by the Authors*. Princeton University Press.

Shneiderman, B. (2016). The dangers of faulty, biased, or malicious algorithms requires independent oversight. *Proceedings of the National Academy of Sciences, 113*(48), 13538–13540. https://doi.org/10.1073/pnas.1618211113

Shorey, S., & Howard, P. N. (2016). Automation, big data, and politics: A research review. *International Journal of Communication, 10*, 5032–5055.

Sipiora, Phillip., & Baumlin, J. S. (2002). *Rhetoric and Kairos: Essays in History, Theory, and Praxis.* State University of New York Press.

Sloane, M., Moss, E., Awomolo, O., & Forlano, L. (2020). Participation is not a design fix for machine learning. *ArXiv Preprint ArXiv:2007.02423.*

Smith, J. E. (1969). Time, times, and the 'Right Time'; Chronos and Kairos. *Monist, 53*(1), 1–13. https://doi.org/10.5840/monist196953115

Smith, P. H. (2004). *The Body of the Artisan: Art and Experience in the Scientific Revolution.* University of Chicago Press.

Standing, G. (2019). The precariat: Today's transformative class? *Development, 61.* https://doi.org/10.1057/s41301-018-0182-5

Stark, D. (2011). The sense of dissonance: Accounts of worth in economic life. In *The Sense of Dissonance.* Princeton University Press. https://doi.org/10.1515/978140 0831005

Staub, A. (2016). Sharing Economy & Platform Cooperativism. *Faculty of Business, Economics and Social Sciences at the University of Bern Institute.*

Sturgis, P., & Allum, N. (2004). Science in society: Re-evaluating the deficit model of public attitudes. *Public Understanding of Science, 13*(1), 55–74. https://doi.org/10.1177/0963662504042690

Susskind, J. (2018). *Future Politics. Living Together in a World Transformed by Tech.* Oxford University Press, 516.

Szabo, N. (1997a). *Nick Szabo—The Idea of Smart Contracts.* https://www.fon.hum. uva.nl/rob/Courses/InformationInSpeech/CDROM/Literature/LOTwinter school2006/szabo.best.vwh.net/idea.html

Szabo, N. (1997b). Formalizing and securing relationships on Public networks. *First Monday.* https://doi.org/10.5210/fm.v2i9.548

Taylor, C. C. W. (2016). *Aristotle on Practical Reason* (Vol. 1). Oxford University Press. https://doi.org/10.1093/oxfordhb/9780199935314.013.52

Miller, Richard W. 1991. Social and Political Theory: Class, State, Revolution. In T. Carver (Ed.), *The Cambridge Companion to Marx* (Vol. 11, Issue 1, pp. 55–105). Cambridge University Press. https://doi.org/10.1017/CCOL0521366259.003

Trump, B. D., Wells, E., Trump, J., & Linkov, I. (2018). Cryptocurrency: Governance for what was meant to be ungovernable. *Environment Systems and Decisions, 38*(3), 426–430. https://doi.org/10.1007/s10669-018-9703-8

Turner, V. (1969). The Ritual Process: Structure and Anti-Structure. In *The Ritual Process Structure an Antistructure.* Aldine Publishing Company.

Turner, V. (1985). Betwixt and between: The liminal period in Rites de Passage. In A. Leymann & J. Myers (Eds.), *Magic, Witchcraft, and Religion: An Anthropological Study of the Supernatural* (pp. 46–55).

van Helden, A. C. (1991). The age of the air-pump. *Tractrix. Yearbook for the History of Science, Medicine, Technology and Mathematics, 3*, 149–172.

Vertesi, J., Lindtner, S., & Shklovski, I. (2011). Transnational HCI. *Proceedings of the 2011 Annual Conference Extended Abstracts on Human Factors in Computing Systems - CHI EA '11*, 61. https://doi.org/10.1145/1979742.1979584

Vostal, F. (2019). Slowing down modernity: A critique. *Time and Society*, *28*(3), 1039–1060. https://doi.org/10.1177/0961463X17702163

Wang, E. M., & Huang, A. Y. (2000). A study on basic metaphors in human-computer interaction. *Proceedings of the Human Factors and Ergonomics Society Annual Meeting*, *44*(1), 140–143. https://doi.org/10.1177/154193120004400137

Wang, Y., & Wang, Y. (2019). The rise of pseudo-public spaces. In *Pseudo-Public Spaces in Chinese Shopping Malls* (pp. 68–112). Routledge. https://doi.org/10.1201/9780429242823-3

Warman, C. (2020). The Atheist's Bible. In *The Atheist's Bible*. Open Book Publishers. https://doi.org/10.11647/obp.0199

Weibel, P., & Latour, B. (Eds.). (2005). *Making Things Public: Atmospheres of Democracy*. MIT Press.

Weiss, A. (2008). Open source hardware. In *NetWorker*, *12*(3), 26. https://doi.org/10.1145/1435535.1435541

Werrett, S. (2001). Wonders never cease: Descartes's Météores and the rainbow fountain. *British Journal for the History of Science*, *34*(2), 129–147.

Bostrom, N. (2006). What is a Singleton? *Linguistic and Philosophical Investigations*, *5*(2), 48–54. Retrieved July 12, 2022, from https://nickbostrom.com/fut/singleton

Whitney, C. (1989). Francis Bacon's Instauratio: Dominion of and over humanity. *Journal of the History of Ideas*, *50*(3), 371–390.

Wiener, P. P. (1940). Leibniz's project of a public exhibition of scientific inventions. *Journal of the History of Ideas*, *1*(1/4), 232. https://doi.org/10.2307/2707335

Wilkie, A. (2010). *Prototypes in Design: Materializing Futures*. ARC Studio.

Wilkie, A., & Ward, M. (2009). Made in criticalland: Designing matters of concern. *Networks of Design: Proceedings of the 2008 Annual International Conference of the Design History Society*, 118–123. https://research.gold.ac.uk/id/eprint/4657/

Williams, R. (2019). 'This shining confluence of magic and technology': Solarpunk, energy imaginaries, and the infrastructures of solarity. *Open Library of Humanities*, *5*(1). https://doi.org/10.16995/olh.329

Wirtz, B. W., Weyerer, J. C., & Geyer, C. (2019). Artificial intelligence and the public sector—Applications and challenges. *International Journal of Public Administration*, *42*(7), 596–615.

Wofford, L., Wyman, D., & Starr, C. W. (2020). Do you have a naïve forecasting model of the future? *Journal of Property Investment and Finance*, *38*(4). https://doi.org/10.1108/JPIF-12-2019-0154

Rosenzweig, R. (2004). *Worshipping Aphrodite*. University of Michigan Press.

Wright, A., & De Filippi, P. (2015). Decentralized blockchain technology and the rise of lex cryptographia. *Available at SSRN 2580664*.

Zacharias, J., & Tang, Y. (2010). Restructuring and repositioning Shenzhen, China's new mega city. *Progress in Planning*, *73*(4), 209–249.

Zielinski, Siegfried. (2006). *Deep Time of the Media: Toward an Archaeology of Hearing and Seeing by Technical Means*. MIT Press.

Zilsel, E. (2000). The social origins of modern science. In D. Raven, W. Krohn, & R. S. Cohen (Eds.), *Boston Studies in the Philosophy of Science* (Issue 200). Kluwer Academic Publishers.

Zuboff, S. (2018). *The Age of Surveillance Capitalism: The Fight for a Human Future at the New Frontier of Power*. Profile Books.

Index

Pages in *italics* refer to figures.

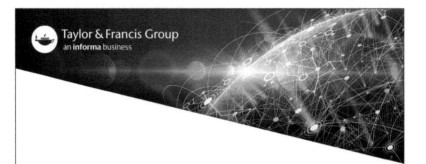